The Birthday Almanac

D0752398

THE BIRTHDAY ALMANAC

Personal Revelations for Every Day of the Year

SOPHIA KENDRICK

THUNDER BAY
P·R·E·S·S

San Diego, California

THUNDER BAY
P · R · E · S · S

Thunder Bay Press
An imprint of Baker & Taylor Publishing Group
10350 Barnes Canyon Road
San Diego, CA 92121
www.thunderbaybooks.com

ISBN-13: 978-1-60710-080-5
ISBN-10: 1-60710-080-0

Library of Congress Cataloging-in-Publication Data available upon request

Printed in China

1 2 3 4 5 13 12 11 10 09

FOR LUCY WOOD,
A LIBRAN LIVE-WIRE AND COOL-HEADED CHARMER

CONTENTS

Introduction

"A MAN'S CHARACTER IS HIS FATE."
On the Universe (fragment 121), Heraclitus (*c*.540–*c*.480 B.C.).

Just as the Greek philosopher Heraclitus deemed every person's fate to be predetermined by his or her character, so astrologers believe that each individual's character is influenced by the position of the planets and constellations overhead at the time of his or her birth on Earth. And while our date of birth determines our zodiacal, or star, sign, that sign's associated ruling planet, element, quadruplicity, and polarity are the basic ingredients that are said to give our characters form and flavor, so that by learning more about them, we can gain a better understanding of ourselves. Remember, however, that although they may have some bearing on what we are like and how we are likely to behave, as well as the types of events that may occur on our birthdays, such astrological birth influences do not have the power to control our destinies. That power ultimately lies with us alone, for perhaps our most potent birthright, and the one that, above all, determines our character is free will.

"MAN IS HIS OWN STAR AND THE SOUL THAT
CAN RENDER AN HONEST AND PERFECT MAN
COMMANDS ALL LIGHT, ALL INFLUENCE, ALL FATE."
John Fletcher (1579–1625).

THE PLANETS

Even today, astronomers are still making new discoveries. But the theories and principles of astrology evolved thousands of years ago, before scientific advances had enabled the nature of the solar system to be understood properly, at a time when it was believed that the heavenly bodies revolved around the Earth, not the Sun. This not only explains why astrology classifies the Sun (actually a star) and the Moon (Earth's satellite) as planets, but why the zodiacal signs of Scorpio, Aquarius, and Pisces are linked with two planets, their primary rulers now being one of the trio of planets that were discovered relatively recently—in astrological terms, at least—namely Uranus, Neptune, and Pluto—with their traditional planetary governors being relegated to secondary-ruler status. The planets are named for Roman deities, apart from the Sun and the Moon, which the ancient Greeks (from whom the Romans derived their pantheon) and Romans nevertheless equated with gods and goddesses.

Although each sign of the zodiac has its own ruling planet (and two in the case of Scorpio, Aquarius, and Pisces) that is said to impart its characteristics to those born under that constellation, all of the planets affect us according to both their positions when we were born and when they move into our zodiacal constellations in real time. You can discover which planet was in which "house," or area of your life, at the time of your birth by drawing up your birth chart or asking an astrologer to do so. The planets are said to bring out, energize, and direct the potential with which our zodiacal signs endow us at birth.

⊙ **THE SUN:** It is easy to understand why ancient astrologers associated such traits as warmth, burning vitality, and a sunny personality with the Sun, and why it can represent a significant man—be it a father, husband, boyfriend, or boss—in a person's birth chart. As the star that dominates the sky, and around which all of the planets revolve, it is not surprising that power, authority, and leadership qualities, or the desire for them, as well as a longing to shine and to be admired as a "star," should be among its attributes. More importantly, perhaps, it is the planet of individuality, identity, and personality, representing as it does the ego, how we feel about ourselves, our outlook on life, and the face that we present to others. It is strongly linked with willpower, self-confidence, and self-esteem, and hence with pride and dignity, along with the self-sufficiency, resilience, and decisiveness of adulthood. The Sun consequently denotes personal integrity, or the ability to remain true to oneself, and suggests that we deal with others in an honorable, principled, and generous way. In addition, the Sun is the planet of personal ambition and blesses us with the determination, energy, and creativity that are necessary if we are to make our aims a reality, whether they be to raise a family, build up a business, or bring any sort of visionary project to fruition. It also gives us a joyful appreciation of life, which may manifest itself as playfulness, exuberance, vigor, and a willingness to experiment and explore new possibilities. More negatively, it can result in someone being egotistical, domineering, and attention-demanding.

Right: In ancient times, the sun was recognized as the crucial force for the creation and maintenance of life. It was associated with intelligence and spirituality as well as warmth and light.

THE MOON: The Moon's appearance in an individual's birth chart can signify an important woman—specifically a mother, or mother figure—in the subject's life or how he or she relates to women in general, but is generally interpreted as denoting that person's inner life, soul, unconscious urges, or instinctual reactions. Because it generates no light of its own, unlike the Sun, whose radiance it subtly reflects, the Moon additionally signifies that we are easily swayed by others, and thus that we are in danger of being gullible or of not knowing our own minds, although the more positive traits of adaptability, openness, and receptiveness, along with empathy and compassion, are also implied. Further gifts of

Left: William Blake's portrait of Hecate, an ancient Greek goddess linked with the Moon, portrays her introspective, sensitive qualities, which are typical of those born under the Moon's influence.

Mother Moon are imagination and innate creativity, both of which can ultimately bring fulfillment should they produce an idea that we find satisfaction in nurturing from conception to fruition. Yet some of the downsides bestowed on us by this "planet" include a tendency to be backward-looking, reactionary, or to live in the past, or a childish or immature attitude. Still more are an overdependence on loved ones for emotional sustenance, which may result in clinginess or neediness; oversensitivity, in turn triggering moodiness when our feelings have been wounded; and a propensity to control those closest to us by means of emotional blackmail, which is usually manifested as guilt-inducing, martyrlike behavior. When under the influence of the Moon, people may also reason or behave irrationally, but this needn't be a negative characteristic, for tapping into the unconscious and acting intuitively, rather than logically, can often have startlingly successful consequences.

☿ **MERCURY:** Because its rate of orbit around the Sun is the fastest of all of the planets at eighty-eight days, Mercury was named for the winged-sandaled, fleet-footed messenger of the Roman gods (whose counterpart was Hermes in Greece). A quick-witted trickster, a silver-tongued charmer and an ingenious inventor, Mercury is linked with siblings, communication, travel, learning, and everyday transactions and commerce (Mercury was the patron deity of Roman merchants). He is also associated with work, service, and health (Mercury's snake-entwined caduceus was said to have healing powers, which is why it is often used to represent medicine, too).

Mercury's appearance in a birth chart indicates how we gather knowledge and then use logic and reason to analyze it. Mercury therefore points to our intellectual ability or cleverness, our schooling, curiosity, and general appetite for learning, along with our capacity for thinking objectively. It also denotes how we communicate our thoughts to others, be it through speech or writing. If we use Mercury's articulacy to the full, we may communicate clearly, fluently, and persuasively, yet also critically (and not everyone appreciates their actions being subjected to the scrutiny of a neutrally minded person whose opinions are unclouded by emotions, and who can therefore lack empathy). Further gifts include the ability to think on one's feet, dextrousness, versatility, adaptability, and a zest for travel. If this desire to be mentally and physically occupied at all times is frustrated, however, restlessness, unreliability, capriciousness, and pranks may result, and it is no coincidence that the word "mercurial" can mean both liveliness and volatility.

Left: *Venus, depicted here by Velázquez, is shown reclining languorously before a mirror. The Roman goddess of love and beauty, her influence can incline her children toward vanity and indulgence.*

♀ **Venus:** Venus points to the things that bring us happiness in life, particularly the ecstasy that we may experience in the arms of a lover, but also light-hearted friendships and the delight that we find in creative endeavors and artistry, be they music, art, the theater, or simply lovely objects. It is partly because the goddess was associated with commerce and prosperity, and partly because she craved ease and opulence, that Venus bestows a talent for money management, a desire for financial security, and an urge to amass material possessions. Romance and sexual desire are Venus' primary province, however, and when this planet appears in a man's birth chart, it may denote his ideal woman, his anima (or the feminine side of his nature), his relationship with his girlfriend or life partner, or else his rapport with women in general; in a woman's chart, Venus may reveal what it is that she wants and needs in a romantic liaison. Venus otherwise signifies a balanced, benevolent, and soft-hearted personality that longs for harmony, hates unpleasantness, and therefore strives to keep the peace when confronted by hostility or arguments, thus encouraging friendly social interaction. People who are influenced by Venus furthermore don't like to rush, typically have deeply sensual and highly developed aesthetic tastes, and believe in indulging themselves and others, as well as in having fun with one another. They also take pride in their appearance and manners and similarly expect others to look well turned-out and to behave graciously. All positives have their flip sides in astrology, however, and less pleasing traits associated with Venus include decadence, promiscuity, narcissism, indolence, extravagance, and jealousy.

♂ **MARS:** Because the iron oxide on its surface causes Mars to glow red, the color of blood and life, the Romans named this planet for their virile and aggressive warrior god (whose Greek counterpart was Ares). This planet is linked with the self, beginnings, and vitality, and also brings its influence to bear on sexual relationships in particular.

The position of Mars in a birth chart signifies what we really want to achieve or possess in life, and how single-mindedly and passionately we set about getting it. It is the planet of self-seeking or selfish behavior, for when we are fueled by a Mars-driven urge to charge toward our goals, we don't care whose feelings we trample over in our driving need to reach our targets. Mars is therefore the planet that fills us with a pioneering spirit, energy, determination, and forcefulness when in pursuit of tangible aims, be they triggered by competitiveness, realizing career ambitions, or making a sexual conquest. This planet infuses us with the stamina required to achieve them, too. When Mars is considered in relation to a man, it can denote a macho mindset or leadership qualities that either already exist or are lacking and longed for, while Mars' significance for a woman may indicate her masculine ideal, her animus (or the male side of her personality), her boyfriend or husband. More generally, Mars can suggest that we should either toughen up or that our emotions and actions have veered toward the thoughtless and violent. This planet can therefore empower us by making us strong-willed, assertive, and fearless, or can destroy all that we hold dear by prompting us to behave in a reckless or violent manner.

4 **JUPITER:** Jupiter is the largest visible planet, which is why the Romans named it for their sky god, the ruler of their lesser deities, and the ultimate lawgiver. Jupiter's Greek equivalent was Zeus, and this planet's sigil describes the Greek letter *zeta,* "Z," Zeus' initial. Jupiter is linked with travel, broadening one's mind and horizons, and also healing and spiritual reflection.

The key word associated with Jupiter is "expansion," be it widening our social circle and making new contacts, traveling farther afield and learning about other cultures, enlarging our knowledge through college, university, or other forms of higher education, or deepening our spirituality, morality, or understanding of the world and our place within it. It is therefore regarded as the planet that has the power

Left: The mighty Jupiter, ruler of the skies, is identified in this painting by his solar crown and the radiant light that emanates from his head.

to bestow an all-embracing, all-encompassing outlook upon us, as well as wisdom, particularly in the fields of religion, ethics, and philosophy. And it is through its association with expansiveness that Jupiter is believed to bring good fortune and prosperity and to create new opportunities by pushing back boundaries, consequently blessing us with optimism, hope, and a "can-do" attitude. Other characteristics that are the gift of Jove, as the Romans also called Jupiter, are joviality and exuberance, generosity and loyalty, and an honorable, just, liberal, or charitable way of judging and dealing with others, particularly those who are less fortunate than themselves. Certain negative traits are attributed to Jupiter, too, however, including a tendency to exaggerate or tell tall tales, greed and intemperance, and misplaced pride, snobbishness, or imperiousness.

♄ **SATURN**: This planet was named for the Roman god of agriculture and time (whose equivalent in Greece was Cronos, or Kronos), who came to be equated with the "grim reaper," or the personification of death who cuts down humans with his sickle. Saturn influences our long-term goals, particularly our career ambitions, and how we apply ourselves to achieving them, and also how we relate to friends and social groups.

Just as the mythological Saturn was a disciplinarian father, so the astrological characteristics associated with this planet include repression and limitation, and sometimes even someone's own father if he was a stern and strict figure who overshadowed that individual's childhood. Indeed, some typical

saturnine traits may include a conservative and coldly realistic, unfeeling outlook, as well as a firm determination to keep us on the straight and narrow. However, these need not be negative qualities, for they also indicate a prudent, serious, and mature attitude, especially toward

Left: Saturn may be seen as as a paternal figure who takes his responsibilities over his charges seriously.

Right: *The planet Uranus was first discovered in the eighteenth century. In astrological terms, it is linked with revolutionary originality.*

others, along with true commitment and devotion, straightforward ambitions, and the understanding that anything worthwhile has to be patiently worked for, and that no corners can be cut in the process. Saturn can therefore be regarded as a wise teacher who slowly and soberly shows us how to live a responsible and productive life, and suggests that we will receive tangible rewards for the sacrifices that we make in so doing. In return for being self-disciplined, tenacious, and diligent in our careers, for instance, we should eventually earn ourselves financial security, an elevated status, the respect of others, and the satisfaction of knowing that our success has been hard won and is consequently well deserved.

URANUS: Perhaps it is because the planet Uranus was unknown to the ancients (discovered, as it was, in 1781) that its astrological associations have next to nothing to do with its namesake deity. Instead, they are tied up both with the planet's extreme tilt and its manner of rotation, which, like that of Venus, is clockwise, or retrograde, while that of the rest of the planets is counterclockwise. As a result of these differences,

Uranus is linked with innovative, unpredictable, and unconventional ways of thinking and behavior, as well as with rebellion against the norm, so that its energy as the "Great Awakener," as it is sometimes called, can result in sudden, radical, and even revolutionary changes, especially where social systems and values are concerned, when they may have either wonderfully beneficial or disastrously destructive consequences. Indeed, at their most extreme, the effects of being under Uranus' sway may include being an eccentric, "antisocial," or anarchic character, or else a brave and inspired social reformer. Uranus' oddball energy can furthermore trigger the most inventive and unusual of ideas, reflecting its status as the "higher octave" of Mercury, the planet of basic intelligence, but one that lacks Uranus' dynamic, transcendental qualities. Because the Uranian mindset is pioneering, experimental, forward-looking, and determined to transcend conventional boundaries, it follows that it embraces new technology and is inspired by its potential, and that it is ever curious and willing to question established beliefs. There are some significant downsides of having an uncompromisingly willful, logical, and independent, Uranian personality, however, such as forever feeling disconnected from, or at odds with, others.

Ψ **NEPTUNE:** Neptune was discovered in 1846, at a time when the Romantic movement was flowering in Europe, a style that encouraged artists, writers, and composers to express their feelings as well as to pay homage to the glories of the natural world. This is one of the reasons why astrologers associate Neptune with the emotions, creativity, and an instinctive search for beauty, which is also why it is called the "higher octave" of Venus, the planet that gives us an appreciation of artistry. Neptune's influence is far more profound than that of Venus, however, not least because its namesake god's watery realm is linked with that of the unconscious in symbolic thought, whose workings can appear as confused and mysterious to the rational mind as the constantly changing nature of the oceans and seas. The Neptunian personality is consequently said to be hard to understand, being nebulous and dreamy, but also, through its connection with the element of water, empathetic, compassionate, and intuitive to the point of having psychic insight. And just as the sea can be calm one moment and turbulent the next, so, under Neptune's influence, we may rapidly switch from feeling composed and content to unstable, muddled, and despairing, a state that we may try to escape by seeking refuge in fantasies and daydreams at best, or mind-altering substances at worst. Yet Neptune's subtle powers can also infuse us with unselfishness and a desire to help others, along with giving us a deep spiritual awareness and an idealistic, if rather imprecise, vision that can enable us to transcend the harsh realities of the real world and pin our hopes on building a better existence, one in which all artificial boundaries have been swept aside and we all live in kindly, happy harmony.

♇ PLUTO: Although Pluto's existence was not confirmed until 1930, the characteristics that astrologists ascribe to the planet are drawn directly from the tales that Greco–Roman mythology tell of the dark deity that ruled the underworld, the abode of the souls of those who had died. Not only was this shadowy place invisible and inaccessible to the living, but Pluto himself tended to hold himself aloof from his fellow deities, with the result that this is said to be the planet of mystery and secrecy, one whose intense influence can cause us to feel isolated or alienated from others, to suffer from power complexes, or to have a tendency to hatch plots and plans behind the scenes. Pluto may have the power to depress, yet its influence can bring astounding reversals of fortune, too, for just as Christians believe that we are reborn through death, and the apparently lifeless natural world is rejuvenated as winter gives way to spring, so this planet gives us the necessary endurance and resilience to survive a long period of hardship and to emerge transformed for the better. So not only is Pluto the planet of death and endings, it is that of birth and beginnings, too, compounded by its association with sexual relationships. Similarly, Pluto is linked with the money that may enable us to make a fresh start, perhaps as the result of a bequest or legacy. As strange as it may sound, gloomy Pluto can therefore be described as a planet that gives us the hope that however dire our existence, if we can just hold out long enough for a complete metamorphosis to be effected, we may be rewarded by a wonderful, life-changing gift, be it self-reinvention, a baby, or a windfall.

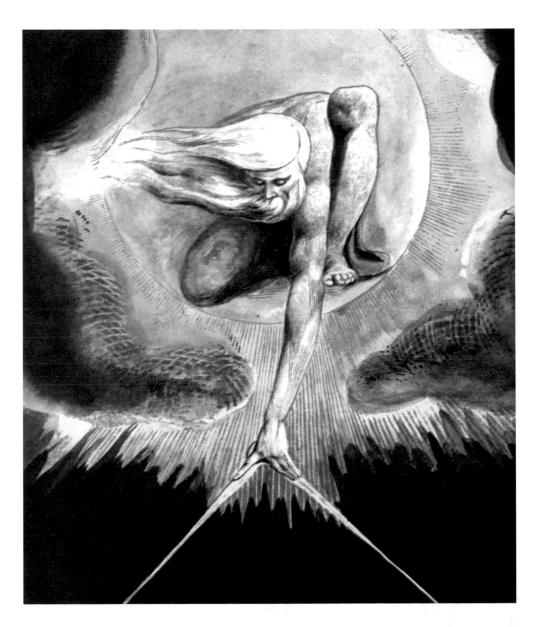

The Elements

For millennia, it was believed that everything in the universe was made up of the four elements—fire, earth, air, and water—in varying degrees. This theory was extended to humans, too, in whom the four elements were thought to take the form of fluids, or "humors," that circulated the body, an imbalance of which could cause specific ailments and personality traits. The element of fire, which supposedly manifested itself as the hot and dry, choleric humor (yellow bile), was said to make someone hot-tempered; the element of earth's cold and dry humor was black bile, or melancholic, an excess of which could cause a person to be gloomy; the element of air was equated with the blood and the hot and moist, sanguine humor, which, if dominant, would result in a confident, cheerful, and optimistic personality; and finally, the element of water was said to flow around the body as the cold and moist, phlegmatic humor, which was associated with a stolid and unemotional personality.

The zodiacal signs were similarly each allocated an element and related characteristics, Aries, Leo, and Sagittarius being equated with fire; Taurus, Virgo, and Capricorn with earth; Gemini, Libra, and Aquarius with air; and Cancer, Scorpio, and Pisces with water. According to astrological belief, the first of the fire, earth, air, and water signs in the zodiacal cycle (Aries, Taurus, Gemini, and Cancer) display the strongest of their element's qualities, which are diluted in the second signs (Leo, Virgo, Libra, and Scorpio), and even more so in the third (Sagittarius, Capricorn, Aquarius, and Pisces).

THE FIRE SIGNS: Those born under the zodiacal signs of Aries, Leo, and Sagittarius are said to have certain characteristics in common. Fiery people are said to be warm-hearted, generous, and magnetic, to relish being the center of attention, and to be stimulated and energized by contact with others. When their imaginations are fired up, they can be highly creative, and when their enthusiasm has been kindled, their vitality, exuberance, ardor, and passion enlivens those around them. Like fire's unpredictable, leaping flames, these individuals are adventurous, outgoing, impulsive, and spontaneous, and often inspirational, experimental trendsetters who are blessed with a masculine polarity's confidence and the courage of their convictions. If a headstrong, fiery character's flame is to burn brightly, he or she needs self-autonomy and freedom of action, however, and watery or earthy influences may dampen or suppress a fiery type's high spirits. Along with having a gift for making things happen, those whose element is fire are furthermore typically honest and optimistic.

Fire can be dangerous, however, and when fueled by excitement, a fiery temperament can often rashly and unthinkingly overstep certain boundaries; or else a spark of annoyance may rapidly escalate into furious rage. Fiery individuals may therefore lack self-control, and are prone to burnout if they are unable, or unwilling, to rein in their energies. They may be hot-tempered, but their heated outbursts are usually short-lived, and once vented, their fury generally quickly subsides. Indeed, despite their often heart-warming demonstrativeness, all have a tendency to be the exhibitionists of the zodiac, which others may find tiresome.

THE EARTH SIGNS: The earth signs are Taurus, Virgo, and Capricorn, and, as their element suggests, all have fundamentally down-to-earth natures. These are level-headed individuals, who are stable and supportive. Even when a personal catastrophe rocks the very foundations of their existence, their resilience and practical approach generally soon reassert themselves, enabling them to rebuild their world steadily and productively. Additionally hardworking, loyal, and dependable, they can be relied upon to see a job through to the end, and, once committed, to remain faithful to those close to them. However, it is no coincidence that "earthy" can mean "sensual," or "lusty," and, indeed, Venus-ruled Taureans have a pronounced relish for indulging their senses. All earth-sign characters enjoy spending time outside, too, for they feel grounded when they are in physical contact with their element.

Some of the disadvantages of having earth as an element include passiveness that it bestows, a characteristic that is compounded by having a feminine polarity, which means that Taureans, Virgoans, and Capricorneans can be somewhat stolid and inactive, and, because they are naturally prudent and cautious, too, may do little on joyous impulse and may rarely take the initiative. They can also be hardheaded materialists who sometimes take greater pleasure in working hard to accumulate the money and possessions that make them feel secure than in simply having fun. Another trait that may irritate others is their slow, considered, plodding approach and refusal to be rushed, even if their thoroughness, attention to detail, and tenacity bring concrete results in the end.

Right: *The element of air represents freedom: those born under an air sign like to fly through life without being tied down.*

THE AIR SIGNS: The zodiacal signs of Gemini, Libra, and Aquarius all have the element of air in common, and because air is associated with the intellect in astrological thought, they are believed to be united in their analytical, logical, and rational way of thinking. These coolly cerebral people are stimulated by ideas, be they those that they think up themselves or those that spring from the minds of others. And just as the air in Earth's atmosphere is both everywhere and moves around freely, so do they, partly because they are constantly in search of new and interesting viewpoints, partly because they are curious about others and enjoy evaluating their personalities, and partly because they are fluent and articulate communicators who feel the urge to impart their news and views. Sociable, amiable, and easygoing, airy individuals have a charming, playful streak and are great fun to be with.

The airy traits of blowing hot and cold, fickleness, unreliability, a resistance to being contained, and a horror of being bored can annoy or wound those who were born under more constant zodiacal signs, as can, at times, the aloof or breezy manner that is also characteristic of the element of air. Airy people can lack empathy and emotional depth, and because they don't often need propping up themselves, can't understand why others may occasionally want or require a tangible gesture of devotion, sympathy, or support. Sometimes lacking in direction, these impractical types are furthermore prone to wandering around with their heads in the clouds, and don't appreciate being torn from their fascinating fantasies should someone try to encourage them to reconnect with the real world by bringing them back down to earth.

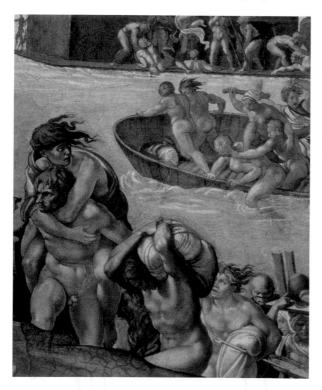

Left: Michelangelo's depiction of Noah's Flood illustrates the rising water levels causing panic. Water-sign people may feel "swamped" by their emotions or "flooded" with insecurity. Yet their element also makes them empathic and helps nurture their imaginations.

THE WATER SIGNS: The element of water (which psychologists associate with the unconscious mind) gives those whose zodiacal signs are Cancer, Scorpio, or Pisces certain shared characteristics, such as profound emotions, genuinely felt compassion, and intuitive insight. Because they also have an introspective, feminine polarity, water-sign individuals often spend much of their time in their personal inner worlds, be it contemplating their feelings, daydreaming, or gradually nurturing the germ of a concept to successful fruition. And just as water supports a host of life forms, so the watery mind is teeming—somewhat chaotically—with creative notions, which may nevertheless rarely come to the surface to face the scrutiny of others, partly because sensitive, watery people can't bear the hurt of being ridiculed or rejected, and partly because their nebulous element sometimes makes it hard for them to express themselves. They have no such difficulty understanding others, however, for they are both born listeners and almost psychically attuned to the emotional signals that they pick up from those around them.

However, they are often beset by insecurities that others may inadvertently trigger. And when they feel wounded, they typically either retreat into themselves or lash out in self-protective retaliation, thereby confirming their reputation as being changeable and moody, and bewildering or upsetting the supposed culprits. Not only that, but they may have a tendency to control those close to them by means of sulking and emotional blackmail, and, after a while, others may think it easier to comply than risk being swamped with tears or buffeted by stormy emotions.

The Quadruplicities

The three quadruplicities—cardinal, fixed, and mutable—are each associated with a set of characteristics that indicate the innate instincts and motivations that underpin our actions. Also termed the qualities (of life) or modes, the quadruplicities are so called because four zodiacal signs are assigned to each. Although two share a masculine (active, or positive) polarity, and two a feminine (passive, or negative) polarity, the four signs that make up a quadruplicity's group are otherwise dissimilar, not least because each has a different element. It is the ancient link between the Sun's annual cycle and the zodiacal cycle, which starts with Aries in the spring, and then marks out the passing of the four seasons as it progresses, that is believed to have given rise to the concept of the quadruplicities, as described by the English astrologer William Lilly in his work *Christian Astrology* (1647).

The Signs again are divided into Moveable [cardinal], Fixed and Common [mutable], Aries, Cancer, Libra, Capricorn are called moveable and Cardinal: moveable, because when the Sun enters into Aries and Libra, the Weather and Season of the Year quickly varies and changes; they are called Cardinal, because when the Sun enters into any of those Signs from that time we denominate the Quarters of the yeer. For from the Sun entering into Aries and Libra the Equinoctial or the Spring and Autumne [fall] arise; from the Sun his entrance into Cancer and Capricorn ariseth the Solstice of Summer and Winter.

The Fixed Signs do in order follow the Equinoctial and Tropicks; and they are called fixed, for that when Sun enters

*into them, the season of the year is fixed, and we do more evi-
dently perceive either Heat or Cold, Moysture or Drinesse. The
fixed Signes are these, Taurus, Leo, Scorpio, Aquarius.*

*Common [mutable] Signes are constitutes between moveable
[cardinal] and fixed, and retain a property or nature, pertaking
both with the preceding and consequent Sign: and they are
Gemini, Virgo, Sagittarius, Pisces. They are called By-corpo-
real or double bodied, because they represent two Bodies: as
Gemini two Twinnes, Pisces two Fishes.*

Right: *Vincent Van Gogh
was born under the sign
of Aries. He displayed not
only fiery creativity, but a
pioneering streak typical
of the cardinal nature.*

THE CARDINAL SIGNS:

The cardinal signs are
Aries (which is masculine
and fiery), Cancer (femi-
nine and watery), Libra
(masculine and airy), and
Capricorn (feminine and
earthy). Each cardinal sign heralds the start of a new season,
Aries (March 21 to April 20) signaling the beginning of spring,
Cancer (June 22 to July 22), that of summer, Libra (September
23 to October 22), the start of fall, and Capricorn (December
22 to January 19), the onset of winter.

Because their zodiacal signs initiate the seasons, cardinal-quadruplicity people are regarded as self-starters who cope well with change. They are also said to be pioneering, enterprising, and, because they usually take the initiative, to have leadership qualities. These decisive and ambitious, active and go-getting characters are motivated by the desire to achieve their goals as quickly as possible, and they channel all of the energy that they can muster into doing so. Their drive to get ahead can also make them rather self-centered, pushy, and bossy, however, and they typically insist on following their own path in life.

Reflecting the influence of the ruling planets, polarities, and elements associated with their respective zodiacal signs, they tend to take dissimilar approaches when asserting themselves: Arien people do so courageously; Cancerian characters, circumspectly; Libran personalities, charmingly; and Capricorn individuals, patiently and deliberately.

THE FIXED SIGNS: The fixed-quadruplicity signs are Taurus (which is feminine and earthy), Leo (masculine and fiery), Scorpio (feminine and watery), and Aquarius (masculine and airy). The reason why each is said to have a "fixed" nature is because its month falls in the middle of a season, when the weather is relatively unchanging: Taurus (April 21 to May 20) in spring, Leo (July 23 to August 22) in summer, Scorpio (October 23 to November 21) in fall, and Aquarius (January 20 to February 18) in winter.

Just as their zodiacal signs hold sway at times when each season is well established, so fixed-quadruplicity individu-

Right: Charles Darwin, born under the sign of Aquarius, demonstrated his fixed-quadruplicity determination during his years of scientific research. He focused his mind on sticking to the evidence as he saw it, rather than following received wisdom, in interpreting his findings.

als are considered to be capable consolidators who are blessed with remarkable powers of concentration. As well as having stable and loyal personalities, they are furthermore dedicated and determined people who hate to give up on anything or anyone to whom they have committed themselves. The downside of having a fixed quadruplicity is that they can be set in their ways, resistant to change, rigid and inflexible, and infuriatingly stubborn or egocentric.

Zodiacal bulls, lions, scorpions, and water-carriers manifest their fixed-quadruplicity characteristics slightly differently: Taureans are steady, but also bull-headed; Leos are constant, yet sometimes egotistical; and although Scorpio people are devoted, they cannot forget a slight; while Aquarians can be both single-minded and dogmatic.

THE MUTABLE SIGNS: The mutable-quadruplicity signs are Gemini (which is masculine and airy), Virgo (feminine and earthy), Sagittarius (masculine and fiery), and Pisces (a feminine, watery sign). "Mutable" means "changeable," and these signs are so named because they prevail at those times of year when the seasons are about to change: Gemini's zodiacal month (May 21 to June 21) coming at the end of spring, Virgo's (August 23 to September 22) occurring when summer is about to give way to fall, Sagittarius' (November 22 to December 21), when winter is on the verge of succeeding fall, and Pisces' month running from February 19 to March 20, when spring is in the winter air.

Mutable-quadruplicity Gemini, Virgo, Sagittarius, and Pisces people are consequently said to be adaptable individuals who are open to change, enjoy variety, and have a visionary's focus on the future. In addition, they are typically sociable, versatile, and cooperative people. Yet they can be so changeable or moody, restless or unstable that it may sometimes seem as though they have split personalities.

Left: Sagittarian Mark Twain loved to travel and get to know new people, impulses that tend to come naturally to those with a mutable quadruplicity.

Certain characteristics are particularly pronounced in those born under the signs of Gemini, Virgo, Sagittarius, and Pisces: Geminis have diverse interests, but tend to be fickle; Virgos are practical problem-solvers who find it hard to make up their minds; Sagittarians are adventurous and unreliable; and Pisceans are flexible, yet emotionally inconstant.

THE POLARITIES

Each zodiacal sign has a polarity, which ancient astrologers described as being either masculine or feminine. Although the words "masculine" and "feminine" still conjure up broadly accurate, if stereotypical, images of the characteristics imparted by the polarities (two opposing sets of attributes), some modern astrologers consider them sexist, and instead prefer to call the masculine polarity "active" or "positive," and the feminine polarity "passive" or "negative." Beginning with masculine-polarity Aries, which is followed by feminine-polarity Taurus, the two polarities alternate through the twelve signs of the zodiac.

The traits with which each polarity is associated, as well as the way in which the two polarities interact with one another, are similar to the yin (masculine, or positive) and yang (feminine, or negative) theory of Chinese Taoist and Confucian belief, namely that everything in the universe consists of these two forces in some measure, and that perfection is achieved when they are equally balanced and thus working in harmony with one another. Similarly, an integrated personality is said to be one in which neither polarity predominates, so that whatever our zodiacal sign's polarity, we should try to develop some of the opposite polarity's qualities.

THE MASCULINE, ACTIVE, OR POSITIVE POLARITY: Aries, Gemini, Leo, Libra, Sagittarius, and Aquarius are all masculine-polarity signs, Aries, Leo, and Sagittarius also being fire signs, and Gemini, Libra, and Aquarius, air signs.

Masculine-polarity individuals are extroverted, active, positive, and energetic types who are typically direct, confident, outgoing, and assertive. These pioneering people tend to act without thinking, behave in a dynamic and uninhibited way, and can be aggressive, forceful, and confrontational, too.

THE FEMININE, PASSIVE, OR NEGATIVE POLARITY: The feminine-polarity signs are Taurus, Cancer, Virgo, Scorpio, Capricorn, and Pisces, of which Taurus, Virgo, and Capricorn are earth signs, and Cancer, Scorpio, and Pisces are water signs.

Feminine-polarity individuals are introverted, passive, negative, and contemplative characters. They consider all of the options before taking action, prefer to work quietly behind the scenes, and have a talent for nurturing, be it others or ideas. Although they are intuitive and receptive, they can be shy, reticent, or withdrawn.

INTERPRETING THE PROFILES IN THIS BOOK

When looking up your birthday, and those of your family and friends, you may be surprised at the familiar descriptions you find associated with each date. Remember, though, that while learning astrology's secrets can help us to understand our personal characteristics and tendencies, planetary influences do not predetermine our destiny.

SYMBOL: THE RAM
CELESTIAL RULER: MARS
ELEMENT: FIRE
POLARITY: POSITIVE (MASCULINE)
QUADRUPLICITY: CARDINAL

ARIES

MARCH 21 TO APRIL 20 ♈

Aries, the zodiacal ram and a cardinal, active sign, gives the wheel of the astrological year a vigorous butt, setting it turning rapidly again after the stagnant winter months. Having kick-started spring with a fire sign's characteristic vitality, the headstrong ram charges ahead with unflagging energy. Those born under this sign are assertive, enterprising, and energetic, and are usually also buzzing with their martial ruling planet's electrifying forcefulness. In their rush to get ahead and achieve their ambitions, they may, however, ruthlessly ride roughshod over weaker souls, may intimidate others with their aggressive attitude, or may lead themselves into trouble through their own recklessness.

MARCH 21

UNCOMPROMISING PIONEERS

If today is your birthday, you have a pioneering mindset, an urgent drive to put forward your progressive ideas, and an uncompromising attitude. "Assertive" is often too mild a tag for someone as forceful as you. You relish a challenge, know no fear, and will not back down, even when—or especially when—the odds are stacked against you. Thankfully, although your brusque manner may sometimes offend others, you typically channel your prodigious energies into acting as a force for good.

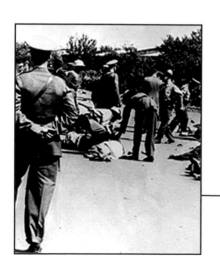

fAMOUS BIRTHS: Johann Sebastian Bach (1685); Antony Hopkins (1921); Gary Oldman (1958); Matthew Broderick (1962)

BRUTAL BLOODSHED
The small, but real, danger that instances of ugly aggression may manifest themselves on this day was tragically demonstrated in 1960, during South Africa's apartheid era, when government troops opened fire on protestors in Sharpeville, killing nearly seventy people.

ARIES

♂ ♈

Adventurous
Energetic
Determined

MARCH
22

FORCEFUL INITIATORS

Those born on March 22 are adventurous instigators whose ambition fires them up and whose energy, stamina, and bravery give them winning potential, especially when a spirit of adversity is added to the mix. Although these people are fiery characters, they possess remarkable self-discipline, too, and will therefore strive to reach their goals with unwavering determination. But brace yourself for roars of fury and frustration when things aren't going a March 22 individual's way. Be afraid!

FAMOUS BIRTHS: Marcel Marceau (1923); Stephen Joshua Sondheim (1930); William Shatner (1931); Reese Witherspoon (1976)

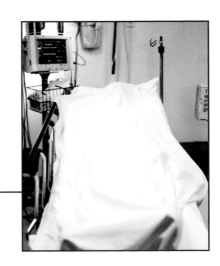

COURAGE AND CONVICTION

The first official "mercy killing" was carried out in Melbourne, Australia, on this day in 1988, illustrating the emotional toughness and willingness to take decisive action in the face of difficult ethical issues that are associated with March 22.

MARCH 23

TIRELESS TRAILBLAZERS

Thanks to their go-getting cardinal mode, March 23 people have the potential to rocket to the forefront of their fields, leaving the pack far behind as they power ahead in pursuit of their ambitious aims. Once they have decided on a course of action, few can match their Mars-bestowed bloody-mindedness, stamina, and courage. Self-centered they may be, yet others are drawn to their fiery charisma and the sizzling energy that crackles from their every pore.

FAMOUS BIRTHS: Juan Gris (1887); Erich Fromm (1900); Joan Crawford (1908); Roger Bannister (1929); Chaka Khan (1953)

STAR WARS
Reflecting the pioneering spirit and bold assertiveness that are linked with March 23, it was on this day in 1983 that President Reagan revealed the USA's Strategic Defense Initiative, an aggressively defensive military program that was popularly dubbed "Star Wars."

ARIES
♂ ♈

Creative
Resilient
Optimistic

MARCH
24

GUTSY GO-GETTERS

If you were born on this day, your fiery element infuses you with plenty of creative flair. But your most pronounced characteristics are probably the "can-do" attitude of a positive polarity, the vision and drive of a cardinal quadruplicity, and the mental toughness of your ruling planet, Mars. As a result, not only are you original and upbeat, but you're resilient and single-minded enough to stick doggedly to your long-term aims, regardless of what others may think of you and your ventures.

FAMOUS BIRTHS: William Morris (1834); Harry Houdini (1874); Steve McQueen (1930); Lara Flynn Boyle (1970)

JAMES THE RESOLUTE

King James VI of Scotland was not a popular successor to Elizabeth I when he assumed the English throne on this day in 1603. Maybe the qualities associated with March 24 assisted him, for he proved a firm ruler.

MARCH 25

*Willful
Creative
Expressive*

SINGLE-MINDED SURVIVORS

While their fiery element provides the spark of creativity that gives March 25 people their talent for expressing often painful life experiences though the medium of art, they are perhaps more remarkable for their Mars-bestowed resilience in the face of adversity. They also display their cardinal ambition and their positive-polarity dynamism. These are people with steely willpower who will bellow furiously when they suffer a body blow, but will then demonstrate true grit in turning the situation around.

FAMOUS BIRTHS: Arturo Toscanini (1867); Béla Bartók (1881); Aretha Franklin (1942); Elton John (1947); Sarah Jessica Parker (1965)

SCOTLAND'S CHAMPION
Robert the Bruce was crowned king of Scotland on this day in 1306, an appropriate date considering that his bravery would win Scotland its independence, despite King Edward I of England branding him a traitorous rebel.

ARIES

♂ ♈

Authoritative
Confident
Trailblazing

MARCH 26

INIMITABLE INDIVIDUALS

If this is your birthday, the powerful presence, uncompromising confidence, and compelling magnetism you exude means that you effortlessly command the attention and respect of others. Your innate authority, fierce individualism, and unshakable self-belief are the result of the interaction of assertive Mars, your uninhibited, positive polarity, and your ego-boosting element of fire. When combined with your self-starting, cardinal nature, this suggests that, as a natural-born trailblazer, you aren't afraid of antagonizing others—and you frequently do.

FAMOUS BIRTHS: Chico Marx (1891); Tennessee Williams (1911); Leonard Nimoy (1931); Diana Ross (1944); Keira Knightley (1985)

A LEADING LADY
Illustrating the pioneering nature of this day, on March 26, 1973, the first female to be hired as a stockbroker in England braved the previously all-male halls of the London Stock Exchange and began trading.

MARCH 27

OUTSPOKEN INDIVIDUALISTS

Two pronounced traits exhibited by those born on March 27 are their strong opinions and tendency to speak their minds, both Martian attributes. These individuals fear neither going out on a limb nor causing offense, so that others sometimes consider them eccentric or aggressive. They may be uncompromising and single-minded, thanks to the influence of Mars and their cardinal quadruplicity, but their fiery element and positive polarity ensure that they are generous, "can-do" livewires, too.

FAMOUS BIRTHS: Gloria Swanson (1897); Sarah Vaughan (1924); Quentin Tarantino (1963); Mariah Carey (1970)

NEW BLOOD
That the first effective, nondirect blood transfusion should have been carried out on this day in 1914 in Brussels, Belgium, is astrologically appropriate, for blood and its color are associated with Mars, the "Red Planet" and its namesake warrior deity.

ARIES

♂ ♈

*Disciplined
Headstrong
Passionate*

MARCH 28

REGIMENTED REBELS

A rebellious streak runs through those born on this day, perhaps because the combination of strong-willed Mars, an uncontainable, fiery element, a self-starting, cardinal quadruplicity, and a forceful, masculine polarity makes them so headstrong and passionate, as well as so resistant to conforming to society's norms. Yet their soldierly planetary ruler also instills self-discipline in his protégés, so that they have the potential to harness their considerable willpower and energy for constructive, not destructive, purposes.

FAMOUS BIRTHS: Maxim Gorky (1849); Flora Robson (1902); Dirk Bogarde (1921); Reba McEntire (1955); Vince Vaughan (1970)

MARTIAL FORCE
Reflecting the day's military-rebel flavor, Madrid fell on March 28, 1939, effectively ending the Spanish Civil War and heralding the fascist dictatorship of General Francisco Franco, whose rebellion against the ruling Popular Front had prompted the war's outbreak in 1936.

MARCH 29

ARIES

♈ ♂

Competitive
Motivated
Focused

AMBITIOUS ATHLETES

Most cardinal-quadruplicity Ariens are intent on getting ahead, and when a positive polarity's drive, a fiery element's energy, and soldier-deity Mars's relish of confrontation are added to the equation, the upshot is that March 29 people's preferred field of battle is often the sporting arena. Just as well, then, that these physical individuals are motivated and determined self-starters. A downside of sharing March 29's astrological makeup, however, is a tendency to turn relationships into rivalries.

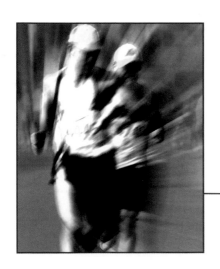

FAMOUS BIRTHS: Cy Young (1867); Eric Idle (1945); Elle MacPherson (1963); Lucy Lawless (1968); Jennifer Capriati (1976)

A MARATHON MISSION
Given this day's sporting affinities, March 29 was an auspicious date on which to launch the first London Marathon, with nearly seven thousand participants speeding, limping, and lurching toward the finishing line on that day in 1981.

ARIES

♂ ♈

Enterprising
Dynamic
Unconventional

MARCH 30

PASSIONATE PERFORMERS

If today is your birthday, true to your fiery and attention-grabbing element, you love being in the spotlight—but you are driven by far more than a desire for admiration. Indeed, your burning passion, enterprising, masculine-polarity dynamism, Martian fearlessness, and cardinal ambition together push you to test the boundaries of convention and, once unfettered, to go to extremes. Some may consider you confrontational and even reckless, but the world would be duller without vibrant livewires like you.

FAMOUS BIRTHS: Vincent van Gogh (1853); Tom Sharpe (1928); Warren Beatty (1937); Eric Clapton (1945); Celine Dion (1968)

CRAZY IN LOVE

Wild, attention-seeking behavior is one of the more unpleasant characteristics associated with this day, which marks the anniversary of John Hinckley's attempted assassination of President Ronald Reagan in 1981 in a deluded bid to impress the actress Jodie Foster.

MARCH 31

EARNEST EXPERIMENTERS

Although March 31 people are just as single-minded as other cardinal-quadruplicity Ariens, they are more likely to channel their fiery energy into encouraging ground-breaking ideas to flare into life than into firing up their tempers. Along with backbone and a fighter's zeal, they have inherited a dash of military discipline from their planetary ruler, making these determined individuals forces to be reckoned with. Yet given their intensity, others may perceive them as being a little humorless.

FAMOUS BIRTHS: Descartes (1596); Joseph Haydn (1732); Christopher Walken (1943); Al Gore (1948); Ewan McGregor (1971)

A TOWERING ACHIEVEMENT
The soaring ambition and enterprising energy that are astrological features of March 31 are epitomized by the Eiffel Tower, which its architect, Gustave Eiffel, unveiled in all of its glory on this day in 1889 in Paris, France.

ARIES

♂ ♈

Committed
Inspirational
Imaginative

STEELY STRATEGISTS

Do not be misled by their birth date: those born on April 1 are far from being fools. Their fiery passion and creativity may be more pronounced in some, while others may demonstrate more of Mars's charisma and leadership skills, but all share a cardinal quadruplicity's far-sighted ambition, as well as a positive polarity's confidence. As a result, these individuals know exactly where they are headed in life, and are utterly determined to succeed.

FAMOUS BIRTHS: Otto von Bismarck (1815); Sergei Rachmaninov (1873); Toshiro Mifune (1920); Debbie Reynolds (1932); Ali MacGraw (1938)

A SHOOTING STAR
Illustrating the pursuit of long-term goals that is favored by this day, it was on April 1, 1956, that Elvis Presley shot his first Hollywood screen test, for Paramount Studios. He went on to make thirty-one movies.

APRIL 2

ARIES
♈ ♂

Strong-willed
Brave
Innovative

fEARLESS fIGHTERS

Whether or not physical confrontation is integral to your life's work, if you were born on this day you're a battler and a true child of Mars, your planetary ruler. You instantly respond to a challenge without regard to the potential risks, a masculine-polarity trait that causes some to consider you reckless. And if your all-or-nothing, fiery element should come to the fore, you may even be self-destructive. Yet wherever you lead as an enterprising, cardinal pioneer, you'll find that others often follow.

fAMOUS BIRTHS: Charlemagne (742); Hans Christian Andersen (1805); Emile Zola (1840); Marvin Gaye (1939); Emmy Lou Harris (1947)

BREAKING BOUNDARIES

April 2 favors exploration and conquest, and maybe it was the day's astrological influences that directed explorer Juan Ponce de León to land on Florida's shore on this date in 1513 and to claim this "new" territory for Spain.

ARIES
♂ ♈

Assured
Resourceful
Impatient

APRIL
3

ENTERPRISING EXTREMISTS

Due to the extreme characteristics inherent in their birth influences, those born on April 3 are often found at opposite ends of the personality spectrum: some may display the smoldering intensity of their fiery element, while others may burn with impatience, for instance. All, however, share their masculine polarity's assertiveness, their cardinal quadruplicity's initiative, and Mars's iron will. Yet if they push the boundaries too far, they may end up being their own worst enemies.

FAMOUS BIRTHS: Washington Irving (1783); Marlon Brando and Doris Day (1924); Helmut Kohl (1930); Eddie Murphy (1961)

DICING WITH DEATH
One of the astrological messages imparted by April 3 is that an extreme lifestyle may result in an extreme end, and it was on this day in 1882 that the U.S. outlaw Jesse James was shot dead by Bob Ford.

APRIL
4

FEISTY FREEDOM-FIGHTERS

Whether it is adverse circumstances or personal demons that they are struggling to overcome, those born on April 4 seem defined by their fighting spirit. This dominant trait is the legacy of Mars, their ruling planet, while their passion is imparted by their element of fire, their polarity gives them their positive outlook, and their cardinal nature gives rise to their single-minded vision. Although their charisma attracts admirers, many April 4 people seem destined to remain loners.

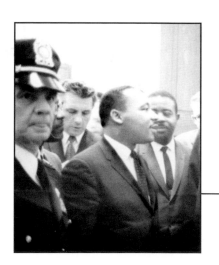

FAMOUS BIRTHS: Muddy Waters (1915); Maya Angelou (1928); Robert Downey, Jr. (1965); David Blaine (1973)

DYING FOR A DREAM

Confrontation and violence are, sadly, twin features of this day, and it was on April 4, 1968, that Dr. Martin Luther King, the segregation-era hero of the U.S. civil-rights' movement, was shot dead in Memphis, Tennessee, by James Earl Ray.

ARIES

♂ ♈

Lively
Cheerful
Driven

APRIL
5

HAWKS TURNED DOVES?

As proud astrological children of the fierce and fearless warrior god Mars, those ambitious individuals born on April 5 often project a forbidding image, particularly in their prime. The passage of the years usually has a mellowing effect on the intimidating traits associated with having a fiery element, however, and as they mature, many become increasingly patient, tolerant, and calm, enabling others better to appreciate their leadership qualities, "can-do," positive-polarity outlook, and cardinal initiative.

FAMOUS BIRTHS: Spencer Tracy (1900); Bette Davis (1908); Gregory Peck (1916); Colin Powell (1937); Agnetha Faltskög (1950)

ROMANTIC RAPPROCHEMENT
On a day that promises peaceful, yet courageous, solutions to inflammatory situations, Pocahontas, daughter of a Powhatan chief, married English settler John Rolfe in Virginia in 1614, a year when hostility between Native Americans and colonists prevailed.

APRIL 6

Creative
Expressive
Fearless

CHARISMATIC CREATIVES

It is the element of fire that gives you your breathtaking creativity, if you were born on April 6. And whether your natural aptitude is for expressing yourself through art, music, drama, or original ideas, you tend to channel your formidable, positive-polarity energy into expressing and promoting your forward-thinking, cardinal ideologies to a wider audience. Although your Mars-inspired fearlessness and outspokenness mark you out as a leader, these same qualities may sometimes arouse the hostility of others.

FAMOUS BIRTHS: Raphael (1483); Walter Huston (1884); André Previn (1929); Merle Haggard (1937); Bob Marley (1945)

OATH OF OFFICE
It was on this Mars-ruled day in 1841 that John Tyler—who had demonstrated outstanding leadership as vice-president—was inaugurated as the tenth U.S. president, following William Henry Harrison's untimely death.

ARIES

♂ ♈

Fiery
Dynamic
Headstrong

APRIL

7

DEMANDING DISCIPLINARIANS

Being children of Mars, April 7 individuals demand obedience from others, but because they are headstrong, cardinal-quadruplicity astrological rams who are fueled by their fiery emotions and turbocharged by their masculine-polarity dynamism, they often find it impossible to toe the line or to contain their temper themselves. Yet their flaws give them the brilliance of rough diamonds, and if they can only enlist, and sustain, Mars's soldierly stamina and self-control, stellar success is within their grasp.

FAMOUS BIRTHS: William Wordsworth (1770); Billie Holiday (1915); Jackie Chan (1954); Russell Crowe (1964)

FIRE AND BRIMSTONE

Mount Vesuvius—the Italian volcano that destroyed Pompeii in A.D. 79—erupted again on April 7, 1906, devastating the nearby town of Naples and graphically demonstrating the explosive nature of this fire-fueled day, and its potential to cause terrible damage.

APRIL 8

ARIES
♈ ♂

Commanding
Ambitious
Energetic

POWERFUL PERSONALITIES

All of those born on April 8 seem to display power in some way, be it by sheer force of personality or by literally flexing their muscles. Their commanding manner is the gift of Mars, their planetary ruler, but it is their cardinal quadruplicity that propels them ever forward. Their masculine polarity supplies them with forceful energy, while their fiery element empowers them to leave any barriers to progress smoldering in their wake.

FAMOUS BIRTHS: Betty Ford (1918); Jacques Brel (1929); Julian Lennon (1963); Robin Wright Penn (1966); Patricia Arquette (1968)

HITTING HOME

Demonstrating the physicality associated with April 8, the Atlanta Braves's "Hammerin'" Hank Aaron smashed the legendary Babe Ruth's record and won a place in the annals of baseball history by hitting his 715th home run on this day in 1974.

ARIES

♂ ♈

Headstrong
Courageous
Determined

APRIL
9

CONTRARY CHARACTERS

Those born on April 9 often exasperate others with their perceived cussedness or contrariness. They do not set out to frustrate or infuriate, however, but because their cardinal quadruplicity makes them headstrong, their masculine polarity, assertive, their fiery element, vital, and their martial planetary ruler, forceful, they sometimes come across as being willfully confrontational. They may be misunderstood, but the unwavering courage and determination that they show when pursuing their goals merits respect.

FAMOUS BIRTHS: Charles Pierre Baudelaire (1821); Hugh Marston Hefner (1926); Dennis Quaid (1954); Cynthia Nixon (1966)

COURAGEOUS CONCESSION
Deeds that demand mental strength are highlighted today, so it is appropriate that General Robert E. Lee should have taken the bitter step of surrendering his Confederate forces to General Ulysses S. Grant in Virginia on April 9, 1865.

APRIL 10

ARIES

♈ ♂

Resolute
Bold
Assured

MASTERFUL MINDS

Men who were born on April 10 exude masculinity, thanks to the influence of macho Mars, their ruling planet, which is reinforced by their masculine polarity, while women whose birthday falls on this day similarly display such traditionally "manly" traits as assertiveness, fearlessness, decisiveness, and drive. These are often hot-blooded types, too, their passion being the gift of their element of fire, but it is their cardinal quadruplicity that is responsible for their awesome determination.

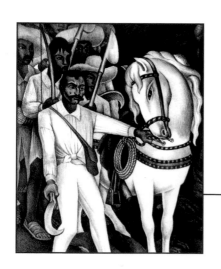

FAMOUS BIRTHS: Joseph Pulitzer (1847); Max Von Sydow (1929); Omar Sharif (1932); Afrika Bambaataa (1960)

DEADLY ACCURACY
Illustrating the brutally direct action that is likely on April 10, and acting on the orders of Mexico's president, Venustiano Carranza, soldiers shot dead the revolutionary leader Emiliano Zapata on this day in 1919, in the Mexican city of Chinameca.

ARIES

♂ ♈

Creative
Pioneering
Daring

APRIL
11

ARDENT ARTISTS

If this is your birthday, the influence of your fiery element is particularly pronounced in your personality. It fires you up with a burning passion to accomplish the challenging goals that, in true cardinal style, you have dared yourself to pursue and achieve. And it is again thanks to fire that you are likely to follow a highly original artistic or creative path through life, aided by the courage, dynamism, and pioneering spirit that are the joint gifts of your ruling planet, Mars, and your positive polarity.

FAMOUS BIRTHS: Charles Hallé (1819); Lizzie Bliss (1864); John Nash (1893); Jane Bolin (1908); Ethel Kennedy (1928)

GOING UP IN FLAMES

In a dazzling demonstration of April 11's fiery nature, the Apollo 13 spacecraft blasted off from Cape Canaveral on this day in 1970. A subsequent explosion in the service module caused the lunar mission to be aborted, however.

APRIL 12

IMPOSING INNOVATORS

Although the steely input of Mars means that April 12 people are prepared to challenge and confront if necessary, they prefer to eschew conflict and instead to channel their electrifying, active-polarity energy into more positive ventures. What's more, the combination of their freedom-seeking element of fire and pioneering, cardinal quadruplicity gives them an appetite for experimentation and an abhorrence of boundaries, the upshot being that these bright sparks have the potential to be creative geniuses.

fAMOUS BIRTHS: Maria Callas (1923); Herbie Hancock (1940); David Letterman (1947); Claire Danes (1979)

PATENTLY PROGRESSIVE
Illustrating the window of opportunity that opens on April 12 for groundbreaking advances, it was on this day in 1988 that a life form was first patented, namely a mouse that had been genetically modified by Harvard scientists.

ARIES

♂ ♈

Impatient
Confident
Intrepid

APRIL 13

DASHING DAREDEVILS

There is an air of danger about the larger-than-life characters whose birthday is April 13, perhaps because their fiery element causes them to crackle with impatience, or maybe because fearless Mars, their planetary ruler, stiffens their sinews and urges them to be adventurous to the point of recklessness. Add their cardinal qualities of ambition and determination to the mix, along with the confidence of a positive polarity, and there's little that these swashbuckling go-getters won't attempt.

FAMOUS BIRTHS: Thomas Jefferson (1743); Butch Cassidy (1866); Samuel Barclay Beckett (1906); Al Green (1946)

DAREDEVIL SPIRIT
Born Robert LeRoy Parker on this day in 1866, Butch Cassidy lived an unusually eventful life that exemplified the reckless, ambitious, and determined characteristics of those ruled by fearless Mars and blazing with fire's vitality.

APRIL 14

DRAMATIS PERSONAE

If all the world's a stage, those born on April 14 are determined to be in the center of it, basking in the limelight, and wowing their audience with their brio and daring. Their attention-seeking tendencies are mainly the result of having fire as an element, while their natural exuberance and extroversion are part and parcel of having a positive polarity. Their desire to tackle challenging roles proves that they are worthy children of Mars.

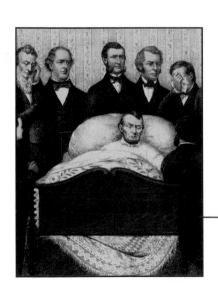

FAMOUS BIRTHS: John Gielgud (1904); Loretta Lynn (1935); Robert Carlyle (1961); Sarah Michelle Gellar (1977)

DEADLY DESTINY?

This day is linked with all things theatrical, but its rulership by Mars threatens bloodshed. Was it therefore inevitable that President Abraham Lincoln should have been assassinated by John Wilkes Booth at Ford's Theater, Washington, D.C., on April 14, 1865?

ARIES
♂ ♈

Motivated
Resilient
Original

APRIL 15

ADVENTUROUS SELF-STARTERS

Of all the astrological influences that contribute to April 15 people's characters, perhaps it is their enterprising, cardinal quadruplicity that is the most evident. For these individuals are motivated self-starters who not only set themselves ambitious goals, but revel in surpassing their own high expectations. In this, they are aided by their masculine-polarity confidence and Mars-derived resilience, and are abetted by their appetite for experimentation, a trait that is associated with the element of fire.

FAMOUS BIRTHS: Leonardo da Vinci (1452); Henry James (1843); Elizabeth Montgomery (1933); Emma Thompson (1959)

A CATASTROPHIC COLLISION
If days had mottoes, "Full steam ahead" would suit April 15. Yet following an undeviating course can cause disaster, as was demonstrated on this day in 1912, when the Titanic collided with an iceberg and sank.

APRIL 16

ECCENTRIC GENIUSES

If this is your birthday, it's just as well that you have inherited the toughness of Mars, that your positive polarity gives you self-belief, and that your cardinal nature enables you to remain focused on your goals. You're probably an ingenious individual, but others often brand you an oddball. It is your element of fire that provides your creative spark, which, like a flickering flame, may lead you in unexpected, but ultimately amazing, directions.

FAMOUS BIRTHS: Wilbur Wright (1867); Charlie Chaplin (1889); Spike Milligan (1918); Martin Lawrence (1965); Selena Quintanilla (1971)

REBELS ROUTED

A battle of one sort or another is always possible on a Mars-governed day, and the last on British soil took place on April 16, 1746, when the Duke of Cumberland's forces defeated the Jacobite army of Bonnie Prince Charlie.

ARIES

♂ ♈

Disciplined
Authoritative
Uninhibited

APRIL 17

AUTHORITATIVE ANTIAUTHORITARIANS

Although remarkably self-disciplined, thanks to their martially minded planetary ruler, the independent individuals born on April 17 rebel against submitting to another's control. Maybe it is due to their freedom-seeking, fiery element that they resist being contained, or perhaps it is their uninhibited polarity that prompts them to challenge authority. The irony is that once in a position of power, they themselves display strong authoritarian tendencies.

FAMOUS BIRTHS: J.P. Morgan (1837); Nikita Khrushchev (1894); William Holden (1918); Sean Bean (1958)

CUBAN CHALLENGERS

That this is a day on which confrontational, antiauthoritarian tendencies may manifest themselves was illustrated on April 17, 1961, when an antirevolutionary band of Cuban exiles landed at the Bay of Pigs, Cuba, intent on overthrowing Fidel Castro, Cuba's leader.

APRIL 18

♈ ♂

Lively
Forceful
Vigorous

AMBITIOUS CREATIVES

Those born on this day combine creativity (the gift of their element of fire) with ambition (a cardinal-quadruplicity characteristic), and frequently to devastating effect. April 18 people know what they want, know how to get it, and are prepared to unleash the full force of their positive-polarity vigor and Mars-bequeathed forcefulness on the world in their quest to achieve their aims. Single-minded and driven they may be, but their vitality and passion attract others.

FAMOUS BIRTHS: Lucrezia Borgia (1480); Hayley Mills (1946); Rick Moranis (1954); Melissa Joan Hart (1976)

ONWARD AND UPWARD
The glamorous actress Grace Kelly had already conquered Hollywood when she married Prince Rainier III of Monaco on this day in 1956, thus illustrating both the stellar potential and the union of artistry and power that are highlighted on April 18.

ARIES

♂ ♈

Courageous
Innovative
Spirited

APRIL
19

CHALLENGERS AND CREATORS

All are energetic and decisive, but two distinct characters are otherwise associated with April 19, depending on which astrological influence predominates. Mars prevails in one personality type, who is typically someone of courage and integrity who is not afraid to stand up for what he or she believes to be right. And the element of fire colors the nature of the other April 19 temperament, resulting in highly creative individuals who defy stereotyping.

FAMOUS BIRTHS: Eliot Ness (1903); Jayne Mansfield (1932); Tim Curry (1946); Paloma Picasso (1949); Ashley Judd (1968)

RIGHTFUL RESISTANCE

April 19, 1775, was the day on which British troops opened fire on minutemen at Lexington, Massachusetts, thus initiating America's Revolutionary War and forcing the colonists to assume the martial traits that are associated with this date.

APRIL 20

CHARISMATIC RISK-TAKERS

If this is your birthday, on the cusp of Taurus, the most forceful elements inherent in each of your birth influences merge within your personality, and you project yourself extremely powerfully. As a result, you may come across as rash, aggressive, uncompromising, headstrong, and self-centered—particularly if Mars has your head. Otherwise, however, you may be adventurous and willing to take risks that more cautious characters would deem unacceptable, but you are still heartwarmingly generous, exuberant, and positive.

FAMOUS BIRTHS: Napoleon III of France (1808); Adolf Hitler (1889); Joan Miro (1893); Jessica Lange (1949); Luther Vandross (1951)

AN AUSTRALIAN ADVENTURE
Illustrating the appetite for exploration that is a feature of April 20, on this day in 1770, English seafarer Captain James Cook first sighted the territory that he subsequently named New South Wales as he skirted Australia aboard the Endeavour.

SYMBOL: The bull
CELESTIAL RULER: Venus
ELEMENT: Earth
POLARITY: Negative (feminine)
QUADRUPLICITY: Fixed

TAURUS

APRIL 21 TO MAY 20 ♉

The sayings "like a red rag to a bull" and "like a bull in a china shop" imply that bulls are invariably easily provoked, aggressive, and destructive. Yet when trying to understand those born under the sign of Taurus, the astrological bull, it's important to remember that bulls are domesticated animals, placid unless threatened. Taureans derive their balanced temperament from Venus, the ruling planet that is also responsible for their occasional indolence, while their passive polarity makes them thoughtful and receptive, but risk-averse. Having earth as an element makes them practical and patient, with a sensual streak. The bullheadedness, or stubbornness, of astrological bulls is a result of their fixed quadruplicity.

APRIL 21

♉ ♀

Tenacious
Hardworking
Charming

STICKLERS WHO SPARKLE

Perhaps the most obvious Taurean trait shared by April 21 people is their remarkable tenacity, caused by the merging of their steady, earthy element and their fixed quadruplicity, which promotes persistence. It is due to these two astrological influences, too, that they are hardworking and committed individuals, who may, however, sometimes seem miserly, inflexible, and, when their passive polarity prevails, overly negative. Yet when they are able to relax, their charming, fun-loving Venusian side becomes delightfully evident.

FAMOUS BIRTHS: Charlotte Brontë (1816); Queen Elizabeth II of Britain (1926); Iggy Pop (1947); Andie Macdowell (1958)

LAYING THE GROUNDWORK

Legend says that it was on this day of the sign of the astrological bull in 753 B.C. that Romulus founded Rome. He marked out the square footprint of his city with a plow that was pulled by a white cow and a white bull.

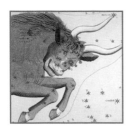

TAURUS

♀ ♉

Committed
Earnest
Dedicated

APRIL 22

COMMITTED CHARACTERS

If those born on this day have one characteristic in common, it is a fixed-quadruplicity's commitment. While the influence of hedonistic Venus may be particularly pronounced in those April 22 individuals who cultivate a party-animal lifestyle, some may demonstrate the earnestness and tenacity that are earthy traits. The type of philosophical thoughtfulness that points to a passive polarity may be especially evident in others. But all remain totally dedicated to their life's work.

FAMOUS BIRTHS: Immanuel Kant (1724); Nikolai Lenin (1870); Yehudi Menuhin (1916); Jack Nicholson (1937)

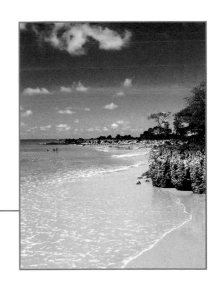

LAND AHOY!

That land is highlighted by this earth-associated day was demonstrated in 1500, when the Portuguese navigator and explorer Pedro Álvares Cabral became the first European to catch sight of the coastline of the territory that would eventually be named Brazil.

APRIL 23

*Artistic
Productive
Introverted*

SELF-CONTAINED ARTISTS

If today is your birthday, you exhibit two outstanding qualities. The first, the gift of Venus, is your artistic talent, and the second is your impressive productivity. For this you have your element of earth to thank, along with your fixed nature, which keeps your nose to the grindstone. Those close to you may chide you for prioritizing your work above your personal life, however, while your passive-polarity introversion can also make you seem uninterested in the people around you.

FAMOUS BIRTHS: William Shakespeare (1564); Joseph Mallard William Turner (1775); Sergei Prokofiev (1891); Michael Moore (1954)

A SCIENTIFIC BREAKTHROUGH
Venus aside, all of April 23's astrological influences aid research, and on this day in 1984 it was announced that a team of U.S. virologists led by Robert Gallo had discovered HIV (then called HTLV-III), the virus responsible for AIDS.

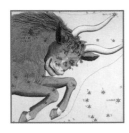

TAURUS

♀♉

Creative
Thoughtful
Persistent

APRIL 24

EARNEST ACHIEVERS

If the influence of Venus is particularly pronounced in those people whose birthday falls on April 24, they may win plaudits for their work in the arts. Whether or not they end up being fêted in this field, however, their thoughtful, feminine polarity, determined, fixed nature, and diligent, earthy element together suggest that it is far more important to them that their views are taken seriously and that their persistence and hard work are recognized.

FAMOUS BIRTHS: William I, Prince of Orange (1533); Shirley MacLaine (1934); John Williams (1941); Barbra Streisand (1942); Jean Paul Gaultier (1952)

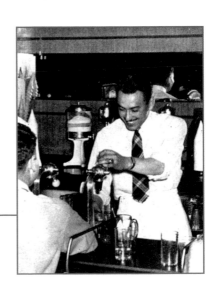

A SPARKLING ACCOMPLISHMENT

April 24 is ruled by Venus, and given her sweet, sensual, and self-indulgent nature, it seems apt that Jacob Ebert, of Ohio, and George Dulty, of West Virginia, should have patented the first soda fountain on this day in 1833.

APRIL 25

Considerate
Resilient
Patient

GRACEFUL SURVIVORS

However tough their early years, and whatever difficulties they encounter later in life, April 25 people have the potential to overcome their problems, and to do so with remarkable grace and good humor, thanks to Venus. They also show plenty of consideration for others, due to their feminine polarity. But these are no doormats, for their fixed nature fortifies them with steely determination, and their earthy element supplies them with endless reserves of resilience, patience, and tenacity.

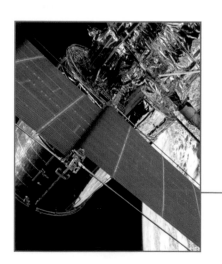

fAMOUS BIRTHS: Oliver Cromwell (1559); Guglielmo Marconi (1874; Ella Fitzgerald (1918); Al Pacino (1940); Renée Zellweger (1969)

STAYING fOCUSED

Perseverance in the face of adversity (a fixed-quadruplicity trait) is starred on April 25, and N.A.S.A. scientists demonstrated this when, following the launch of the Hubble Space Telescope on this day in 1990, a disastrous—but fixable—focusing fault became apparent.

TAURUS

♀ ♉

Introspective
Resolute
Imaginative

STUBBORN STAYERS

If this is your birthday, you have been blessed with the artistic streak that is a hallmark of Venus, your ruling planet. Your softer side may be reinforced by your inward-looking, feminine polarity, but you are nevertheless a real tough cookie. Having a fixed nature means that you are staunchly change-resistant, while your element of earth supplies your steady resolve. All in all, saying that you stick to your guns is quite an understatement!

FAMOUS BIRTHS: Marcus Aurelius (AD 121); Ferdinand Delacroix (1798); Rudolf Hess (1894); Duane Eddy (1938); Bobby Rydell (1942)

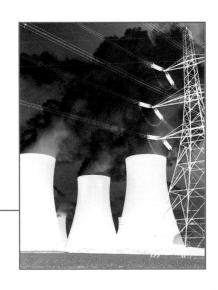

DOGGED DENIALS

When a catastrophic explosion occurred at a Ukrainian nuclear power station in Chernobyl, then part of the U.S.S.R., on April 26, the day's negative polarity and fixed quadruplicity were evident in the authorities' repeated denial of the accident's disastrous consequences.

APRIL 27

Logical
Practical
Contemplative

CAPABLE COORDINATORS

If April 27 individuals have anything in common, it is their calm, logical, and hands-on approach to life. Their down-to-earth personalities and practical bent are down to their earthy element, while their passive polarity is responsible for the caring and contemplative characteristics that surface every so often, and the gifts of their fixed quadruplicity include a flair for coordination and consolidation. It's not all hard work, though, for Venus contributes a craving for, and appreciation of, creature comforts.

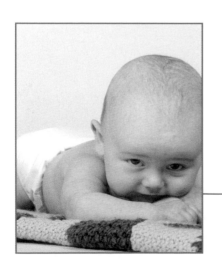

FAMOUS BIRTHS: Mary Wollstonecraft Godwin (1759); Samuel Morse (1791); Ulysses S. Grant (1822); Mica Paris (1969)

PATENTLY PRACTICAL

Its association with the element of earth suggests that April 27 has a practical "personality," which is why it is not surprising that R.C. Duncan should have patented "Pampers," the disposable diaper that he invented, on this day in 1965.

TAURUS

♀ ♉

Forward-thinking
Gracious
Committed

APRIL 28

OUTSTANDING ORGANIZERS

That you are a are born organizer, if you were born on this day, is due to the interaction of all of your birth influences. While you derive your talent for planning, your patience, and your productivity from your earthy element, your fixed nature keeps you committed to a project, whatever problems may arise. It is thanks to your feminine polarity, and to Venus, that you usually remain graciously receptive to others' suggestions while steering your steady onward course.

FAMOUS BIRTHS: James Monroe (1758); Saddam Hussein (1937); Jay Leno (1950); Penelope Cruz (1974); Jessica Alba (1981)

AN UNCOMPROMISING CLASH
April 28 is a fixed-quadruplicity day, and maybe its obstinacy was especially pervasive in 1789, when the crew of H.M.S. Bounty, led by Fletcher Christian, mutinied against William Bligh, the ship's commander, who lacked Venus's conciliatory charm.

APRIL 29

TAURUS

♉ ♀

*Energetic
Meticulous
Cautious*

RESPECTED ROLE MODELS

Others tend to respect those born on this day because of their phenomenal, earthy productivity and meticulousness, as well their fixed-quadruplicity staying power. That they are sometimes regarded as being sticks-in-the-mud is a misperception, because there is no question that Venus prompts them to relax, let their hair down, and have fun when appropriate. Due to the fact that their feminine polarity makes them shy and cautious, though, they only loosen up when they are with people whom they trust.

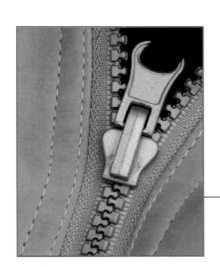

FAMOUS BIRTHS: Arthur Wellesley, Duke of Wellington (1769); Jerry Seinfeld (1955); Daniel Day-Lewis (1957); Uma Thurman (1970)

A HOOKLESS HELPER

Bearing in mind that April 29 is influenced by practical earth, it seems apt that Gideon Sundbach, a Swedish–American engineer, should have patented the "Hookless 2," today better known as the zipper, on this day in 1913.

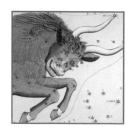

TAURUS

♀ ♉

Peacable
Straightforward
Obstinate

APRIL 30

INDIVIDUALS OF INTEGRITY

There is enough of Venus in your personality, if this is your birthday, to ensure that you are peaceable and shrink from offending others, and your passive polarity makes you open to others' opinions. But when push comes to shove, you will always remain true to yourself. While it is your earthy element that causes you to be as straight as an arrow (and therefore also a little predictable), it is your fixed mode that gives you your iron firmness and your obstinacy.

FAMOUS BIRTHS: Willie Nelson (1933); Bobby Vee (1943); Merrill Osmond (1953); Jane Campion (1954); Kirsten Dunst (1982)

NO SURRENDER!

The German dictator Adolf Hitler and his bride, Eva Braun, committed suicide on April 30, 1945, in Berlin rather than surrender to Soviet troops. Was Hitler's uncompromising action, and his wife's loyal one, influenced by this day's fixed quadruplicity?

MAY
1

TAURUS
♉ ♀

Sensible
Constant
Caring

POLISHED PRAGMATISTS

If you were born on this day, the sensible, level-headed approach to life that is characteristic of your element of earth, along with your fixed qualities of determination and commitment, cause you to be someone upon whom others can always rely for advice and support. Although the additional input of Venus can give you an aura of sophistication that makes you seem a little unapproachable, underneath your polished persona lies a rather shy and caring, feminine-polarity center.

FAMOUS BIRTHS: Joseph Addison (1672); Mary Jones (1830); Jack Paar (1918); Joseph Heller (1923); Joanna Lumley (1946)

FIRM FOUNDATIONS
The combination of Venus's urbane esthetic tastes and the solidly supportive foundations provided by the element of earth can be seen in the Empire State Building, New York's Art Deco icon, which was officially opened on May 1, 1931.

TAURUS

♀ ♉

Artistic
Grounded
Capable

MAY 2

DOWN-TO-EARTH DOERS

The Venusian glamour that many of those born on this day exude—be it due to their immaculately groomed appearance or their affinity with all things artistic—often masks their fundamentally down-to-earth natures. Not only do May 2 people enjoy rolling up their sleeves and setting to work in typically grounded, earthy, hands-on fashion, but their passive polarity makes them thoughtful and cautious, while their fixed quadruplicity ensures that they are both capable and committed.

FAMOUS BIRTHS: Empress Catherine II (the Great) of Russia (1729); Jerome K. Jerome (1859); Bianca Jagger (1945)

A TRIUMPH OF PLANNING
In Britain, the Labour Party swept to victory in the general election that was held on this day in 1997, a feat that many attributed to its exemplary planning, dedication, receptiveness, and polished image (earthy, fixed, feminine, and Venusian characteristics).

MAY 3

♉ ♀

Pragmatic
Ambitious
Diligent

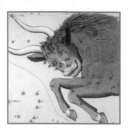

HARD-WORKING HEDONISTS

If this is your birthday, you appear to be a happy hedonist due to the influence of Venus—but appearances can deceive. While you are blessed with the goddess's grace and artistry, you are, at heart, a hard-nosed pragmatist. Your ambition and diligence are due to your earthy element, which, in combination with your introspective, passive polarity, make you a formidable planner. You will follow the career or life path that you have set yourself in your own unwavering, fixed-nature way.

FAMOUS BIRTHS: Niccolo Machiavelli (1469); Dodie Smith (1896); Bing Crosby (1904); Sugar Ray Robinson (1921); James Brown (1928)

LOOKING AHEAD
The astrological influences that prevail on this day, and earth in particular, aid organization, and it was on May 3, 1988, that the White House confirmed that First Lady Nancy Reagan often consulted astrologers when planning President Ronald Reagan's schedule.

TAURUS

♀ ♉

Stylish
Polite
Self-contained

MAY
4

STEELY CHARMERS

When they first encounter May 4 individuals, people are generally charmed by their stylish appearance and exquisite manners, evidence that their planetary ruler is Venus. Others may be impressed by their air of self-containment—a feminine-polarity trait—or by their remarkable efficiency, the hallmark of the element of earth. That said, and although they may not be immediately obvious, perhaps among the strongest May 4 characteristics are a fixed quadruplicity's unshakeable determination and bullish stubbornness.

FAMOUS BIRTHS: Sylvia Pankhurst (1882); Eric Sykes (1923); Audrey Hepburn (1929); Keith Haring (1958); Mike Dirnt (1972)

LADIES' DAY
Margaret Thatcher was officially proclaimed Britain's first female prime minister on this goddess-ruled, feminine-polarity day in 1979. Maybe May 4's fixed quadruplicity and earthy element contributed to the "Iron Lady's" resolute, no-nonsense premiership style.

MAY 5

♉ ♀

Consistent
Focused
Level-headed

STEADFAST SOFTIES

If you were born on May 5, it is thanks to your fixed quadruplicity that you remain staunchly true to whatever is most important to you, be it your loved ones, your career, or your beliefs—or all of the above. This birth influence is primarily responsible for your awesome powers of concentration, too, while your earthy element causes you to be a clear-sighted realist. You may be a pragmatist, but Venus and your feminine polarity make you surprisingly soft-hearted and indulgent on occasions, too.

FAMOUS BIRTHS: Søren Aabye Kierkegaard (1813); Karl Marx (1818); Tammy Wynette (1942); Annette Bening (1959)

FOREVER AFTER
When the exiled Napoleon Bonaparte died on this day in 1821, his dying words were: "France, the Army, head of the Army, Joséphine..." His devotion—to his country, his soldiers, and his ex-wife—is a fixed-quadruplicity characteristic.

TAURUS

♀ ♉

Seductive
Stubborn
Responsible

COMPELLING CHARACTERS

Those born on May 6 attract others' attention—and because they have an inward-looking, feminine polarity, often quite unconsciously so—whether it be on account of their seductive, Venusian charm or their stubborn, fixed-nature refusal to budge from a firmly held view. Their astrological birthright includes many blessings and benefits, but because these people's element is hardworking, responsible earth, they tend to be grounded grafters and givers rather than airy idlers and takers.

fAMOUS BIRTHS: Sigmund Freud (1856); Rudolph Valentino (1895); Orson Welles (1915); Tony Blair (1953); George Clooney (1961)

GOING UNDERGROUND
The element of earth is associated with this day, making May 6 an apt choice for the official opening, in 1994, of the Channel Tunnel, the marvel of engineering that was bored through the seabed to link England and France.

MAY 7

TAURUS

♉ ♀

Determined
Romantic
Dreamy

THINKERS AND DREAMERS

If today is your birthday, you probably conform to one of two types, or else have two distinct sides to your character. On the one hand, you may be a logical and practical thinker who demonstrates dogged determination, thanks to your earthy element and fixed nature. On the other hand, you may be a romantic, artistic child of Venus, your feminine-polarity gentleness causing you to shrink from conflict and, if necessary, to take refuge in delicious, sometimes escapist, daydreams.

FAMOUS BIRTHS: David Hume (1711); Johannes Brahms (1833); Peter Ilich Tchaikovsky (1840); Maria Eva Perón (1919)

A VICTORY FOR VENUS

One of the qualities associated with Venus is a desire for peace, and maybe the goddess's conciliatory influence prevailed on this day in 1945, when Germany surrendered to the Allies, thus ending World War II in the European theater.

TAURUS

♀ ♉

Resolute
Nurturing
Responsible

SENSIBLE SUPPORTERS

May 8 personalities are typically the product of the inter-action between their "hard" and "soft" birth influences. While their element of earth and fixed quadruplicity together cause these individuals to be straightforward and resolute, Venus and their feminine polarity ensure that they are both tolerant and nurturing when need be. As a result, others often turn to them for valuable direction and support, and although they are reluctant leaders, their sense of responsibility usually prevails.

FAMOUS BIRTHS: Harry S. Truman (1884); David Attenborough (1926); Sonny Liston (1932); Alex Van Halen (1955)

JAW-JAW, NOT WAR-WAR
The planet Venus is said to exert a peace-promoting influence over earthlings, so it is not surprising that Cuba and the Soviet Union should have established diplomatic relations on May 8—a date that is ruled by Venus—in 1960.

MAY 9

 TAURUS

Cautious
Eloquent
Obstinate

PRUDENT POETS

Having a caution-bestowing, feminine polarity, and, in earth, an element that prompts them to believe that actions speak louder than words, means that May 9 individuals tend to keep their opinions to themselves. When they do feel compelled to speak out, however, their Venusian side often becomes evident, be it in their conciliatory approach or their elegant language. But it is their fixed nature that dominates when they flip into their obstinate mode.

FAMOUS BIRTHS: John Brown (1800); J.M. Barrie (1860); Howard Carter (1873); Alan Bennett (1934); James L. Brooks (1940); Candice Bergen (1946); Billy Joel (1949)

FEMALE EMANCIPATION
May 9 has both a feminine polarity and a goddess for a planetary ruler, and it consequently seems fitting that women were first permitted to vote, and stand, in a Bahraini election (for municipal councils) on this day in 2002.

TAURUS

♀ ♉

Creative
Supportive
Realistic

MAY 10

ACCIDENTAL ACTIVISTS

If this is your birthday, you are Venus-influenced and artistically inclined. You probably don't intend to become a campaigner for a common cause, but that could well be your destiny. Thanks to your feminine polarity and earthy element, you are a good listener with a supportive streak, and when you're approached for help, you will spend long hours patiently thinking up a practical solution to a pressing problem. You will then strive to implement this in characteristically adamant, fixed-quadruplicity style.

FAMOUS BIRTHS: John Wilkes Booth (1838); Fred Astaire (1899); David O. Selznick (1902); Sid Vicious (1957); Bono (1960)

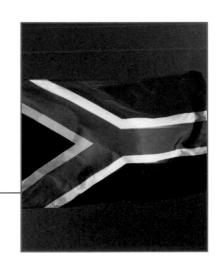

AN APPEASING PRESIDENT

On Nelson Mandela's inauguration as the first black president of South Africa—which occurred on May 10, 1994, a date presided over by peace-bringing Venus—he vowed to work tirelessly for the reconciliation of his post-apartheid-era, "rainbow nation's" citizens.

MAY 11

TAURUS

Courteous
Calm
Loyal

CHARMING CONCILIATORS

Venus's influence is particularly pronounced in those whose birthday falls on May 11, be it on account of their artistic flair, their beautiful manners, their chic appearance, or their desire to bring harmony wherever there is conflict. As well as admiring such Venusian accomplishments, their friends are often grateful for May 11 individuals' passive-polarity interest in others and earthy level-headedness and loyalty. Even so, there are occasions when their fixed-nature stubbornness is utterly infuriating.

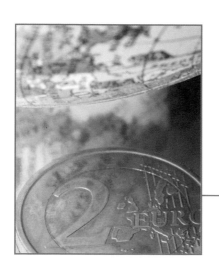

FAMOUS BIRTHS: Irving Berlin (1888); Salvador Dalí (1904); Phil Silvers (1912); Randy Quaid (1950); Natasha Richardson (1963)

COINING IT

With Venus, May 11's ruling planet, being associated with harmony and materialism, maybe it was no coincidence that the first euro—the basic unit of the European Economic and Monetary Union's currency—should have been minted on this day in 1998.

TAURUS

♀ ♉

Sensual
Pensive
Lazy

MAY 12

ROBUST ROMANTICS

If you were born on this day, Venus has cloaked you with such polish, and has given you such a romantic air of mystique, that your steely core is not immediately obvious. Yet you are a personality of substance, ranging from your earthy, no-nonsense, yet sensual, approach to life through your feminine-polarity pensiveness and fixed-quadruplicity determination. That you can also be lazy to the point of inertia is down to the combination of all four birth influences.

FAMOUS BIRTHS: Dante Gabriel Rossetti (1828); Katharine Hepburn (1907); Burt Bacharach (1929); Jason Biggs (1978)

A WHITE WEDDING
The goddess Venus is a real romantic, so her planetary namesake must have beamed down on Rolling Stone Mick Jagger and Bianca Perez Morena de Macias when they married on this Venus-ruled day in St. Tropez, France, in 1971.

MAY 13

FIGURES OF FORTITUDE

Life isn't always easy for those born on May 13, not least because these conscientious, earthy types believe in doing things right and consequently won't cut corners or take short-cuts. However, their patience and fixed-nature perseverance are usually rewarded—and applauded. And thanks to Venus, these people never forget how to laugh and have fun, however grim their circumstances, nor do they lose the gentle, caring qualities that come from having a feminine polarity.

FAMOUS BIRTHS: Georges Braque (1882); Daphne du Maurier (1907); Harvey Keitel (1939); Stevie Wonder (1950)

FOUNDING FATHERS

That May 13's element is earth was underlined on this day in 1607, when river-borne members of the English London Company selected the North American site on which they would found "James Cittie," which subsequently evolved into Jamestown, Virginia.

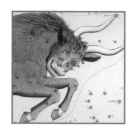

Taurus

♀ ♉

Well-prepared
Diligent
Amicable

MAY 14

COMMITTED CONSOLIDATORS

Maybe it is due to their fixed quadruplicity that May 14 people take a long-term view of life. They are certainly ambitious, due to their element of earth, which makes them sensible and diligent, too, so that they will typically work hard over time to build up a solid body of work. And although, having a passive polarity, they are not especially outgoing, Venus encourages them to form relaxed relationships, and to enjoy entertaining others.

fAMOUS BIRTHS: Gabriel Daniel Fahrenheit (1686); George Lucas (1944); David Byrne (1952); Tim Roth (1961); Cate Blanchett (1969)

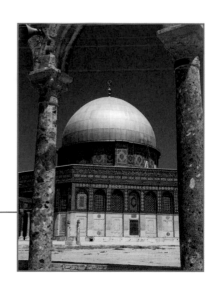

BUILDING A NATION
The qualities associated with this day include an earthy element's groundwork and a fixed quadruplicity's dedication, and it therefore seems apt that David Ben-Gurion should have announced the establishment of the state of Israel on May 14, 1948.

MAY 15

DEDICATED CRAFTSPEOPLE

The unique interaction of your birth influences gives you deep distinction, if today is your birthday. First, there is Venus, who instills an attraction to the arts in you; then there is your feminine polarity, which encourages introspection. Add your earthy element to the mix, and you are a patient personality who is good with your hands; and finally, factor in your fixed quadruplicity, and concentration and commitment stand out as further formidable qualities of yours.

FAMOUS BIRTHS: L. Frank Baum (1856); James Mason (1909); Jasper Johns (1930); Brian Eno (1948); Mike Oldfield (1953)

MOVING IN HARMONY
Was it solely due to serendipity that, in 1618, on a day ruled by Venus, the planet associated with harmony, German astronomer Johannes Kepler should have discovered his third law of planetary motion, which he published in Harmonices Mundi (1619)?

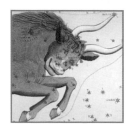

TAURUS

♀ ♉

Amusing
Passionate
Thorough

MAY 16

GENUINE ENTERTAINERS

Having the art-loving, people-pleasing Venus as a fairy godmother indicates that May 16 personalities are born entertainers. It is not that they are attention-craving lightweights—on the contrary, their passive polarity can give them an aversion to the limelight—but rather that they have fallen under art's spell, and if others appreciate their passion, all well and good. Take their earthy thoroughness and fixed-nature dedication into account, and there is real substance behind these people's charming style.

FAMOUS BIRTHS: Henry Fonda (1905); Liberace (1919); Pierce Brosnan (1953); Krist Novoselic (1965); Tori Spelling (1973)

OSCAR NIGHT
That Venus, this day's planetary ruler, is linked with artistic appreciation was emphasized on May 16, 1929, when the winners of the very first Academy Awards were announced at a banquet held at the Hollywood Roosevelt Hotel in Los Angeles.

MAY 17

♉ ♀

Unbending
Considerate
Diplomatic

DOGGED DIPLOMATS

The fact that you can seem uncompromising is mainly down to your fixed nature, if today is your birthday. Your solid and straightforward, earthy element also contributes to your unwillingness to embrace alternative viewpoints. Yet others admire your tenacity and impeccable logic, particularly when it is clear that you have given your position much thought (feminine-polarity style). And when you so wish, your light, Venusian touch in diffusing a potentially explosive disagreement without giving ground is simply masterly.

FAMOUS BIRTHS: Ayatollah Ruhollah Khomeini (1900); Dennis Hopper (1936); "Sugar" Ray Leonard (1956); Enya (1961)

MAKING MONEY

This was a propitious date on which to found the New York Stock Exchange, as occurred when the Buttonwood Agreement was signed on May 17, 1792, for Venus imbues this day with her financial acumen, and earth, with its productivity.

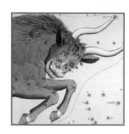

TAURUS

♀ ♉

Contemplative
Persistent
Artistic

TENACIOUS DOERS

Although they have a passive polarity, this predisposes May 18 individuals to thinking hard before taking action rather than to taking no action at all. Having an earthy element and fixed quadruplicity means that those born on this day are practical people who derive satisfaction from being physically occupied and from pushing on with a project until it has been completed. And because their ruling planet is Venus, they generally share her artistic inclinations.

FAMOUS BIRTHS: Czar Nicholas II of Russia (1868); Frank Capra (1897); Perry Como (1912); Margot Fonteyn (1919); Chow Yun-Fat (1955)

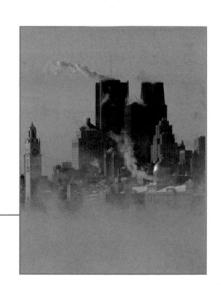

MONTREAL IN THE MAKING

Sowing, building, and consolidating are favored on May 18, a day whose character is flavored by earth and a fixed quadruplicity, and it was on this date in 1642 that French colonists founded "Ville-Marie," today the Canadian city of Montreal.

MAY 19

Resistant
Tolerant
Receptive

CREATURES OF CONVICTION

It is just as well that those born on this day are fortified with earth's resilience, and that Venus's gift is a healthy dose of self-regard, because the uncompromising influence of their fixed quadruplicity means that their firmly held views often cause conflict with others. It is not that they see things in black and white, because Venus makes them tolerant, and their feminine polarity, receptive; just that their instinct always leads them to stick to their guns.

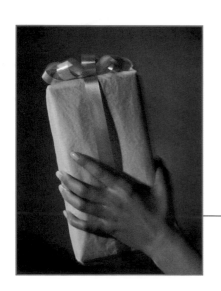

FAMOUS BIRTHS: Nancy and Waldorf Astor (1879); Ho Chi Minh (1890); Malcolm X (1925); Grace Jones (1952); Joey Ramone (1954)

BIRTHDAY TRIBUTE

On May 19, the goddess Venus's rule of the sky is drawing to an end, and on this date in 1962, screen goddess Marilyn Monroe performed her own swansong, singing "Happy Birthday" to J.F.K. at Madison Square Garden, New York.

TAURUS

♀ ♉

Intuitive
Straightforward
Grounded

MAY 20

EARTHY INDIVIDUALS

The down-to-earth influence of your earthy element is especially evident in your personality, if this is your birthday, even when the artistry and tastefulness that are characteristic of Venus, and the intuition that comes of having a feminine polarity, are also clearly present. Rather than displaying Venus's delicate sensibilities and a feminine polarity's shrinking sensitivity, you are a very robust, no-nonsense, and unashamedly sensual type, and your groundedness is given extra strength by the stability of your fixed nature.

FAMOUS BIRTHS: Honoré de Balzac (1799); James Stewart (1908); Joe Cocker (1944); Cher (1946); Busta Rhymes (1972)

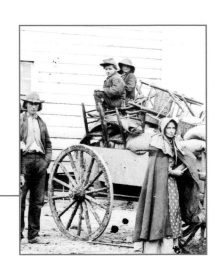

ON HOME GROUND

May 20 has strong connections with the element of earth, which may be why it was on this day in 1862 that President Abraham Lincoln signed the Homestead Act, enabling settlers to claim their own farmland in the American West.

SYMBOL: TWINS
CELESTIAL RULER: MERCURY
ELEMENT: AIR
POLARITY: POSITIVE (MASCULINE)
QUADRUPLICITY: MUTABLE

GEMINI

MAY 21 TO JUNE 21 ♊

With curious, communicative Mercury as their ruling planet, a variety-loving, mutable quadruplicity, an outgoing, positive polarity, and breezy, sociable air as their element, those born under the sign of Gemini are anything but shy and retiring. Yet as much as they are stimulated by intellectual challenges, and by constant changes of companions and scenery, these are also self-contained, emotionally detached individuals who can feel suffocated by others' neediness or possessiveness. Just as real-life twins are two individuals, so those who are astrological twins can appear to have two distinct personalities: one easygoing, lively, uninhibited, and flexible, and the other critical, impersonal, aggressive, and fickle.

GEMINI

☿ ♊

Curious
Communicative
Confident

MAY 21

SHARP-EYED OBSERVERS

If today is your birthday, the combined influence of Mercury and air is particularly pronounced in you. Your constant curiosity and eagerness to learn drive you to observe everything that goes on (and your eclectic range of interests is down to your mutable nature, too). Once you have analyzed what you've seen and reached your shrewd conclusions, your active polarity gives you the confidence to communicate your thoughts to a wide audience, unafraid of criticism.

FAMOUS BIRTHS: Albrecht Dürer (1471); Alexander Pope (1688); "Fats" Waller (1904); Mr. T (1952); Notorious B.I.G. (1972)

AN AERONAUTICAL ACHIEVEMENT

May 21's element is air, so it is fitting that it should mark the anniversary of U.S. aviator Charles Lindbergh's solo nonstop flight from New York to Paris in his single-engine monoplane, Spirit of St. Louis, in 1927.

MAY 22

DARING TO BE DIFFERENT

Their mutable nature makes them versatile and interested in a wide range of pursuits, but May 22 people have Mercury and air to thank for their inquisitive natures. With their masculine-polarity courage added into the mix, they love to enter and explore uncharted territory—be it actual or intellectual—and then try to make sense of their situation and solving the challenging questions that confront them there. More conventional souls may feel that they go too far, however, and should stay more grounded.

FAMOUS BIRTHS: Richard Wagner (1813); Mary Cassatt (1844); Laurence Olivier (1907); Morrissey (1959); Naomi Campbell (1970)

ALIEN TERRITORY
Horizon-broadening travel is highlighted on this Mercury-ruled day, on which, in 1972, Richard Nixon landed at Moscow's Vnukovo Airport, ready to begin his state visit to the Soviet Union, the first by a U.S. president.

GEMINI

☿ ♊

Indecisive
Restless
Cheerful

MAY 23

VARIABLE VARIETY-LOVERS

If you were born on this day, you have the potential to excel at whatever you turn your bright, Mercurial, air-influenced mind to. Your variety-loving, mutable nature makes it hard for you to decide on your life's purpose, though, and you tend to head off in many directions at once. The combination of your ruling planet, element, and quadruplicity can also make you exceptionally restless and unable to stick at anything for long. But wherever the winds of change blow you, you remain upbeat, your moods as positive as your polarity.

fAMOUS BIRTHS: Scatman Crothers (1910); Rosemary Clooney (1928); Joan Collins (1933); Drew Carey (1958); Jewel (1974)

DEAD-ON DETECTION

That Mercury and air infuse this day with an information-gathering, analytical flavor was illustrated on May 23, 1934, when a police posse ambushed and executed the outlaws Bonnie and Clyde, the F.B.I.'s investigative operation having tracked them down to Louisiana.

MAY 24

GEMINI

♊ ☿

Analytical
Good-humored
Dynamic

COOL-HEADED CHARMERS

Your dynamic, positive polarity and changeable, mutable quadruplicity can merge so powerfully in you, if this is your birthday, that you occasionally blunder into action with both feet. Usually, however, your head firmly rules your heart. Having analytical air as an element and critical Mercury as a ruling planet means that you're constantly assessing your circumstances and considering your next move. You sometimes seem cool and calculating, but few can resist your good-humored charm.

FAMOUS BIRTHS: Queen Victoria of Britain (1819); Bob Dylan (1941); Priscilla Presley (1945); Kristin Scott Thomas (1960)

A CODED COMMUNICATION

May 24's planetary ruler is Mercury, whose namesake is the Roman messenger god. It was on May 24, 1844, that U.S. academic Samuel Morse sent the first Morse-code message, by telegraph from Washington, D.C., to Baltimore.

Incisive
Articulate
Forceful

fLUENT COMMUNICATORS

With clever Mercury and articulate air among their birth influences, May 25 people are incisive thinkers who are especially notable for their natural gift of eloquence. Their expressiveness may take a variety of forms, thanks to their mutable nature—so that their preferred medium may be the written word one moment and music the next, for example—but they invariably "speak" to others effectively. And because their masculine polarity makes them forceful, people are always impressed by their conviction.

fAMOUS BIRThS: Ralph Waldo Emerson (1803); Miles Davis (1926); Ian McKellan (1939); Mike Myers (1963); Lauryn Hill (1975)

A WIT'S CONVICTION
Articulacy and intelligence are both hallmarks of this air- and Mercury-influenced day, as well as of the Anglo–Irish writer Oscar Wilde. Despite his passionately argued defense, he was sentenced to two years' imprisonment for "gross indecency" on May 25, 1895.

MAY 26

ELOQUENT ENTERTAINERS

Their people-oriented, mutable nature and sociability-encouraging element of air ensure that those born on this day thrive in the company of others. Mercury makes them witty and communicative, and their positive polarity gives them confidence and removes their inhibitions. Their sparkling conversational skills delight others, and their entertaining anecdotes often attract an admiring audience. The trouble is, their need to be center of attention can make it difficult for them to limit themselves to one-on-one relationships.

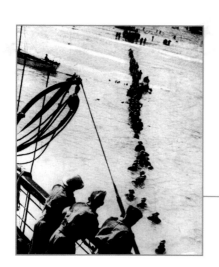

FAMOUS BIRTHS: Al Jolson (1886); John Wayne (1907); Peggy Lee (1920); Lenny Kravitz (1964); Helena Bonham-Carter (1966)

OPERATION DYNAMO

May 26's influences promote daring and communication, as demonstrated in 1940 when privately owned small ships implemented British Admiral Ramsey's plan to evacuate British and French soldiers from Dunkirk.

Gemini

☿ ♊

Upbeat
Gregarious
Fickle

May 27

Neutral Negotiators

Many of Mercury and air's characteristics are very similar and seem to combine, thrive, and burgeon within the May 27 psyche. Indeed, to say that these people are bright would be an understatement, and they are exceptionally analytical, articulate, and people-oriented, too. They are thus gifted negotiators, particularly when their upbeat, positive polarity kicks in. They may, however, come across as cool, detached, and critical, and when their mutable nature reinforces their innate restlessness, they can be quite fickle.

Famous Births: "Wild Bill" Hickock (1837); Christopher Lee (1922); Henry Kissinger (1923); Joseph Fiennes (1970); André 3000 (1975)

Bridging the Gap
That Mercury, this day's ruling planet, favors travel, was illustrated in San Francisco, California, on May 27, 1937, when the Golden Gate Bridge was opened, initially to pedestrians, and the next day to automobiles.

MAY 28

Outgoing
Adaptable
Engaging

POLISHED PERFORMERS

It is your positive polarity that makes you such a confident and outgoing person, if you were born on May 28. Your mutable nature enables you to adapt readily to changing circumstances. Throw the communicative talents that are the combined gift of Mercury and air into the mix, and you are a gifted entertainer with the rare ability to review your own performance objectively, identify your faults, and eliminate them. Boredom and lack of staying power may prevent you from ever achieving perfection, however.

FAMOUS BIRTHS: Thomas Moore (1779); Ian Fleming (1908); Gladys Knight and Rudolph Giuliani (1944); Kylie Minogue (1968)

ASTRONOMICAL MATTERS

Mercury encourages dissemination of information and, in 1998, prompted California's Extra Research Corporation, to share the discovery of a "candidate young" planet, provisionally called TMF-1C, outside our solar system.

Gemini
☿ ♊

Extroverted
Versatile
Charming

May 29

Smooth Operators

Although their positive polarity is clearly visible in May 29 people's extrovert personalities, and their mutable mode makes them versatile types with many strings to their bows, it is, perhaps, the combination of Mercury and air that is most evident in these clever characters. Above all else, those born on this day are consummate charmers, whose curiosity gives them a real interest in others. They may seem detached and lacking in genuine empathy, though.

Famous Births: G.K. Chesterton (1874); Bob Hope (1903); John F. Kennedy (1917); Annette Bening (1958); Rupert Everett (1959); Melissa Etheridge (1961)

To Boldly Go
The Roman god Mercury was an intrepid explorer, so it seems apt that Edmund Hillary and Tensing Norgay became the first people to set foot on the summit of Mount Everest on one of "his" days, namely May 29, 1953.

MAY 30

Enthusiastic
Flexible
Eloquent

MATCHLESS MESSENGERS

If this is your birthday, perhaps the only language with which you don't have an instinctive affinity is the language of love—you tend to be unemotional. But, whether your talent is for English, Spanish, business, or science, the articulacy that you receive from air and Mercury makes you a master of communication. And because you have a mutable mode and a positive polarity, you are able to adapt your message and fire up any audience, so you'd make a highly effective teacher.

FAMOUS BIRTHS: Peter Carl Fabergé (1846); Pierre Janet (1859); Mel Blanc (1908); Benny Goodman (1909); Wynona Judd (1964)

EXTRATERRESTRIAL COMMUNICATION

Aided by Mercury, air carries all manner of messages, and perhaps even extraterrestrial ones. Real or imagined, these were the undoing of Joan of Arc, who was executed for heresy and sorcery in Rouen, France, on May 30, 1431.

GEMINI

☿ ♊

Adventurous
Communicative
Astute

MAY 31

PERCEPTIVE PERSONALITIES

Whether or not they chose acting as a career, May 31 individuals certainly possess the necessary qualities. Their positive polarity provides the confidence to express themselves freely; their mutable nature makes them versatile; and their airy element blesses them with articulacy. Mercury's contribution includes inquisitiveness and analytical skills, which are invaluable aids in researching and understanding a character. But sometimes they seem to be playing a role rather than being themselves when trying to please their loved ones.

fAMOUS BIRTHS: Walt Whitman (1819); Clint Eastwood (1930); Sharon Gless (1943); Brooke Shields (1965); Colin Farrell (1976)

BREAKING fREE

The influence of its freedom-seeking, airy element is especially strong on this day, which may be why it was on May 31, 1961, that South Africa—previously a sovereign state within the British Empire—declared itself an independent republic.

June 1

CAPTIVATING CHAMELEONS

The greatest gift that their mutable quadruplicity has bequeathed to those born on this day is potentially also their downfall, namely their changeability. When combined with the quick-wittedness of Mercury, the gregariousness of air, and the confidence of their positive polarity, the result is people who are able to adapt to, and shine within, any social group. Yet flip the coin, and the same influences can produce individuals who are unreliable, capricious, directionless, and unthinking.

FAMOUS BIRTHS: Brigham Young (1801); Marilyn Monroe (1926); Edward Woodward (1930); Morgan Freeman (1937); Ron Wood (1947)

SUPERNATURAL BRETHREN?

The first issue of Action Comics, published on June 1, 1938, introduced Superman to readers. Was it mere coincidence that the superhero shared the supersonic speediness of winged-sandaled Mercury, the deity for whom this day's ruling planet was named?

GEMINI

☿ ♊

Convivial
Rational
Inquisitive

JUNE

2

STUDENTS OF HUMANITY

Perhaps their fascination with what makes others tick is due to the combination of objective Mercury and rational air, causing June 2 people to be rather dispassionate types, as well as incorrigibly inquisitive. Add their mutable nature and active polarity to this already convivial combination, and the result is exceptionally outgoing individuals, who are as accomplished at listening as they are at conversing, and who make excellent use of the information that they gather.

FAMOUS BIRTHS: Comte Donatien de Sade (the Marquis de Sade) (1740); Thomas Hardy (1840); Edward Elgar (1857)

A CROWNING MOMENT
Queen Elizabeth II of the United Kingdom was crowned at Westminster Abbey, London, on June 2, 1953. Maybe the globetrotting influence exerted by Mercury was especially powerful on that day, because she subsequently traveled farther afield than any other monarch.

JUNE 3

♊ ☿

Uninhibited
Intelligent
Animated

ECCENTRIC ENTHUSIASTS

If today is your birthday, you often go off at tangent. Thanks to your mutable nature, you're easily diverted, and, with your positive polarity, you're completely free of inhibitions. You are intelligent and original, and you don't care what others think of your sudden enthusiasms, which is just as well, because having Mercury and air among your birth influences means that you are consumed with an irresistible need to find out what's happening and where it's at.

FAMOUS BIRTHS: Jefferson Davis (1808); Tony Curtis (1925); Allen Ginsberg (1926); Curtis Mayfield (1942); Suzi Quatro (1950)

WHAT'S IN A NAME?

Insensitive comparisons may be made on this air-infused day, on which, in 1946, Louis Reard's two-piece bathing costume made its debut in Paris, France. His "explosive" invention was named after Bikini Atoll, where the USA was testing deadly atom bombs.

GEMINI

☿ ♊

Independent
Assertive
Adaptable

JUNE
4

FORCEFUL FREE-THINKERS

So powerful is the union of questioning Mercury, independent air, and their assertive, active polarity within those whose birthday falls on June 4 that they are determined to go their own way, regardless of what others think. But because they have a changeable, mutable quadruplicity, their path is unlikely to be straightforward. Luckily, they are not only adaptable enough to cope with their ever-changing circumstances, but they positively thrive on variety.

FAMOUS BIRTHS: King George III of Great Britain (1738); Bruce Dern (1936); Noah Wyle (1971); Angelina Jolie (1975)

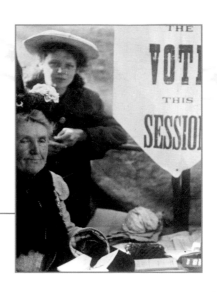

RIGHT TO VOTE

Air, June 4's element, is associated with freedom of thought, word, and deed. This combination was demonstrated on this day in 1919 when the 19th Amendment was passed, guaranteeing women the right to vote.

JUNE 5

Rational
Experimental
Bold

LOGICAL LIBERTARIANS

If this is your birthday, you have a wide variety of interests, thanks to your mutable mode. You approach each of these in the same way, harnessing a streak of Mercury's logic, a dash of air's independence, and a dose of your positive polarity's abundant self-assurance. You are consequently a rational, experimental, and bold researcher and developer of ideas. You also have a flair for communication, which helps you to make the case for your theories, however surprising they may be, to the wider world.

FAMOUS BIRTHS: Adam Smith (1723); Francisco Pancho Villa (1878); Federico García Lorca (1898); Mark Wahlberg (1971)

UP, UP, AND AWAY!

That June 5's element is air was highlighted in 1783, when the inventive French brothers Joseph and Jacques Montgolfier test-launched the first hot-air balloon over Annonay, France. Made of linen and paper, it floated overhead for ten minutes.

Analytical
Cerebral
Energetic

RATIONAL INDIVIDUALISTS

Although their changeable, mutable quadruplicity can make it appear as though there are many sides to the June 6 personality, those born on this day are fundamentally children of their element of air, being clear-thinking, analytical types who are very much their own people. Mercury reinforces many of their cerebral qualities, also contributing an appetite for travel, while their active polarity gives them the pioneering energy that provides these independent individuals their get-up-and-go.

FAMOUS BIRTHS: Diego Velázquez (1599); Nathan Hale (1755); Aleksandr Sergeyevich Pushkin (1799); Bjorn Borg (1956)

AIRBORNE LIBERATORS
June 6, 1944, was D-day, the day on which the Allied forces launched their invasion of France in order to defeat Hitler's Germany and liberate Europe. On this "airy" date, the participation of airborne troops was, of course, vital.

JUNE 7

Fun-loving
Free-thinking
Confident

IDIOSYNCRATIC INDIVIDUALS

If you were born on June 7, your element of air not only makes you sociable and fun-loving, but a free-thinking individualist who makes up your own mind rather than following the herd. Just as well, then, that objective Mercury encourages you to think things through, and that your positive polarity gives you the courage to take an unpopular stance. Under the influence of your inconstant, mutable quadruplicity, you change your opinions frequently anyway.

FAMOUS BIRTHS: Paul Gauguin (1848); Dean Martin (1917); Tom Jones (1940); Liam Neeson (1952); Prince (1958); Anna Kournikova (1981)

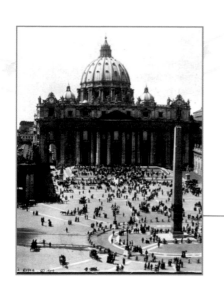

STATE OF INDEPENDENCE
Independence is an attribute of air, this day's element, and it was on June 7, 1929, that the Lateran Pacts were ratified between the kingdom of Italy and the Holy See, thereby bringing the independent Vatican City State into being.

Gemini

Impatient
Curious
Dynamic

June 8

Impatient Livewires

The electrifying combination of all of their birth influences energizes those born on June 8 to such an extent that they simply cannot sit still. Their mutable nature gives them a craving for constant change; Mercury's contribution is a lust for travel; their airy element gives them an interest in everything, and their positive polarity makes them dynamic. In short, it matters not whether they are using their brain or body, as long as they are always on the go.

Famous Births: Robert Schumann (1810); Frank Lloyd Wright (1869); Joan Rivers (1933); Nancy Sinatra (1940); Lindsay Davenport (1976)

Political Parity

The element of air promotes equality, as shown on this day in 1929, when, in the United Kingdom, socialist politician Margaret Bondfield was made minister of labor, becoming the first female member of the British Cabinet.

JUNE 9

WITTY WORDSMITHS

The double dose of communication skills that is Mercury and air's gift to Geminians is particularly well developed in those who were born on June 9. Their witty way with words gives them the power to wow or to wound with a lightning response. Having the confidence of a masculine polarity means that they don't mind too much what others think of them, but then air and their mutable quadruplicity predispose them to being adaptable people-pleasers who would rather be considerate than hurtful to others.

FAMOUS BIRTHS: Cole Porter (1893); Charles Saatchi (1943); Michael J. Fox (1961); Johnny Depp (1963); Natalie Portman (1981)

A PIONEERING PROTOTYPE

June 9 is an auspicious date for space travel on account of its association with air and Mercury, and it was on this day in 1931 that U.S. rocket pioneer Robert H. Goddard patented a design for a rocket-fueled aircraft.

GEMINI

☿ ♊

Articulate
Active
Outgoing

BREEZY BROADCASTERS

If you were born on this day, you're a natural-born broadcaster. This doesn't necessarily mean that you are destined for the stage or studio, but rather that you're a lively and articulate child of Mercury and you're in your airy element when communicating with others and taking center stage. You're certainly not an introspective, shrinking violet: your active polarity makes you a doer more than a thinker, while your breezy sociability and mutable mode cause you to thrive as the life of the party.

FAMOUS BIRTHS: James Stuart, the "Old Pretender" (1688); Judy Garland (1922); Robert Maxwell (1923); Elizabeth Hurley (1966)

A MULTIPURPOSE SPACE

Multifunctionalism is a mutable characteristic that prevails on June 10, as it did in 1793, when the Jardin des Plantes was established in Paris, France. This botanical garden was also destined to serve as the first public zoo.

JUNE 11

ENERGETIC LEARNERS

Those born on this day are likely to have many interests, thanks to their variety-seeking, mutable mode, and to pursue each in the same enthusiastic spirit of exploration and discovery. Inquisitiveness and itchy feet—traits associated with Mercury and air—are particularly pronounced within June 11 people, while their active polarity gives them the urge and energy to throw themselves into a bold (or, as some would say, reckless) mission to find out the lowdown on everything and everybody.

FAMOUS BIRTHS: John Constable (1776); Richard Strauss (1864); Jacques Cousteau (1910); Gene Wilder (1935)

A DANGEROUS DISCOVERY
Mercury, June 11's ruling planet, promotes exploration, and it was on this day in 1770 that British explorer Captain James Cook discovered the Great Barrier Reef, in the Coral Sea, when his ship, the Endeavour, ran aground on it.

GEMINI

☿ ♊

Self-confident
Objective
Persuasive

JUNE 12

RESTLESS REPRESENTATIVES

You often end up being the spokesperson for others, if this is your birthday. This is partly because your positive polarity gives you the confidence to speak out fearlessly, and partly because the combination of objective Mercury and articulate air gives you an effective gift for expressing a viewpoint dispassionately and persuasively. You are amiable and you're happy to help out occasionally, but you dislike being overburdened by responsibility, largely because you have a restless, mutable mode and are easily bored.

FAMOUS BIRTHS: Alexandre Tansman (1897); George Bush (1924); Vic Damone (1928); Anne Frank (1929); Chick Corea (1941)

RESISTING RESTRICTION
The astrological flavor that pervades June 12 results in a hatred of being hemmed in, as was illustrated in 1923 by escapologist Harry Houdini, who wriggled out of a straitjacket while hanging upside down, 40 feet above the ground.

JUNE 13

EXPRESSIVE EXPERIMENTERS

Their eloquence may take a variety of forms, often depending on their mutable mood swings, but there is no doubting June 13 people's facility for free-thinking, cheerful sociability, or great gift for communication. They have Mercury, their ruling planet, and air, their element, to thank for these qualities. Their minds are always ticking over, and it is their outgoing, positive polarity that encourages them to talk openly to friends and family about whatever is on their mind, without fear of seeming foolish.

FAMOUS BIRTHS: W.B. Yeats (1865); Dorothy L. Sayers (1893); Tim Allen (1953); Ally Sheedy (1962); Mary-Kate and Ashley Olsen (1986)

A FREEFALL FIRST
June 13's element is air, making it an auspicious date for aeronautical feats. It was on this day in 1912 that Captain Albert Berry made the first successful parachute jump in the USA, from an airplane above Jefferson, Mississippi.

GEMINI

☿ ♊

Aloof
Logical
Active

LOGICAL LONERS

All of your birth influences—particularly your sociable, mutable quadruplicity—cause you to enjoy company, if this is your birthday. But you still tend to hold yourself apart from the crowd. Your aloofness is due partly to your airy emotional disengagement and partly to your Mercurial habit of observing and judging people. This makes you a shrewd operator, your thoughts mostly unclouded by emotion. And because you have a positive polarity, you're confident and often unwittingly intimidate people into keeping their distance.

FAMOUS BIRTHS: Harriet Beecher Stowe (1811); Che Guevara (1928); Donald Trump (1946); Yasmine Bleeth (1968); Steffi Graf (1969)

A STAR-SPANGLED BANNER
Stars are set in space, or air, this day's element, so it is appropriate that the Continental Congress, meeting in Philadelphia, should have proclaimed the Stars and Stripes the United States' national flag on June 14, 1777.

JUNE 15

COOL CUSTOMERS

Others are enchanted by your cool charm, if today is your birthday, and the fact that you can seem a little aloof merely adds to your irresistible allure. Your appeal is partly down to your airy element's easygoing approach, which is delightfully complemented by your Mercurial liveliness, active-polarity confidence, and mutable love of variety. But when a cloud casts a disagreeable shadow over your life, you can change in a moment and become unpleasantly critical, aggressive, fickle, or moody.

FAMOUS BIRTHS: Edvard Hagerup Grieg (1843); Helen Hunt (1963); Courtney Cox–Arquette (1964); Ice Cube (1969)

A FLASH OF INSPIRATION
Notable events are likely to occur in the air on this day, and it was on June 15, 1752, that U.S. scientist Benjamin Franklin flew his kite in a thunderstorm and proved that lightning is a form of electricity.

GEMINI

☿ ♊

Rational
Persuasive
Adaptable

JUNE
16

PIONEERING PERSUADERS

The powerful interaction between Mercury and air within June 16 characters tends to make them avid learners, enthusiastic students, and brilliant trivia buffs. Their rational, analytical minds make them logical and able to express themselves clearly and persuasively to others. The influence of their masculine polarity means that their opinions are likely to be original and bold, and possibly controversial. With their flexible, mutable mode, they are interested in other people—provided they don't discuss their emotions.

FAMOUS BIRTHS: John Cheke (1514); Stan Laurel (1890); Enoch Powell (1912); Joyce Carol Oates (1938); Tupac Shakur (1971)

ULYSSES DAY
June 16's astrological influences suggest that it has an intellectually experimental flavor, and sure enough, this is the date (in 1904) selected by Irish author James Joyce on which to set the events of his wildly original novel Ulysses (1922).

JUNE 17

Shrewd
Self-assured
Fun-loving

PLAYFUL PIONEERS

If today is your birthday, you are playful and tend to make light of everything. But this can mask your sharp mind, because air, reinforced by Mercury, also gives you a shrewd, calculating brain. Your active polarity fills you with self-assurance, so that whenever you have something to say, however outrageous, you say it without hesitation. Because you have a versatile, mutable nature, you have the potential to be innovative and you enjoy company, but you have difficulty forming deeper, lasting relationships.

FAMOUS BIRTHS: Igor Fyodorovich Stravinsky (1882); M.C. Escher (1898); Barry Manilow (1946); Venus Williams (1980)

AN ENGLISH EXPLORER

Mercury was an inveterate explorer, so maybe his spirit was guiding English navigator Sir Francis Drake when he landed at a port in San Francisco Bay on this day in 1579, named it "New Albion," and claimed it for England.

GEMINI

☿ ♊

Direct
Flexible
Eloquent

SKILLFUL SPEAKERS

It is the fusion of air with their other three birth influences that gives those born on June 18 their inimitable charm. Air and Mercury are responsible for their silver-tongued communication skills. Their active polarity makes them direct and to the point, and their mutable nature enables them to adapt to most circumstances. Because of all these qualities, June 18 people make excellent, confident public speakers, who enjoy being the center of others' attention.

FAMOUS BIRTHS: Edouard Daladier (1884); Jeanette MacDonald (1901); Paul McCartney (1942); Isabella Rossellini (1952)

A CAPITAL CONNECTION
Mercury, this day's ruling planet, aids everything to do with travel and communication, and may consequently have had a hand in ensuring that Waterloo Bridge, which spans the Thames River in London, England, opened to the public on June 18, 1817.

June 19

TALKATIVE TYPES

Maybe it is because you have a confident, positive polarity that you aren't too concerned what others think of you, if today is your birthday. Or perhaps it is because air makes you dispassionate. Either way, the bond between objective Mercury and communicative air prompts you to express the truth exactly as you see it, without worrying about causing offense—though you prefer not to. Because your mutable quadruplicity gives you a variety of interests, you have something to say on just about every subject.

FAMOUS BIRTHS: King James I of England and Scotland (1566); Salman Rushdie (1947); Kathleen Turner (1954); Paula Abdul (1962)

As Free as Air
The element of air signifies freedom, so it is apt that the U.S. Congress should have prohibited slavery in U.S. territories on June 19, 1862, and that slaves should have been emancipated in Texas on this "Juneteenth" day in 1865.

GEMINI

☿ ♊

Versatile
Restless
Confident

JUNE 20

FLEXIBLE FLIRTS

The influence of their versatile, variety-relishing, mutable quadruplicity is particularly evident in June 20 people, who, aided by their confident, positive polarity, seem destined to succeed in all that they attempt. That said, because Mercury and air's combined influence results in them being coolly detached types who prefer a meeting of minds to one of hearts—and because one-on-one relationships make them restless and suffocated—they like to flirt, but often lack the golden touch when it comes to love.

FAMOUS BIRTHS: Errol Flynn (1909);
Brian Wilson (1942); Lionel Richie
(1949); John Goodman (1952);
Nicole Kidman (1967)

TEEN QUEEN
Maybe independence-giving air had a hand in Queen Victoria's ascension to the British throne on this day in 1837. Her new status at last liberated the eighteen-year-old from subservience to her bossy mother, the duchess of Kent.

JUNE 21

♊ ☿

Easygoing
Cooperative
Thoughtful

CHALLENGERS OF CONVENTION

If this is your birthday, you're no rebel, because the joint influence of air and your mutable nature makes you easy-going and cooperative. But you're not a conventional thinker, either. Mercury encourages you to question everything and to make up your own mind, while your positive polarity gives you the courage of your convictions. You won't go along with anything that you consider hidebound, unfair, or illogical. Being on the cusp of Cancer, you also have a splash of that sign's watery capacity for forming deep bonds.

FAMOUS BIRTHS: Jean Paul Sartre (1905); Jane Russell (1921); Juliette Lewis (1973); Prince William of Great Britain (1982)

DEATH'S DISCLOSURE
Mercury imparts the desire to learn the truth on this day, and it was on June 21, 1985, that pathologists announced that tests on bones exhumed in Brazil had revealed them to be those of the Nazi fugitive Josef Mengele.

Symbol: The crab
Celestial Ruler: The moon
Element: Water
Polarity: Negative (feminine)
Quadruplicity: Cardinal

CANCER

JUNE 22 TO JULY 22 ♋

Think of a crab, of its armorlike shell protecting the soft tissue beneath, of its vicious-looking pincers, and of its scuttling, evasive, sideways movement, and you have an inkling of the apparently contradictory Cancerian character. While Cancer's cardinal quadruplicity causes its children to be self-centered, this "hard" quality is outweighed by the "softer" influences of Cancer's planetary ruler, the Moon, its emotional element of water, and its contemplative, passive polarity. Yet so sensitive and fearful of being wounded are they that caring, cautious, human crabs tend to hide their vulnerability under a façade of toughness, and may deliver a self-defensive nip when a breach of their defenses occurs.

JUNE 22

Receptive
Sensitive
Creative

SENSITIVE RECEIVERS

If you were born on June 22, your receptiveness is the joint contribution of the Moon and your feminine polarity. Your sensitivity may prove both a curse and a blessing: repeated knocks may take their toll, flooding you with the insecurity that is inherent in your watery element, and maybe prompting you to lash out with pre-emptive, cardinal, aggressive–defensive strikes. If buoyed up by supportive relationships, however, you will respond by allowing your creativity to blossom and your nurturing instincts to thrive.

FAMOUS BIRTHS: John Dillinger (1903); Billy Wilder (1906); Kris Kristofferson (1936); Meryl Streep (1949); Carson Daly (1973)

DEAD TO THE WORLD

There is a link between the Moon, water signs, and turbulent emotions, and it was on June 22, 1969, that U.S. actress Judy Garland succumbed to a fatal overdose of sleeping pills.

CANCER

Ambitious
Caring
Demanding

JUNE 23

DEMANDING NURTURERS

June 23 people have a strong desire to make something of themselves, spurred on by their cardinal quadruplicity. And because their ruling planet is the family-oriented Moon, and their element is nurturing water, their overriding goal is to provide security and comforts for their nearest and dearest. Yet these same birth influences can make them seem overly controlling, and whenever they are resisted or challenged, wounded, feminine-polarity crabs will typically respond by withdrawing into their shells.

FAMOUS BIRTHS: Bob Fosse (1927);
June Carter Cash (1929);
Frances McDormand (1957);
Selma Blair (1972)

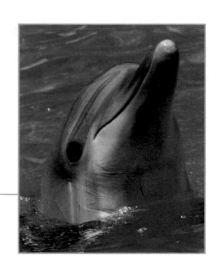

A WATERY WORLD

Water is June 23's element, making any aquatic venture scheduled for this date well-starred, and boding well for Marineland, a beach-front, marine-life theme park in St. Augustine, Florida, that opened to the public on this day in 1938.

JUNE 24

Emotional
Responsive
Kind

ARMOR-PLATED SOFTIES

Maybe your lunar insight gives you an instinctive understanding of exactly how emotionally vulnerable you are, if today is your birthday. This trait is the consequence of having a receptive, passive polarity, sensitivity that is heightened by your watery element, and, of course, the love-hungry Moon as a planetary ruler. In any case, so convincing is the driven, cardinal persona that you adopt that it is generally only your most trusted confidants who appreciate how kind and caring you are underneath.

FAMOUS BIRTHS: Horatio Herbert Kitchener (1850); Jack Dempsey (1895); Jeff Beck (1944); Mick Fleetwood (1947)

SAFEGUARDING SCOTLAND

June 24's astrological influences suggest that violence may be used in defense of home territory, and this was the day, in 1314, on which Robert the Bruce and his Scottish army defeated the invading English at the Battle of Bannockburn.

CANCER

☾ ♋

Empathetic
Intuitive
Contemplative

JUNE 25

TENDER, YET TOUGH

Mother Moon's gifts to her June 25 infants include deep empathy. Their watery element fills them with intuition, and their passive polarity makes them contemplative, and the combination enhances their creativity. Small wonder that these individuals are so sensitive, but then having such gentle and receptive natures lays them open to feeling perceived slights deeply. Little crablets soon learn to protect their soft hearts under an increasingly hard veneer of cardinal-quadruplicity self-centeredness, however.

FAMOUS BIRTHS: George Orwell (1903); Sidney Lumet (1924); Carly Simon (1945); George Michael (1963)

FIGHTING BACK

Emulating the behavior of crabs, which will defend themselves if provoked, it was on this Cancerian day in 1876 that Chief Sitting Bull's Native American forces routed General George Custer's U.S. Cavalry division at the Battle of Little Big Horn.

June 26

Perceptive
Attuned
Driven

WELL-ATTUNED ARTISTS

Three of the four astrological influences that together provide the birthright of June 26 people are linked with receptivity, namely the Moon, water, and their passive polarity, so it is not surprising that they are so finely attuned to others' feelings. Because the fourth influence is their cardinal nature, which gives them initiative, it is not unusual for June 26 individuals to channel their gift for responding to people's emotions into careers like teaching, counseling, and pyschology.

fAMOUS BIRTHS: Abner Doubleday (1819); "Colonel" Tom Parker (1909); Chris Isaak (1956); Chris O'Donnell (1970)

SOARING STRUCTURE

A cardinal quadruplicity plus the supportive element of water equals, in architectural terms, a pioneering, free-standing building, such as the CN Tower in Toronto, Canada—at 1,815 feet, then the world's tallest—which opened on June 26, 1976.

CANCER

Imaginative
Impressionable
Aware

JUNE
27

INTUITIVE INTERPRETERS

Your passive polarity's responsiveness, and the infusion of intuition from both the Moon and water, make you deeply sensitive to others, if you were born on this day. Because these influences make you empathetic, they can mirror and magnify the negative emotions that others offload on you, sometimes to an unhealthy extent. With your cardinal mode, you should soon learn to toughen up, reserving your intuitive and caring gifts for the benefit of your family and real friends.

FAMOUS BIRTHS: Helen Keller (1880); H. Ross Perot (1930); Isabelle Adjani (1955); Tobey Maguire (1975)

A KILLER CRAB

Cancer, the disease, was named for the zodiacal crab because a vein-radiating tumor resembles a crab's body and limbs. It was on this Cancerian day in 1957 that the British Medical Research Council stated its conclusion that smoking causes lung cancer.

JUNE 28

CANCER

69 ☾

Artistic
Thoughtful
Enterprising

CREATIVE CHARACTERS

The Moon and water are both givers of creativity, which is why those born on this day are such imaginative individuals. Sensitive, too, and also very receptive, so that the mere germ of an idea will find a fertile breeding ground in a June 28 person's contemplative, feminine-polarity psyche. Because these individuals are enterprising, they also possess the initiative and drive to follow up their new projects. While they're not party animals, they are caring people who form deep and fulfilling relationships.

FAMOUS BIRTHS: King Henry VIII of England (1491); Richard Rodgers (1902); Mel Brooks (1926); Kathy Bates (1948); John Cusack (1966)

SOVEREIGNTY REGAINED

The crescent symbolizes both the Moon, this day's ruling planet, and Islam, and it was on June 28, 2004, that the United States restored sovereignty to Iraq (whose state religion is Islam) following its invasion of the country in 2003.

CANCER

☾ ♋

Original
Patient
Dynamic

JUNE
29

INNOVATIVE INCUBATORS

If this is your birthday, the interaction of your birth influences makes you likely to dream up and develop some extremely original ideas. Your creativity comes from your watery element, while Mother Moon and your feminine polarity encourage your thinking process. With your cardinal nature, you have the potential to act on your intuition and follow up your gifts. Others find you patient, kind, and a genuine friend who always has time to listen and be supportive.

FAMOUS BIRTHS: Peter Paul Rubens (1577); Robert Schuman and James Van Der Zee (1886); Antoine de Saint-Exupéry (1900)

SUSTENANCE IN SPACE
The joint influence of the Moon and water means that supportiveness is a strong June 29 trait, and it was on this day in 1995 that the U.S. space shuttle Atlantis successfully delivered supplies to Mir, the Russian space station.

JUNE 30

CANCER

69 ☾

Motivated
Determined
Cerebral

DRIVEN DREAMERS

From a very young age, June 30 people have cherished a dream, which their three "feminine" birth influences—the Moon, water, and their passive polarity—have nurtured and kept alive, even if others have ridiculed it as being far-fetched. Their cardinal mode helps motivate them to work to make their dream come true, too. Others find these characters thoughtful and helpful, though, far from just dreamy. They are family-minded and loyal friends.

FAMOUS BIRTHS: Lena Horne (1917); Mike Tyson (1966); Brian Bloom (1970); Ralf Schumacher (1975); Michael Phelps (1985)

A PROTECTIVE "PLANET"

The Moon regulates the tides, and maybe the protective influence of this day's ruling planet over its element—water—helped French tightrope-walker Charles Blondin to cross the Niagara Falls unscathed on June 30, 1859.

CANCER

Gentle
Adaptable
Compassionate

JULY

1

EMPATHETIC EXAMPLES

If you were born on this day, people sometimes underestimate you, mistaking your passive gentleness, lunar adaptability, and watery compassion for weakness. In fact, you're highly motivated and can be quite pushy when in pursuit of something—or someone—on which you have set your heart. Go-getting you may be, but you lead by example in your caring, helpful actions. However, you have the potential to become hurt, even bitter, when you discover that not everyone is as unselfish and understanding as you are.

fAMOUS BIRTHS: Deborah Harry (1945); Carl Lewis and Diana, Princess of Wales (1961); Pamela Anderson (1967); Missy Elliot (1971); Liv Tyler (1977)

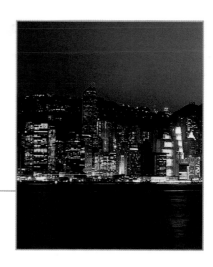

BACK IN THE fOLD
Although China is its motherland, Hong Kong became a British crown colony in 1842. Britain returned it to China on July 1, 1997, an appropriate date, given its rulership by Mother Moon.

July 2

CARING CREATIVES

There are typically two July 2 personalities. One is especially influenced by the interaction between water and their passive polarity, so that these people are imaginative, introspective souls. The combination of the Moon and their cardinal mode prevails in the other, the result being that these are family-oriented types who push themselves hard to provide for their loved ones. Despite these distinctions, all July 2 people are kindly, sensitive, and creative characters.

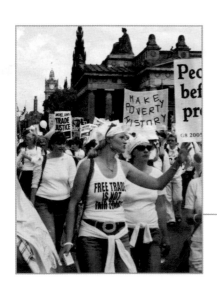

FAMOUS BIRTHS: Herman Hesse (1877); Thurgood Marshall (1908); Vicente Fox (1942); Jerry Hall (1960); Lindsay Lohan (1986)

FEED THE WORLD!

The Moon and water donate compassion to this day; a cardinal quadruplicity provides determination; and a passive polarity makes for nonviolent instincts. No wonder that 225,000 campaigners marched under the banner "Make Poverty History" in Edinburgh, Scotland, on July 2, 2005.

CANCER

Imaginative
Responsive
Pensive

JULY
3

COMPETENT CARERS

It is largely thanks to your element that you're blessed with a richly imaginative inner world, if this is your birthday. You often retreat into it, feminine-polarity style, for a soothing spell of introspection. But the Moon gives you a strong sense of connection to others, and your fellow-feeling may cause you to utilize your cardinal initiative in forging a career from your talent for understanding the human condition. You would be effective in campaigning, aid work, nursing, or other caring professions.

FAMOUS BIRTHS: Franz Kafka (1883); Leos Janácek (1854); Tom Stoppard (1937); Montel Williams (1956); Tom Cruise (1962)

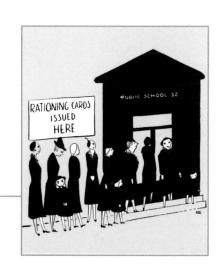

NURTURING A NATION

This day's feminine polarity, lunar ruling planet, and element of water are all associated with nurturing, making July 3, 1954, a highly appropriate date on which to end the World War II-induced rationing of food in Britain.

JULY 4

Dreamy
Considerate
Ambitious

PURPOSEFUL VISIONARIES

Of all of your birth influences, your watery element and cardinal mode manifest themselves the most strongly in you, if you were born on this day. The former gives you a caring mindset, while the latter provides the necessary determination to turn your dreams into reality. You come across as an ambitious self-starter, but having a feminine polarity, as well as the Moon as a planetary ruler, means that you are, at heart, shy, vulnerable, and emotionally needy.

FAMOUS BIRTHS: Nathaniel Hawthorne (1804); Calvin Coolidge (1872); Louis B. Mayer (1885); Eva Marie Saint (1924)

HAPPY BIRTHDAY, USA!

The influence of July 4's pioneering, cardinal quadruplicity must have been especially powerful in 1776, for this date marks the anniversary of the American colonies' adoption of the Declaration of Independence (from Britain), and hence the birthday of the USA.

CANCER

Go-getting
Thoughtful
Intuitive

JULY
5

INSTINCTIVE INITIATORS

Those born on July 5 may give the impression of being go-getting, self-interested characters—and, to a certain extent, so they are, thanks to their cardinal quadruplicity—but there is far more to them than that. Indeed, having a feminine polarity means that they are thoughtful types, whose hidden depths are awash with the profound emotions generated by their watery element. Their intuitive instincts are further magnified by the influence of the Moon. They always find time to provide a shoulder for others to cry on.

FAMOUS BIRTHS: Phineas Taylor Barnum (1810); Jean Cocteau (1889); Huey Lewis (1951); Edie Falco (1963)

HELLO, DOLLY!
The Moon has always been associated with reproduction, and it was on this lunar-ruled day in 1996 that Dolly, the sheep, the first mammal to be cloned from an adult cell, was born at the Roslin Institute, Edinburgh, Scotland.

JULY 6

♋ ☾

Compassionate
Introspective
Pushy

PRIMARILY PROTECTORS

Although all July 6 children have identical birth influences, circumstances can push one or more to the fore, resulting in seemingly different characters. When the Moon, water, or their feminine polarity prevail, the July 6 psyche is likely to be sensitive, compassionate, and introspective. If their cardinal qualities predominate, these crabs will appear pushy and driven. But whatever their personality type, July 6 people are deeply devoted to, and overpoweringly protective of, their loved ones.

FAMOUS BIRTHS: the Fourteenth Dalai Lama (1935); Sylvester Stallone (1946); George W. Bush (1946); 50 Cent (1976)

PROVIDING IMMUNITY
The combination of the Moon, water, and a feminine polarity makes protectiveness a July 6 characteristic. It was on this day in 1885 that scientist Louis Pasteur began injecting his ultimately successful antirabies vaccine.

CANCER

☾ ♋

Creative
Empathetic
Motivated

JULY
7

CREATIVE CATALYSTS

That July 7 people are the source of an inexhaustible stream of ideas is due to the exceptionally fruitful union of the Moon and water. With their passive polarity, these sensitive individuals can pick up subtle signals from others, sometimes appearing uncanny in their ability to tune into what people are really feeling. As well as being creative and ambitious, they are therefore irreplaceable in the affections of their lifelong friends and those in their beloved family circle, for whom they would do anything.

FAMOUS BIRTHS: Gustav Mahler (1860); Marc Chagall (1887); Pierre Cardin (1922); Ringo Starr (1940); Shelley Duvall (1949)

FLOODWATER CONTROL
Water-related activities have a high chance of success on any day whose element is water, and it was on July 7, 1930, that construction began on the Boulder Dam (today known as the Hoover Dam), in the mighty Colorado River.

JULY
8

PHILANTHROPIC PERFORMERS

The joint effect of the sympathetic Moon and your empathetic, watery element makes you unusually compassionate, if today is your birthday. Thanks to your passive polarity, you give much thought to alleviating instances of need and suffering in the world—which is not to say that you are all thought and no action. On the contrary, your cardinal nature gives you initiative and drive, however you choose to express, or act on, your fellow-feeling.

FAMOUS BIRTHS: John D. Rockefeller (1839); Percy Grainger (1882); Billy Eckstine (1914); Anjelica Huston (1951); Kevin Bacon (1958)

A WATERY END

Water, this day's element, may be associated with creativity, but is also dangerous, as was demonstrated on July 8, 1822, when English poet Percy Bysshe Shelley drowned following the sinking of his schooner, Ariel, in the Bay of Spezia, Italy.

Cancer

☽ ♋

Sympathetic
Introverted
Moody

JULY
9

MULTIFACETED PORTRAYERS

Were you born on this day? If it weren't for your enterprising, cardinal mode, the combination of an introspective, passive polarity, sensitive element of water, and intuitive lunar ruler would make you a dreamy introvert with a reluctance to engage with the wider world. As it happens, though, your "softer" birth influences make you artistic. It comes naturally to you to connect with others, often through your preferred means of creative expression—which may be anything from music to photography, quilting, carpentry, or cooking.

FAMOUS BIRTHS: David Hockney (1937); O.J. Simpson (1947); Tom Hanks (1956); Courtney Love (1964); Fred Savage (1976)

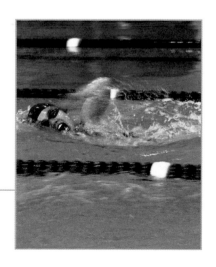

A SWIMMING SENSATION

July 9 is an auspicious date for water-related ventures, and it was on this day in 1922 that U.S. swimmer Johnny Weissmuller became the first person to swim 100 meters freestyle in under a minute in Alameda, California.

JULY 10

Determined
Committed
Contemplative

CONDUITS OF CREATIVITY

It is due to their cardinal traits that July 10 individuals are born ambitious and determined to make something of themselves. Their motivation stems more from their lunar-derived desire to provide for their loved ones than from a craving for personal power or glory, however. It is the intuitive Moon, sensitive water, and their contemplative, feminine polarity that give them the means with which to make their mark on the world, through their creative endeavors.

FAMOUS BIRTHS: Camille Pissarro (1830); James Abbott McNeill Whistler (1834); Arthur Ashe (1943); Jessica Simpson (1980)

THE MOTHER OF HUMANKIND
This day's planetary ruler is the Moon, whose leading symbolic association is with motherhood. On July 10, 1997, scientists in London, England, announced that all humans are descended from a single, African "Eve."

CANCER

☽ ♋

Nurturing
Defensive
Gentle

GENTLE-HEARTED GUARDIANS

If today is your birthday, you're not naturally aggressive—indeed, far from it, given your passive polarity, caring element of water, and nurturing, lunar ruler. But your cardinal mode means that you won't hesitate to launch a pre-emptive strike in self-defense, or to protect your nearest and dearest. You will probably develop a tough façade that belies the gentle, sensitive, and compassionate nature within you. Those who know you well, however, arc always aware of your thoughtful, giving, soft center.

FAMOUS BIRTHS: Robert the Bruce,
King of Scotland (1274);
John Quincy Adams (1767);
Giorgio Armani (1934)

FRIENDLY ARRIVALS
July 11 has pioneering associations, while its influences are linked with non-violence, making this an apt date, in 1656, for the arrival of the first Quaker immigrants—Ann Austin and Mary Fisher—in the American colonies.

JULY 12

CONSIDERATE CONTEMPLATORS

Their passive polarity prevails in those born on July 12, so that they are typically reticent, introspective individuals, which is not to say that they shut others out. This birth influence, along with the Moon and water, make these sensitive souls exceptionally receptive and reactive to the views and moods of those around them. Thoughtful and empathetic they may be, but their cardinal nature means that they're capable of asserting themselves forcefully when necessary.

FAMOUS BIRTHS: Henry David Thoreau (1817); Oscar Hammerstein II (1895); Pablo Neruda (1904); Bill Cosby (1937)

A CANAL'S COMPLETION
It was on this water-influenced day in 1920 that the Panama Canal was formally dedicated. Constructed to link the Pacific and Atlantic oceans, the 51-mile-long canal crosses the Central American Isthmus of Panama.

CANCER

☾ ♋

Intuitive
Kind
Creative

JULY 13

CREATIVE CONTRIBUTORS

While the Moon is responsible for giving caring July 13 people their public-service instincts, it is their passive polarity's receptiveness that enables them to detect even unspoken cries for help. Their element of water contributes the creativity that enables them to make a contribution to the world. With their cardinal traits, they usually translate their dreams into reality, too. All in all, they keep a healthy balance between observing their own needs and those of others.

FAMOUS BIRTHS: Sir George Gilbert Scott (1811); Patrick Stewart (1940); Harrison Ford (1942); Erno Rubik (1944); Cheech Marin (1946)

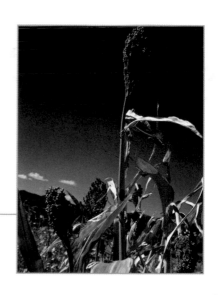

FOOD FOR ALL

The empathy and creativity of the Moon and water worked wonders on this day in 1985, when the Live Aid concerts in London and Philadelphia raised around $140 million for famine relief in Africa.

July 14

Inclusive Initiators

If this is your birthday, the combined influence of the compassionate Moon and empathetic water prompts you to think about your fellow human beings, particularly life's underdogs. With your feminine polarity, you're a good listener and a deep thinker. You also have the cardinal determination and drive to follow up your interests and make a success of yourself. This combination of influences means that you're probably a natural-born educator, politician, or social worker.

Famous Births: William Hanna (1910); Gerald R. Ford (1913); Ingmar Bergman (1918); Maulana Karenga (1941)

An Independent Initiative
Maybe it was July 14's go-getting, cardinal quadruplicity that gave Parisians the initiative to march on, and storm, the Bastille—a prison and symbol of France's monarchy—on this day in 1789, kicking off the French Revolution.

CANCER

☾ ♋

Artistic
Traditional
Introverted

ENTERPRISING TRADITIONALISTS

Their watery element may make July 15 individuals dreamers (especially when their passive polarity switches them to introspective mode), but it is from this birth influence, reinforced by their ruling planet's creative powers, that they derive their artistic streak. Although their cardinal nature gives them initiative, these people are not innovative: the Moon gives them a traditionalist's affinity with the past that is evident in both their personal style and working approach. They are genuine and loyal friends.

FAMOUS BIRTHS: Inigo Jones (1573); Rembrandt Harmenszoon van Rijn (1606); Forest Whitaker (1961); Brian Austin Green (1973)

A MARGARIC INSPIRATION

The Moon, this day's ruler, can be said to be margaric, which means "like pearl," and it was this word that inspired a French chemist to name the butter substitute that he patented on July 15, 1869, margarine.

July 16

Shy
Tender
Ambitious

DREAMY DOERS

Just as real-life crabs protect their vulnerable organs under a tough carapace, so July 16 crabs tend to hide their passive-polarity shyness, tender, water-enhanced feelings, and Moon-derived, emotional neediness by cultivating the go-getting, cardinal-quadruplicity aspect of their characters. This—often unconscious—strategy of diverting attention from their soft, sentimental side through action may have both advantages and disadvantages in terms of their relationships, but certainly helps July 16 people to make their dreams come true.

FAMOUS BIRTHS: Mary Baker Eddy (1821); Roald Amundsen (1872); Ginger Rogers (1911); Michael Flatley (1958); Will Ferrell (1967)

AN AQUATIC ADVANCE

The prevailing element on July 16 is water, making this a fitting date on which to publish the world's first underwater, color photographs. The images, which were shot near the Florida Keys, appeared in National Geographic magazine in 1926.

CANCER

Protective
Supportive
Persistent

JULY
17

SYMPATHETIC SUPPORTERS

Although their cardinal quadruplicity infuses those born on July 17 with the urge to make a success of their careers, they are not usually motivated by personal ambition, but by the desire to ensure that they and their loved ones are financially secure. Indeed, the combined influence of the family-oriented Moon, nurturing water, and their introspective, passive polarity causes July 17 individuals to prefer to play a supporting role, in their private lives, at least.

fAMOUS BIRTHS: James Cagney (1899); Donald Sutherland (1934); Diahann Carroll (1935); Camilla, Duchess of Cornwall (1947); David Hasselhoff (1952)

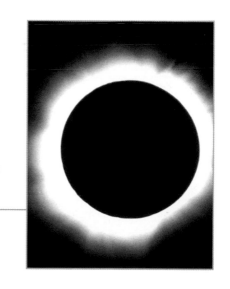

A DAY IN THE SUN
The Moon takes precedence over all other "planets" on this day, and it is therefore appropriate that the first recorded total eclipse of the Sun by the Moon was recorded in China as having occurred on July 17, 709 B.C.

July 18

Imaginative
Understanding
Creative

COMPASSIONATE CHARACTERS

With three-quarters of their birth influences—their feminine polarity, water, and the Moon—heightening their powers of receptiveness, intuition, and empathy, it is small wonder that July 18 individuals are so understanding, and forgiving, of others' human emotions and weaknesses. How they act on their responsiveness is down to the individual—some may enter the caring professions or volunteer work, while others may express their compassion through creativity—but in so doing, all demonstrate their characteristic determination.

FAMOUS BIRTHS: Nelson Mandela (1918); Martha Reeves (1941); Vin Diesel (1967); Lottie van Grieken (1995)

AN IMAGINATIVE INKLING
Of this day's influences, the Moon, water, and its feminine polarity are all linked with intuition and creativity, and maybe they were at work when, in 1877, U.S. inventor Thomas Edison conceived an idea that would evolve into the phonograph.

CANCER

☾ ♋

Complex
Patient
Goal-oriented

JULY
19

RECEPTIVE ACHIEVERS

If you were born on July 19, it is the contrast between your passive polarity and go-getting, cardinal nature that makes you such a complex individual. Your character components aren't necessarily contradictory, however, but complementary. Your receptive polarity makes you patient, and your lunar planetary ruler and watery element give you thoughtful, kind qualities. You only become pushy or controlling when you're acting on something you really care about, which is usually the best interests of those you love.

FAMOUS BIRTHS: Samuel Colt (1814); Edgar Degas (1834); Lizzie Borden (1860); George McGovern (1922); Anthony Edwards (1962)

A SISTERLY STAND
The Moon is associated with womanhood, as is its feminine polarity, both of which must have asserted themselves when the First Woman's Rights Convention opened on July 19, 1848, in Seneca Falls, New York.

JULY 20

♋ ☾

Focused
Supportive
Original

EMPATHETIC ENCOURAGERS

Your cardinal drive focuses your mind on achievement, if this is your birthday. You are instinctively supportive of others, though, so you aren't likely to put your own ambitions first. Because the Moon, water, and your passive polarity give you extraordinary creativity, your persistence may one day bring you great acclaim. In the meantime, you are happy to devote your energies to building up a happy and secure family life and being a thoughtful and sympathetic friend to those you've become close to.

FAMOUS BIRTHS: Francesco Petrarch (1304); Sir Edmund Hillary (1919); Diana Rigg (1938); Carlos Santana (1947); Chris Cornell (1964)

A FEMININE FIRST

July 20 has a feminine flavor, as was evident on this day in 1960, when Sirimavo Bandaranaike became Sri Lanka's (and the world's) first female prime minister. Her leadership inspired Sri Lankan women to new challenges.

CANCER

Contemplative
Dynamic
Encouraging

JULY 21

SYMPATHETIC STRIVERS

It is the interaction between their contemplative, passive polarity and ambitious cardinal mode that results in those born on July 21 giving their life's goals such serious consideration. They will pursue them with all their energies and passion. Yet these are no ruthless go-getters, because the Moon ensures that their most cherished aims are concerned with the well-being of family and friends. Water supplies them with compassion and creativity, too, so that their success is rarely won at others' expense.

fAMOUS BIRTHS: Ernest Hemingway (1899); Isaac Stern (1920); Cat Stevens (1948); Robin Williams (1952); Josh Hartnett (1978)

WALKING ON THE MOON

Did mysterious, lunar influences play a part in ensuring that when humankind—represented by the U.S. astronaut Neil Armstrong—first set foot on the Moon, this momentous event would occur on a Moon-ruled day, namely July 21, 1969?

JULY 22

CANCER

69 ☾

Artistic
Receptive
Imaginative

APPROACHABLE ARTISTS

All of your birth influences provide you with the ingredients to make a gifted artist, if this is your birthday. You might express your creativity in a professional or domestic context, or both. Your passive polarity works with the Moon to help you to absorb outside influences, and water sets your fertile imagination to work. When the seed of an idea germinates, you will be motivated to pursue it with cardinal drive—and a touch of the fire that flickers around the cusp of Leo.

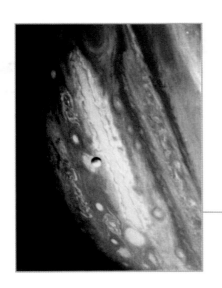

FAMOUS BIRTHS: Bob Dole (1923); Danny Glover and Don Henley (1947); Willem Dafoe (1955); Rufus Wainwright (1973)

MULTIPLYING MOONS?

The Moon governs reproduction, and it was on this lunar-ruled day in 2000 that astronomers from the University of Arizona and Smithsonian Astrophysical Observatory announced that they had discovered a new moon (now named Callirrhoe) orbiting Jupiter.

SYMBOL: The lion
CELESTIAL RULER: The sun
ELEMENT: Fire
POLARITY: Positive (masculine)
QUADRUPLICITY: Fixed

Leo

JULY 23 TO AUGUST 22 ♌

The lion's golden mane once caused it to be identified with the radiant Sun, a symbolic link underlined by the old belief that the lion is "king" of the beasts, just as the Sun outshines all other "planets." The astrological influences on the Leonine character can similarly be likened to aspects of either the dazzling Sun or a dominant, alpha male. These are the Sun itself, which makes Leos proud and vital, if egotistical; a masculine, positive, or active polarity (the names say it all, although "aggressive" could be added to the list); a fiery element, which supplies creativity and overheated emotions; and a fixed quadruplicity, whose contribution includes stability and inflexibility.

July 23

CHARISMATIC COMMANDERS

The influence of the Sun is especially evident in July 23 people, whose vitality and self-certainty impress those who are less sure of themselves, and whose sunny smiles and expansive generosity warm the hearts of those who enter their orbit. Yet their fixed natures makes them intransigent. If anyone refuses to bend to their strong will, then the headstrong, confrontational tendencies that are part and parcel of having a fiery element and masculine polarity may make these lions see red.

FAMOUS BIRTHS: Raymond Chandler (1888); Ras Tafari Makonnen, Haile Selassie (1892); Woody Harrelson (1961); Slash (1965)

GOOD DAY, SUNSHINE!

The Sun rules July 23. How apt, then, that when the U.S. nuclear-powered submarine Nautilus *set off from Pearl Harbor on this day in 1958, its mission—to become the first vessel to cross the North Pole—was given the name "Operation Sunshine."*

Leo

⊙ ♌

Confident
Attention-seeking
Uninhibited

JULY 24

SELF-ASSURED STARS

Taking your cue from your planetary ruler, you radiate sunny self-confidence, if this is your birthday. And if you accept others' approval as your due, Sun-style, it is your fiery element that is responsible for your occasionally outrageous, attention-demanding behavior. Your positive polarity removes your inhibitions whenever you're surrounded by an admiring audience. But your fixed nature exerts a steadying influence over you, so that while you may often get carried away, you rarely go too far.

FAMOUS BIRTHS: Simón Bolívar (1783); Alexandre Dumas, (1802); Amelia Earhart (1897); Lynda Carter (1951); Jennifer Lopez (1970); Anna Paquin (1982)

CITY OF THE SUN

On this solar day in 1911, U.S. archeologist Hiram Bingham discovered Machu Picchu, the Peruvian "lost city" built by the Incan emperor Pachacuti, who, his subjects believed, was the divine descendant of the Sun.

JULY 25

LEO
♌ ☉

Committed
Adventurous
Spontaneous

ADVENTUROUS OPTIMISTS

Those born on this day typically derive their sunny natures from their planetary ruler, and their steady commitment—be it to their families, friends, or career—from their fixed mode. It is the combination of their fiery element and positive polarity that gives them their wild, adventurous streak. As a result, while the Sun ensures that they retain their dignity, and their polarity keeps them anchored, they love partying and behaving in a spontaneous, uninhibited fashion, within these parameters.

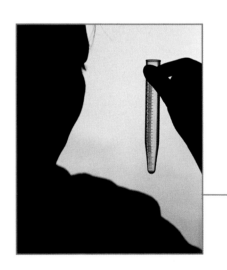

FAMOUS BIRTHS: Walter Brennan (1894); Estelle Getty (1924); Walter Payton (1954); Iman (1955); Matt LeBlanc (1967)

A SUN-BLESSED BABY?

The Sun, which rules this day, is symbolically associated with experimentation, children, and identity, so was it merely a coincidence that Louise Brown, the world's first "test-tube baby," should have been born on July 25, 1978, in Oldham, England?

Leo

☉ ♌

Melodramatic
Charismatic
Proud

July 26

Self-respecting Trailblazers

Having an attention-seeking element in fire makes July 26 individuals people who hate to be ignored, so it is just as well that their positive polarity pushes them into becoming trailblazing pioneers, and that their Sun-bestowed charisma draws all eyes upon them. Yet their planetary ruler is also responsible for their pride, which is a powerful influence on them, while their fixed nature gives them a longing for stability, so that they would never seriously jeopardize their social standing or support structures.

Famous Births: George Bernard Shaw (1856); Carl Jung (1875); Aldous Huxley (1894); Stanley Kubrick (1928); Mick Jagger (1943); Kevin Spacey (1959)

The Sun and Moon
Apollo was the Greco–Roman Sun god who gave his name to the U.S. space project charged with lunar landings. And it was on this solar day in 1971 that Apollo 15 blasted off Moonward from Cape Canaveral, Florida.

JULY 27

PASSIONATE PERFORMERS

If today is your birthday, the ego-enhancing Sun can make you believe that you were born to be the focus of others' admiration. Your remaining birth influences, however, ensure that you deserve it. Your element not only blesses you with creativity, but animates your creations with fire and passion, which often motivates others, too. Your positive polarity makes you enterprising and confident. But, crucially, it is your fixed mode that gives you the concentration and persistence to work hard at achieving success.

FAMOUS BIRTHS: Bobbie Gentry (1944); Peggy Fleming (1948); Maureen McGovern (1949); Alex Rodriguez (1975)

A FIERY DEBUT

July 27's element is fire, which may have given extra energy to the British-manufactured de Havilland Comet, the world's first jet-propelled commercial airliner, when it made its maiden flight over England on this day in 1949.

Leo

☉ ♌

Committed
Creative
Direct

FAITHFUL FIGURES

It may be evident in their personal style, or it may shine through in the creative nature of their work, but most July 28 individuals combine the flair inherent in their fiery element with the directness that they derive from their active polarity to dazzling effect. Their planetary ruler is responsible for their pronounced sense of honor, while their fixed nature supplies commitment, making them people who rarely renege on a pledge. These are vibrant, brave, generous characters who won't let you down.

FAMOUS BIRTHS: Beatrix Potter (1866); Rudy Vallee (1901); Jacqueline Kennedy Onassis (1929); Bill Bradley (1943); Jim Davis (1945)

ACTION STATIONS!

Leo's confrontational, active polarity was in evidence on July 28, 1914, when Austria–Hungary declared war on Serbia, following the latter's rejection of an Austro-Hungarian ultimatum, triggering the outbreak of World War I.

JULY 29

♌ ☉

Energetic
Pioneering
Confident

MAGNETIC LEADERS

Something about July 29 individuals encourages others to follow their example. Maybe it is the self-belief, or sheer star quality, with which the Sun has blessed them, or perhaps it is the inspirational flair and blazing energy that they share with their fiery element. Whatever the source of their magnetism, these are people who delight in taking the lead, and do so in energetic, positive-polarity fashion. Lively and irresistible as they are, though, they also demonstrate their fixed predictability in their routines.

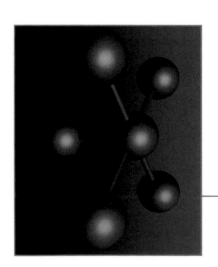

FAMOUS BIRTHS: Benito Mussolini (1883); Dag Hammarskjold (1905); Elizabeth Dole (1936); Sally Gunnell (1966)

GOING NUCLEAR

The Sun's energy is generated by nuclear fusion. It's fitting that it was on this Sun-ruled day in 1957 that the U.N. established the International Atomic Energy Agency to promote the positive use of nuclear power.

Leo

☉ ♌

Cheerful
Determined
Headstrong

JULY 30

CHALLENGERS OF CONVENTION

Your planetary ruler and fiery element may together give you a disarmingly warm and cheerful disposition, if you were born on July 30. These same influences are responsible for your formidable willpower and determination and your disregard for the bounds of convention. Reinforcing these traits, your fixed nature kicks in to set you on an unswerving path and your positive polarity supplies your inexhaustible energy. You are a headstrong, creative trendsetter who will keep forging ahead until you drop.

FAMOUS BIRTHS: Emily Brontë (1818); Henry Ford (1863); Arnold Schwarzenegger (1947); Lisa Kudrow (1963); Hilary Swank (1974)

A LOYAL LEGISLATURE

It was on July 30, 1619, that members of the House of Burgesses—the first legislative assembly in colonial North America—demonstrated their fixed-quadruplicity dedication by convening in Jamestown, Virginia.

JULY 31

LOYALISTS WITH INTEGRITY

Although the combination of the Sun and their element of fire breathes great creativity into those born on this day, July 31 people are often more remarkable for their fixed dedication, be it to a cause, to a commitment, or to their personal relationships or responsibilities. During times of adversity, or when their loyalty is truly tested, their active-polarity readiness to assume a confrontational stance, and their Sun-given integrity, become apparent. Others can only marvel at their drive and success.

FAMOUS BIRTHS: George Henry Thomas (1816); Curt Gowdy and Primo Levi (1919); Geraldine Chaplin (1944); Wesley Snipes (1962); J.K. Rowling (1965)

A LEONINE DEBUT
This day falls under the auspices of Leo, making it the perfect date for Leo, the lion, to roar his first introduction to an M.G.M. movie—the U.S. company's first "talkie," White Shadows on the South Seas—in 1928.

Leo

$\odot \, \Omega$

Creative
Confident
Optimistic

AUGUST
1

INFLEXIBLE INDIVIDUALISTS

So strong is the Sun's egocentric influence on you that you have an instinctive need to stand alone, if you were born today, and an inbuilt resistance to being part of the crowd. It is therefore fortunate that your fiery element endows you with the creativity and confidence to blaze your own trail though life, and that your positive polarity gives you plenty of optimism and energy. Your fixed inflexibility may, however, cause the path you tread to become a lonely one, unless you work hard at your relationships.

FAMOUS BIRTHS: Francis Scott Key (1779); Herman Melville (1819); Dom DeLuise (1933); Yves Saint Laurent (1936); Jerry Garcia (1942); Coolio (1963)

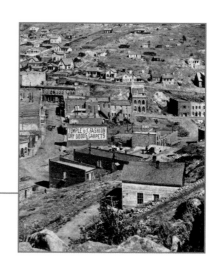

A CENTENNIAL UNION

August 1's quadruplicity is fixed, making consolidation appropriate. Colorado became the United States of America's thirty-eighth state on this day in 1876, on the day of the nation's centenary.

AUGUST 2

♌ ☉

Principled
Adventurous
Energetic

TRUTHFUL TRAILBLAZERS

There are typically two distinct sides to the charismatic personalities of those born on August 2. One results from the combination of the Sun and their fixed mode, which gives them integrity, generosity, and unwavering adherence to their guiding principles. The other is the product of the fusion between fire and their positive polarity, which causes adventurous August 2 individuals to be beacons of creativity, whose activities are fueled by seemingly inexhaustible supplies of enterprising energy.

FAMOUS BIRTHS: James Baldwin (1924); Peter O'Toole (1932); Wes Craven (1939); Edward Furlong (1977)

A SUNNY INSPIRATION

Maybe the color of August 2's planetary ruler influenced the decision to test yellow baseballs during the major-league baseball game played between the Dodgers and Cardinals at Ebbets Field, New York, on this day in 1938.

Leo
☉ ♌

Confident
Creative
Persistent

AUGUST
3

CONFIDENT CONSOLIDATORS

Your trendsetting creativity—the gift of the Sun and fire—will win you the attention of an admiring audience, if you were born on August 3. Your other astrological influences are likely to help bring you enduring success. Your Sun-bestowed self-belief, for instance, along with your positive-polarity confidence and fixed persistence, suggest that you're a fiercely determined individual set on building a career and home life to be proud of. You won't let anything intimidate or discourage you in the process.

FAMOUS BIRTHS: Tony Bennett (1926); Stephen Berkoff (1937); Martin Sheen (1940); Martha Stewart (1941); John Landis (1950)

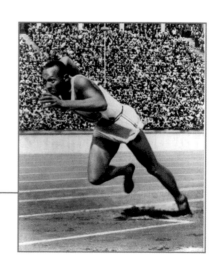

A GOLDEN BOY
When U.S. athlete Jesse Owens won his first gold medal on August 3, 1936, in Berlin, Germany, the day's astrological influences came to the fore: determination (fixed quadruplicity), energy (masculine polarity), inspiration (fire), and confidence (the Sun).

AUGUST 4

ENTHRALLING EXTROVERTS

Having a positive polarity means that August 4 people are usually unafraid of striking out on their own in life, while their fixed nature helps keep them true to their chosen path. It is the combined influence of their planetary ruler, the Sun, and their element of fire, however, that causes them to radiate such charisma and warmth that others can't help but be drawn into their orbit. Because these fiery types feed on flattery, they bask in their admirers' ego-boosting approval, but they may bristle at criticism.

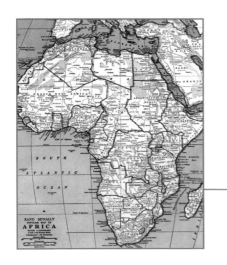

FAMOUS BIRTHS: Louis Armstrong (1901); Yasser Arafat (1929); Billy Bob Thornton (1955); Barack Obama (1961)

A NEW IDENTITY

Identity and integrity are qualities associated with the Sun, and it was on August 4, 1984, that the name of the African country formerly known as Upper Volta was changed to Burkino Faso, or "The Land of Honest Men."

Leo

$\odot \, \Omega$

Loyal
Enterprising
Authoritative

AUGUST
5

DEDICATED ADVENTURERS

Whatever your chosen career or focus in life, having a fixed nature suggests that you will remain loyal to it, if this is your birthday. You won't allow yourself to stagnate or become bored, though. Your passion and vitality are gifts of your element of fire, whose adventurousness fuels the enterprising inclinations contributed by your active polarity. Occasional recklessness is always a risk when you get carried away, but the proud Sun ensures that you never compromise your dignity, or your air of authority.

FAMOUS BIRTHS: John Huston (1906); Neil Armstrong (1930); Maureen McCormick (1956); Patrick Ewing (1962); Adam Yauch (1964)

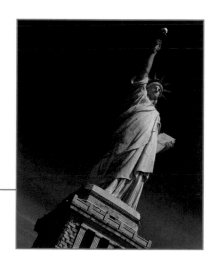

LADY BOUNTIFUL

Traits imparted by the Sun include dignity, pride, and generosity, while a fixed quadruplicity provides commitment, all qualities represented by the Statue of Liberty, the cornerstone for which was laid on Bedloe's Island, New York Harbor, on August 5, 1884.

AUGUST 6

UNCONVENTIONAL CONVENTIONALISTS

Their fixed quadruplicity can make August 6 individuals seem somewhat rigid and unwilling to embrace change. However, when fired up by their element and energized by their positive polarity, they may demonstrate that they are actually quite adventurous, experimental types after all. And because the Sun, their ruling planet, fills them with self-belief, they have the courage to stand up for what they believe to be right, even if it is contrary to convention or the majority view—and even if they suffer for it.

FAMOUS BIRTHS: Lucille Ball (1911); Robert Mitchum (1917); Andy Warhol (1928); Michelle Yeoh (1962); M. Night Shyamalan (1970)

AN ATOMIC ATTACK

The fusion of the day's astrological influences make fiery acts of aggression a sad, but definite, possibility on August 6, the date, in 1945, on which the U.S. Air Force dropped an atomic bomb on Hiroshima, Japan.

Leo

☉ ♌

Confident
Impulsive
Inspirational

SELF-CONFIDENT CHANCERS

If you were born on this day, the powerful interaction between the Sun and your fixed nature gives you a feeling of utter self-certainty and a dogged devotion to your guiding principles. Not only that, but because you also have a positive polarity, you are rarely troubled by doubts, while your fiery element encourages you to act on impulse. The upshot is that you will either be regarded as an inspirational example, or, if you're not careful, as a misguided risk-taker who should learn some humility.

FAMOUS BIRTHS: Mata Hari (1876); Ralph Bunche (1904); David Duchovny (1960); Charlize Theron (1975)

RISKY RACER
Dario Resta broke the 100mph barrier on this day in 1915 when he raced in the 100-mile Chicago Cup Challenge at Maywood Board Speedway. His average speed was 101.86mph.

AUGUST 8

LEO

♌ ☉

*Enthusiastic
Adventurous
Committed*

ACTIVE ADVENTURERS

The combined effect that their active polarity and adventurous element of fire has on August 8 people usually grabs others' attention—in fact, it's impossible to ignore characters who are so full of energy and enthusiasm. Despite being fun-loving, too—even if the overpowering Sun sometimes gives them a domineering edge—these are not frivolous types. Their fixed nature ensures their deep commitment to the people and things that they hold dear in life, and they make generous, warm friends and lovers.

FAMOUS BIRTHS: Matthew Henson (1866); Dustin Hoffman (1937); Keith Carradine (1949); Roger Federer (1981)

LATTER-DAY LEADERSHIP

The Sun's rulership of August 8 highlights leadership issues. The appointment, following the slaying of Joseph Smith, of the Quorum of the Twelve Apostles, headed by Brigham Young, to lead the Mormon Church, occurred on this day in 1844.

Leo

☉ ♌

Confident
Assertive
Commanding

AUGUST
9

AUTHORITATIVE ACTORS

If this is your birthday, regardless of whether you become a professional actor (and your fire-bestowed craving for attention suggests this likelihood), your sunny air of self-confidence makes it seem as though you are starring in your own biopic, from the second you awake to the moment you fall asleep. Your commanding presence, which is reinforced by the assertiveness of your masculine polarity and the firmness of your fixed nature, may impress, but it also intimidates and discourages intimacy.

FAMOUS BIRTHS: Robert Shaw (1927); Melanie Griffith (1957); Whitney Houston (1963); Eric Bana (1968); Gillian Anderson (1968); Audrey Tautou (1978)

A SUN KING
Power, authority, and leadership are all associated with the Sun, making August 9, 1902, a fitting date for the coronation of Queen Victoria's eldest son and successor, Edward VII, king of the United Kingdom.

AUGUST 10

$\Omega \odot$

Proud
Passionate
Spontaneous

SERIOUS SWASHBUCKLERS

Among the contributions that the Sun makes to the characters of those born on August 10 are a concern with their image, a sense of pride, and a need to be respected. Their fiery element, in combination with their active polarity, causes them to project a passionate, positive, spontaneous, almost swashbuckling persona. Meanwhile, their committed, fixed nature helps them build a career that the highest of achievers would be proud of. They can make generous, loyal, and lively friends and life companions.

FAMOUS BIRTHS: Herbert Hoover (1874); Eddie Fisher (1928); Bobby Hatfield (1940); Rosanna Arquette (1959); Antonio Banderas (1960)

GRAVEN IMAGES

Having the Sun as its ruler links August 10 with both leadership and image, making this day in 1927 an appropriate one for work to begin on the carving of four presidential faces into Mount Rushmore, South Dakota.

Leo

☉ ♌

Playful
Pioneering
Persistent

AUGUST
11

PLAYFUL PIONEERS

It is due to the Sun, your ruling planet, that you project a playful, good-natured persona, if today is your birthday. Your element of fire makes you happiest when you're the center of attention. But appearances can be misleading, because the same two astrological influences give you terrific willpower and a refusal to be constrained, while your active polarity provides a pioneering mindset and your fixed nature supplies remarkable persistence. Fun you may be, but you're also a force to be reckoned with.

FAMOUS BIRTHS: Anna Maria Luisa de' Medici (1667); Alex Haley (1921); Steve Wozniak (1950); Hulk Hogan (1953); Richie Ramone (1957)

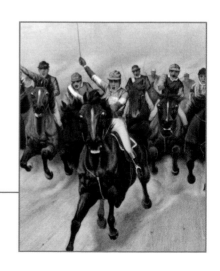

A DAY AT THE RACES

This day's pioneering, competitive, determined, and limelight-seeking influences augured well for competitors in the first race meeting at Ascot, England, taking place in 1711.

AUGUST 12

♌ ☉

Determined
Passionate
Persistent

AUTONOMOUS ASPIRANTS

The self-sufficiency, self-belief, and determination that are just a few of the qualities bequeathed to them by their ruling planet typically prompt young August 12 individuals to vow to become both self-supporting and stars of their chosen field. And their chances of succeeding look promising, given that their fixed nature makes them stick to their guns, their positive polarity banishes self-doubt, and their fiery element provides passion. But they sometimes suffer from overheated emotions and are prone to arrogance.

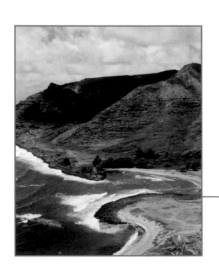

FAMOUS BIRTHS: Cecil B. DeMille (1881); Cantinflas (1911); William Goldman (1931); George Hamilton (1939); Pete Sampras (1971)

RAISING THE FLAG

August 12's fixed quadruplicity encourages acts of consolidation, so it was no coincidence that it was on this day in 1898 that the USA annexed Hawaii and made it a U.S. territory (it became a U.S. state in 1959).

Leo

☉ ♌

Assertive
Charismatic
Confident

AUGUST 13

DOMINATING DIRECTORS

The combination of their unbending, fixed ways, an assertive, active polarity, and their Sun-bestowed self-belief causes those born on August 13 to be charismatic characters with a commanding presence. These big cats certainly like to take charge, and is the interaction of these three birth influences with the fourth, their volatile element of fire, that generally determines whether others warm to their cheery confidence or are brought to boiling point by their perceived highhandedness.

fAMOUS BiRTHS: Annie Oakley (1860); John Logie Baird (1888); Alfred Hitchcock (1899); Fidel Castro (1926); Don Ho (1930)

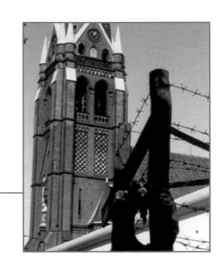

OBDURACY MADE MANifEST
One of this day's traits is the inflexibility imparted by its fixed quadruplicity, as was evident on August 13, 1961, when East German forces blocked access to West Germany by erecting a barrier between East and West Berlin.

AUGUST 14

LEO

♌ ☉

Creative
Extroverted
Attention-seeking

EXUBERANT ENTERTAINERS

Like their element, those Sun-ruled individuals born on August 14 burn ever more brightly when fueled by the oxygen of attention. And when all eyes are upon them, these creative, engaging personalities ensure that they remain in the spotlight by switching into entertaining mode. But being active-polarity extroverts and having a fixed quadruplicity's rigidity means that their fury may flare all too fiercely if there is no one to spark off, or if others won't go along with them. Their egos can be too much.

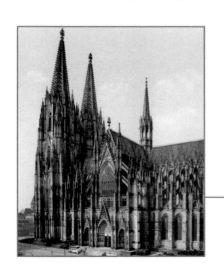

FAMOUS BIRTHS: Doc Holliday (1851); Steve Martin (1945); Gary Larson (1950); Earvin "Magic" Johnson (1959); Halle Berry (1968)

A DISPLAY OF DEVOTION

Determination and perseverance are qualities associated with this day's fixed quadruplicity, and both were demonstrated in Cologne, Germany, on this day in 1248 and 1880, when rebuilding work on the city's striking cathedral respectively began and ended.

Leo

☉ ♌

Challenging
Confrontational
Warm-hearted

AUGUST
15

CONFIDENT COMMANDERS

If this is your birthday, so powerful is the influence of the commanding Sun over you that you have been challenging others to defy you from the cradle. When people go along with your wishes, they are typically rewarded with sunny smiles and the delightful warmth inherent in having fire as an element—but should they refuse, they might find themselves feeling the full force of your confrontational masculine polarity, unbending, fixed mode, and searing anger. You should learn to control your temper.

FAMOUS BIRTHS: Napoleon Bonaparte (1769); Princess Anne of the United Kingdom (1950); Debra Messing (1968); Ben Affleck (1972)

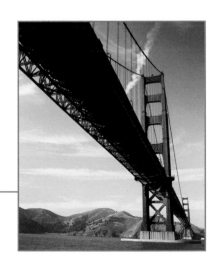

LOOK AT ME!

Demonstrating the daring, attention-seeking behavior associated with August 15's influences, on this day in 1949 Robert L. Niles performed the first successful stunt leap off San Francisco's Golden Gate Bridge.

AUGUST 16

SINGLE-MINDED TRENDSETTERS

Having the Sun as their planetary governor may mean that August 16 people come across as being self-regarding egotists, but then they have the talent, energy, and perseverance to merit being the focus of others' attention, as well as their own. Their fiery element gives them trailblazing creativity and trendsetting instincts, while their positive polarity gives them dynamism. Their fixed nature infuses them with unwavering determination: all told, an electric, extremely effective, combination.

FAMOUS BIRTHS: Gabriel Lippmann (1845); James Cameron (1954); Madonna and Angela Bassett (1958); Timothy Hutton (1960)

A HEARTBREAKING END

The Sun confers majesty, while the heart is said to be vulnerable to Leo's influence. It is therefore sadly fitting that Elvis Presley, the "King of Rock and Roll," should have had his fatal heart attack on August 16, 1977.

Leo

☉ ♌

Charismatic
Uninhibited
Stubborn

AUGUST 17

IMPRESSIVE IMPRESARIOS

Be they male or female, those whose birthday falls on August 17 are born showmen, for, like the alpha-male lions that they are, they give off waves of charismatic self-assurance, thanks to the Sun. They also exert a magnetic pull on others, courtesy of their impossible-to-ignore, fiery element, which is also responsible for their limelight-loving lust for staging a performance. Further attention-attracting characteristics include their masculine-polarity lack of inhibition and fixed-quadruplicity stubbornness.

FAMOUS BIRTHS: Davy Crockett (1786); Mae West (1893); Robert De Niro (1943); Sean Penn (1960); Donnie Wahlberg (1969)

A fiERY fLIGHT
Harnessing the power of fire, in 1978, Americans Max Anderson, Ben Abruzzo, and Larry Newman completed the first successful transatlantic crossing by hot-air balloon when they landed in Miserey, France.

AUGUST 18

UNCOMPROMISING LEADERS

Their fixed-quadruplicity obduracy marks out those born on August 18 as individuals who will remain true to themselves, and will not be browbeaten into behaving otherwise. Flattery may work, though, for these Sun-ruled, fiery people have stellar levels of self-esteem, making them predisposed to warm to anyone who praises their character or capabilities. But as essentially tough-minded leaders, with a masculine-polarity's assertiveness, they need no one's approval to act as they see fit.

FAMOUS BIRTHS: Meriwether Lewis (1774); Shelley Winters (1922); Roman Polanski (1933); Robert Redford (1937); Christian Slater (1969); Edward Norton (1969)

A RISING STARR

While the Sun, August 18's planetary ruler, hints at glory, fire infuses this day with a performer's passion and exuberance, making it a fitting date for British drummer Ringo Starr to join the Beatles, which he did in 1962.

Leo

$\odot$ ♌

Pioneering
Creative
Intelligent

AUGUST
19

GENIAL GENIUSES

If today is your birthday, the combination of a pioneering, positive polarity, a concentration-enhancing, fixed nature, and solar creativity gives you genius potential. This will only be fulfilled, however, if perfect conditions enable a spark of inspiration from your fiery element to kindle a latent idea. Genius or not, the Sun blesses you with good humor, with fire contributing warmth, making you a popular personality—although these characteristics can, at times, be transformed into aggression and stubbornness.

FAMOUS BIRTHS: Orville Wright (1871); Ogden Nash (1902); Gene Roddenberry (1921); Bill Clinton (1946); Matthew Perry (1969)

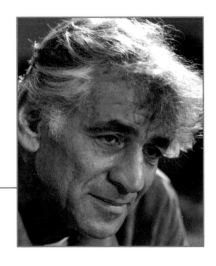

A GOLDEN FAREWELL

"Leonard" means "hard lion," and it was on this Leonine day in 1990 that U.S. musician Leonard Bernstein gave his last public performance, bowing out in a blaze of glory by conducting the Boston Symphony Orchestra at Tanglewood, Massachusetts.

August 20

Pioneering Performers

While it is the commanding Sun that gives its August 20 protégés such presence, it is their fiery element that provides their passion for performing, and their positive polarity that urges them to push back the boundaries of possibility. It goes without saying that these individuals usually possess both self-confidence and courage aplenty, but it may come as a surprise to some that they can be so rigidly resistant to change, due to their fixed nature. This also makes them endearingly loyal, though.

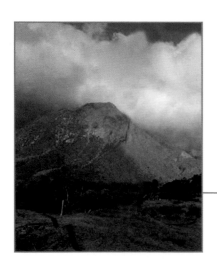

Famous Births: Benjamin Harrison (1833); H.P. Lovecraft (1890); Don King (1931); Isaac Hayes (1942); Robert Plant (1948); Joan Allen (1956); Fred Durst (1971)

A Fiery Hazard

August 20's fiery element was emphatically emphasized on this day in 1997, when the increasing danger presented by the Soufriere Hills Volcano forced evacuation of the citizens of the Caribbean island of Montserrat.

Leo

⊙ ♌

Brave
Challenging
Dramatic

AUGUST
21

COURAGEOUS CHARACTERS

If there is one characteristic that August 21's astrological influences have in common, it is courage, which is why bravery is always evident in those born on this day. Be it because they make a fixed-mode stand against a popular innovation, because they launch a masculine-polarity challenge against an abuse of power, because their element fires them up to give a provocative performance, or because the Sun compels them to display leadership, these are plucky personalities who will make their mark.

FAMOUS BIRTHS: Aubrey Beardsley (1872); Count Basie (1904); Shimon Peres (1923); Wilt Chamberlain (1936); Kenny Rogers (1938); Kim Cattrall (1956)

ART ATTACK

When courage is not matched by judgment, an impulse to foolhardy behavior can emerge on August 21. In 1911, an employee of the Louvre Museum, Paris, stole the world's most famous painting on this day.

AUGUST 22

Leo
♌ ☉

Authoritative
Self-Sufficient
Enthusiastic

POWERFUL PERSONALITIES

If today is your birthday, the Sun beams down on you, giving you an aura of authority and inner strength that sets you apart as being both special and self-sufficient. Not only that, but your fixed nature supplies determination, your positive polarity infuses you with purpose, and your fiery element contributes vitality and enthusiasm. As intimidating as you are impressive, others may be afraid to approach you, but they'll be amply rewarded when they do—provided that you show them your generous, sunny side.

FAMOUS BIRTHS: Claude Debussy (1862); Dorothy Parker (1893); Deng Xiaoping (1904); John Lee Hooker (1917); Tori Amos (1963)

LONG LIVE THE KING!

August 22 is *ruled by the Sun, a kingly symbol, so it is fitting that it should mark the death of one English king, Richard III, and the accession of another, Henry VII, at the Battle of Bosworth Field in 1485.*

Symbol: A virginal woman
Celestial Ruler: Mercury
Element: Earth
Polarity: Negative (feminine)
Quadruplicity: Mutable

Virgo
August 23 to September 22 ♍

If you're a Virgoan, you may have contradictory aspects to your personality. Your ruling planet and your mutable quadruplicity give you a sociable, communicative side, but the combination of your passive polarity and earthy element can make you introverted and cautious. If all four astrological influences are interacting harmoniously, you may be analytical and articulate, amiable and adaptable, receptive and thoughtful, and hardworking and supportive. If there is an imbalance, though, you might be excessively critical and carping, changeable and capricious, negative and withholding, sluggish and miserly—someone who simply cannot be pleased.

AUGUST 23

Sociable
Ambitious
Articulate

AMBITIOUS NETWORKERS

That August 23 people have a gregarious, mutable nature is especially evident when they go off-duty, when they enjoy being exposed to different personalities and viewpoints. Having an ambition-enhancing, earthy element means that they spend most of their time diligently furthering their careers, however. They are helped in their aim to make a comfortable living by their analytical minds and effortless articulacy (Mercury's contribution), and by the thoughtfulness that comes of having a feminine polarity.

FAMOUS BIRTHS: Georges Cuvier (1769); Gene Kelly (1912); Shelley Long (1949); River Phoenix (1970); Kobe Bryant (1978)

A FREEDOM FIGHTER FALLS
A combination of earthy pragmatism and analytical political calculation influenced Edward I of England's tactical execution of the charismatic Scots patriot and warrior William Wallace on this day in 1305.

VIRGO
☿ ♍

Logical
Gregarious
Pragmatic

AUGUST 24

PRACTICAL PHILOSOPHERS

Mercury, the logic-enhancing, intelligence-sharpening ruler of those born on this day, and their rumination-encouraging, feminine polarity form a strong bond within the August 24 psyche, creating deep, incisive thinkers who are blessed with phenomenal powers of expression, thanks to Mercury. Yet their element ensures that they are down-to-earth types, rather than airy-fairy intellectuals, while their mutable personality gives them a taste for mixing, so that they can communicate with anyone.

FAMOUS BIRTHS: Aleksey Konstantinovich Tolstoy (1817); Jorge Luis Borges (1899); Yasser Arafat (1929); Paulo Coelho (1947); Steve Guttenberg (1958)

SPREADING THE WORD

Mercury, August 24's ruling planet, is concerned with communication, which may be why it was on this day in 1456 that Johann Gutenberg completed his Bible, the first printed book.

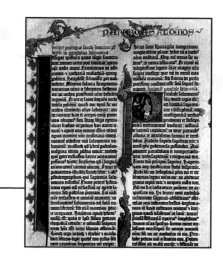

AUGUST 25

Determined
Practical
Eclectic

CAPABLE CAREERISTS

If you were born on August 25, you tend to keep your feet firmly on the ground and rarely lose your head, however far your ambition takes you. Your determination, diligence, and straightforward outlook are down to your earthy element, but it is the influence of Mercury that is responsible for your objectivity, while your quadruplicity tempts you to change direction every so often. Despite being generally level-headed, your negative polarity makes you prone to the occasional gloomy spell.

FAMOUS BIRTHS: Leonard Bernstein (1918); Sean Connery (1930); Gene Simmons (1949); Elvis Costello (1954); Tim Burton (1958); Claudia Schiffer (1970)

EARTH'S EMISSARY

The Roman messenger god Mercury rules this day, on which, in 1989, the U.S. spacecraft Voyager 2 beamed back the first close-up images of Neptune and its satellites.

VIRGO
☿ ♍

Communicative
Analytical
Helpful

OBJECTIVE SUPPORTERS

There are two distinct strands running through the August 26 pysche. The first derives its curious, objective flavor and urge to communicate from both Virgo's ruling planet, Mercury, and its mutable quadruplicity, which contributes cooperative instincts. The second is influenced by the union of the supportive element of earth and this day's nurturing, feminine aspect. The result is typically bright, unprejudiced individuals who are predisposed to helping others, particularly by providing practical assistance.

fAMOUS BIRTHS: Antoine Lavoisier (1743); Peggy Guggenheim (1898); Christopher Isherwood (1904); Macaulay Culkin (1980)

fEMALE fRANCHISE
Maybe August 26's feminine polarity helped to ensure that the Nineteenth Amendment to the U.S. Constitution was adopted on this day in 1920, for it was this that gave American women the right to vote.

AUGUST 27

Independent
Inquisitive
Practical

IMPARTIAL OBSERVERS

You probably take a keen interest in your fellow humans if you have an August 27 birthday, due partly to your mutable quadruplicity and partly to inquisitive Mercury. But your judgment is usually unclouded by feelings, and not just because Mercury makes you objective and dispassionate: your earthy element means that you prefer to provide practical, rather than emotional, help when support is needed. Because you have an inward-looking, feminine polarity, you tend to need your own space, too.

FAMOUS BIRTHS: Man Ray (1890); Lyndon B. Johnson (1908); Mother Teresa (1910); Barbara Bach (1947); Pee-wee Herman (1952)

MIGHT IS RIGHT?

On this day in 1896, the Anglo-Zanzibar War was fought. The shortest war in world history, it lasted only from 9:02 to 9:40 a.m., when Zanzibar surrendered, and discussions took over from hostilities—perhaps due to Mercury's influence.

VIRGO

☿ ♍

*Broad-minded
Sensible
Flexible*

AUGUST 28

FLEXIBLE FRIENDS

Two characteristics become increasingly evident as August 28 people age: firstly, their versatility (the gift of their mutable mode), and, secondly, their wide-ranging outlook (the input of Mercury)—which may be literally so, if they have the opportunity to travel, or may otherwise describe their mental viewpoint. But their earthy element grounds them, too, and their passive polarity gives them caution, thereby tempering the fickle and flighty tendencies inherent in their quadruplicity and planetary ruler.

FAMOUS BIRTHS: Johann von Goethe (1749); Elizabeth Ann Seton (1774); Leo Tolstoy (1828); David Soul (1943); Shania Twain (1965); LeAnn Rimes (1982)

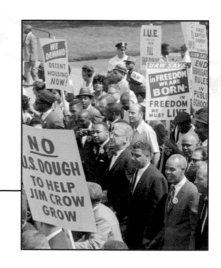

I HAVE A DREAM
On this day in 1963, Dr. Martin Luther King, Jr., delivered his powerful speech at a rally in Washington, DC. Always a gifted communicator, Mercury's powerful influence may have inspired him.

AUGUST 29

Friendly
Self-sufficient
Successful

CIRCUMSPECT COMMUNICATORS

Some August 29 traits seem confusingly contradictory. For while Mercury instills in those born on this day the desire to communicate, and their mutable mode makes them highly sociable, these outgoing tendencies are tempered by their passive-polarity desire for privacy. It is earth that reconciles their often conflicting instincts by, for example, combining their polarity's natural caution with Mercury's logic. Their element also supplies a steadying and career-promoting dose of diligence and ambition.

FAMOUS BIRTHS: Ingrid Bergman (1915); Charlie "Bird" Parker (1920); Richard Attenborough (1923); Elliott Gould (1938); Michael Jackson (1958)

STORM SURGE
On this mutable-quadruplicity day in 2005, Hurricane Katrina's unpredictable course and enormous power devastated much of the U.S. Gulf Coast, with storm surges in its wake that swept away entire communities.

VIRGO
☿ ♍

Quirky
Level-headed
Thoughtful

AUGUST
30

SENSIBLE, BUT SURPRISING

If the August 30 personality were represented as a balance sheet, ranged on one side would be Mercury, earth, and a feminine polarity, while a mutable quadruplicity would appear on the other. Their ruling planet, element, and polarity interact to produce people who are objective, level-headed, and prudent—and thus individuals who think for themselves, weigh up their options carefully, and are risk-averse. Their quadruplicity, on the other hand, supplies a dash of surprisingly unpredictable quirkiness.

FAMOUS BIRTHS: Mary Wollstonecraft Shelley (1797); Huey Long (1893); Ted Williams (1918); Frank "Tug" McGraw (1944); Cameron Diaz (1972); Andy Roddick (1982)

TERRITORIAL CONCERNS

August 30 was the earthy-element date in 1945 on which the territory of Hong Kong was liberated from Japan by British armed forces in the late stages of World War II.

AUGUST 31

Persuasive
Rational
Charitable

PRACTICAL PERSUADERS

It is due to your feminine aspect that you are a deep thinker and caring character, if you were an August 31 baby. Mercury supplies your objectivity and helps you to spread the word effectively when you choose to champion a cause. And it is your earthy element that is responsible for your practical streak, as well as your dependability—which is not to say that you are dull, because your variable, mutable quadruplicity causes you to sparkle socially and gives you an eclectic range of interests.

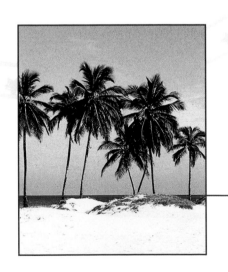

FAMOUS BIRTHS: James Coburn (1928); Eldridge Cleaver (1935); Van Morrison (1945); Richard Gere (1949); Chris Tucker (1972)

INDEPENDENT ARCHIPELAGO

Twenty-three small Caribbean islands, including Trinidad and Tobago, together became a single independent state on this earth-governed day in 1962, when the UK ceded power under its decolonization plan.

VIRGO
☿ ♍

Family-oriented
Home-centered
Adaptable

SEPTEMBER
1

HARDWORKING HOMEBODIES

Inquisitive, itchy-footed Mercury may send those born on September 1 out and about at regular intervals, but having a feminine polarity and earth as an element means that they crave a secure family background and a comfortable home to return to. And it is in order to build and maintain these domestic support structures that they typically channel their earthy diligence into furthering their careers, encouraged in this aim by their mutable quadruplicity's versatility and adaptability.

FAMOUS BIRTHS: Edgar Rice Burroughs (1875); Rocky Marciano (1923); Lily Tomlin (1939); Barry Gibb (1946); Dr. Phil McGraw (1950); Gloria Estefan (1957)

A SUCCESSFUL SEARCH
September 1 derives its probing character from Mercury, and this was the day, in 1985, when oceanographic investigators finally discovered the wreck of R.M.S. Titanic.

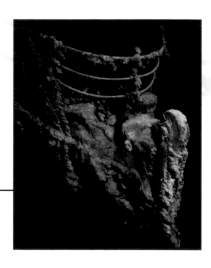

September 2

Ambitious Planners

It is largely down to their earthy element that many September 2 people formulated a life plan as children, and have stuck tenaciously to it ever since. And being resolutely earthy types, the desired reward for their hard work is likely to be financial security, to which end they employ their formidably sharp, Mercury-influenced intellect. Yet their feminine polarity can make these apparently stolid types shy, while their mutable quadruplicity contributes indecisiveness, but also cooperativeness.

Famous Births: Jimmy Connors (1952); Keanu Reeves (1964); Lennox Lewis (1965); Salma Hayek (1966)

Scorched Earth

On this day in 1666 the overcrowded city of London burst into flames that blazed relentlessly for three days, destroying more than 10,000 buildings in its capricious, destructive path and claiming many lives.

VIRGO
☿ ♍ ♍

Moody
Cautious
Restless

SEPTEMBER
3

VOLATILE WORRIERS

Were you born on September 3, and are your moods changeable? You may not always be anxious, especially when you have succumbed to earth's influence and are in a grounded phase, but not only do your mood swings rival a seesaw's, due to your mutability, but having a caution-bestowing, feminine polarity can make you a terrible worrier. It is dispassionate, objective Mercury that supplies your calmness and confidence, however, often by sending you on a vacation or giving you a new project.

FAMOUS BIRTHS: Ferdinand Porsche (1875); Dick Motta (1931); Al Jardine (1942); Steve Jones (1955); Charlie Sheen (1965)

TERRITORIAL CONFLICT
On this earth-ruled day in 1939, Neville Chamberlain, Britain's prime minister, took to the airwaves to announce his declaration of war on Germany, following the invasion of Poland two days previously.

SEPTEMBER 4

VIRGO
♍ ☿

Mercurial
Caring
Grounded

FICKLE FRIENDS

Those who come into contact with September 4 individuals often see two sides to their characters, not least because their mutable quadruplicity makes them so changeable. On the one hand, steady earth and their guarded, feminine polarity make those born on this day generally stable and sensible types. On the other, when clever, curious Mercury and that restless, mutable nature hold sway, their impatient quest for interesting diversions or new projects and friends causes them to be surprisingly impulsive.

FAMOUS BIRTHS: Richard Wright (1908); Henry Ford II (1917); Dick York (1928); Mitzi Gaynor (1930); Beyoncé Knowles (1981)

HEAVEN ON EARTH

Territorial ventures are highlighted on earthy September 4, the day on which, in 1781, Spanish settlers established "El Pueblo de Nuestra Senora La Reina de Los Angeles de Porciuncula"—or the Californian city of Los Angeles.

VIRGO
☿ ♍

Inquisitive
Home-centered
Easily bored

SEPTEMBER
5

RESTLESS, BUT ROOTED

If you were born on September 5, the combination of Mercury, your information-hungry, travel-loving, ruling planet, and your variable, mutable mode fills you with the desire to see the world and experience constant changes of scenery. But having a stable home base is also very important to the earthy side of your character. And it is usually only in the privacy of your own home that you feel able to soften your no-nonsense image and allow your gentle, feminine-polarity side to emerge.

FAMOUS BIRTHS: Jesse James (1847); John Cage (1912); Raquel Welch (1940); Loudon Wainwright III (1946); Freddie Mercury (1946)

A CLOSE SHAVE
Demonstrating the logic and hands-on approach that are hallmarks of Mercury and earth, Tsar Peter the Great of Russia personally shaved off his officials' beards on September 5, 1698, deeming this "new look" vital for promoting a modernizing mindset.

SEPTEMBER 6

NIGGLING NITPICKERS

If this is your birthday, it is mainly from your element of earth that you derive your ambition, determination, and perseverance, as well as your ultimate aim, which is probably to be financially secure for life. In pursuit of this goal, you are helped by your adaptability-providing, mutable nature, as well as by Mercury, whose contribution includes cool objectivity and a gift for communication. As for your feminine polarity, that supplies thoughtfulness, but sometimes also a negative, pessimistic outlook.

FAMOUS BIRTHS: Joseph P. Kennedy (1888); Michael Winslow (1960); Rosie Perez (1964); Greg Rusedski (1973); Tim Henman (1974)

WYOMING WOMEN

On this earthy, perseverance-rewarding day in 1870, Louisa Ann Swain of Laramie, Wyoming, became the first woman officially to cast a vote in a United States national election, following local legislation enacted the previous year.

VIRGO
☿ ♍ ♉

Indecisive
Anxious
Flexible

SEPTEMBER
7

WARM-HEARTED WORRIERS

September 7's birth influences often pair up to give those born on this day drastically different public and private personas. When intelligent, communicative Mercury teams up with the stable element of earth, the personality that sallies forth into the world typically appears quick-witted, detached, practical, and persistent. But when their changeable, mutable nature combines with their inward-looking, passive side, the result is often an indecisive worrier, even if a cooperative and caring one.

FAMOUS BIRTHS: Elizabeth I of England (1533); Grandma Moses (1860); Elia Kazan (1909); Buddy Holly (1936); Richard Roundtree (1942); Gloria Gaynor (1949)

LADY DAY
This day's feminine polarity was especially influential on September 7, 1921, for this date marks the anniversary of the first Miss America beauty pageant, held in Atlantic City, New Jersey, and was won by Margaret Gorman.

SEPTEMBER 8

Clever
Sociable
Productive

HARDWORKING HEDONISTS

Although those born on September 8 share Mercury's shrewdness, as well as their passive polarity's tendency to turn inward every so often for some quiet contemplation, it is the influence of their remaining two birth influences that is especially evident to others. For while their productivity-enhancing, earthy element is at the root of their prodigious work rate (as well as their sensuality), it is their mutable quadruplicity that is responsible for their sociable streak—and, sometimes, moodiness.

FAMOUS BIRTHS: Antonin Dvorak (1841); Peter Sellers (1925); Patsy Cline (1932); Henry Thomas (1971); Pink (1979)

LONGING FOR LEARNING

Demonstrating the thirst for knowledge with which Mercury infuses this date, it was on September 8, 1636, that the Massachusetts Bay Colony voted Harvard University (then called New College) into being.

VIRGO
☿ ♍

Private
Considerate
Practical

SEPTEMBER
9

INTUITIVE INTROVERTS

Your thoughtfulness, intuition, and inborn tendency to worry that are part of your feminine-polarity birthright are particularly pronounced if your birthday is September 9. You also have an endearing gentleness about you, but these "soft" qualities are balanced by the "harder" traits bestowed on you by your ruling planet, element, and quadruplicity. Mercury provides your logical mindset, earth gives you a practical outlook, and your mutable nature causes you to be drawn to the company of others.

FAMOUS BIRTHS: Cliff Robertson (1925); Otis Redding (1941); Michael Keaton (1951); Hugh Grant (1960); Adam Sandler (1966)

A BABY QUEEN
The element of earth's influence over September 9 indicates that land- and power-related events are particularly likely to occur on this day, on which, in 1543, nine-month-old Mary Stuart was crowned "Queen of Scots."

September 10

Flexible
Innovative
Self-starting

EQUABLE ENTREPRENEURS

September 10 individuals have entrepreneurial potential. While objective, commercially minded Mercury prompts them to identify a gap in the market, and their feminine polarity causes them to reflect carefully on everything they learn, it is the element of earth that encourages the germ of an idea to take root and provides the calm, constructive approach that enables it to flourish. Add their versatile, mutable nature to the equation, and these people typically have many strings to their bows.

FAMOUS BIRTHS: Elsa Schiaparelli (1890); Arnold Palmer (1929); Karl Lagerfeld (1938); Joe Perry (1950); Dan Castellaneta (1958); Ryan Phillippe (1974)

FINAL CUT
The events of the French Revolution made the executioner's guillotine infamous. But in 1977, on a day governed by the feminine trait of compassion, the guillotine was used for the last time in the nation that invented the device.

VIRGO
☿ ♍

Contemplative
Communicative
Practical

SEPTEMBER
11

PRACTICAL COMMUNICATORS

Your creativity may not be of the fiery, crackling type if you were born on this day, but the combination of your intuitive, contemplative, feminine polarity and your industrious element of earth makes you thoughtful and hands-on, and your ventures typically bear tangible fruit. You are also helped in all you undertake by the logical thinking and excellent communication skills of Mercury, as well as by the adaptable nature that is one of the benefits of having a mutable quadruplicity.

fAMOUS BIRTHS: D.H. Lawrence (1885); Brian DePalma (1940); Moby (1965); Harry Connick, Jr. (1967); Ludacris (1977)

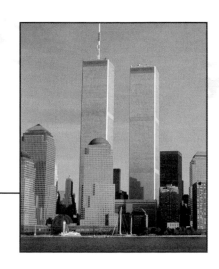

AIRBORNE ASSASSINS

Astrological forces did not cause the terror attacks on 9/11/2001, but detailed planning and unquestioning determination are both characteristics of the astrological element of earth, and Mercury has travel connections.

SEPTEMBER 12

VIRGO

♍ ☿

Selfless
Cooperative
Supportive

SELF-EFFACING SUPPORTERS

It is partly because they have nurturing, feminine-polarity instincts and partly because they have a dependable element that others frequently rely on September 12 people, especially for practical support. The input of adaptable Mercury and a flexible nature makes them cooperative, and sometimes indecisive, types, too. Their tendency to go along with others means that they sometimes neglect their own desires, perhaps because they don't always know exactly what they want for themselves.

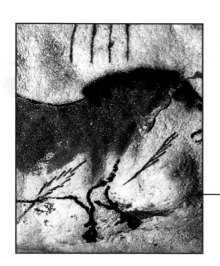

FAMOUS BIRTHS: Maurice Chevalier (1888); Jesse Owens (1913); Linda Gray (1940); Barry White (1944); Benjamin McKenzie (1978)

UNEARTHING THE PAST
This day's influences include exploratory Mercury and the element of earth, their link being made explicit on September 12, 1940, when four inquisitive boys discovered Paleolithic-era paintings adorning the walls of an underground cave in Lascaux, France.

VIRGO
☿ ♍

Practical
Persuasive
Gregarious

SEPTEMBER
13

EARTHY ENTERTAINERS

Having a feminine polarity means that September 13 people have plenty to think about and are comfortable in their own company, but they also have a curiosity-heightening planetary ruler in Mercury, as well as a sociable, mutable nature. As a result, they usually enjoy hearing what others have to say. Because their earthy element compels them to be productive, no-nonsense types, they may express what they have learned through their work, thereby instructing or entertaining others.

FAMOUS BIRTHS: John J. Pershing
(1860); Claudette Colbert (1903);
Roald Dahl (1916); Jacqueline
Bisset (1944); Nell Carter (1948)

FLEET OF FOOT

Mercury, the messenger god, rules this day, while the first marathon was run in 490 B.C. by the message-carrying Greek soldier Pheidippides, making September 13, 1970, an apt date for the the first New York Marathon.

September 14

Inquisitive
Analytical
Hardworking

Logical Learners

September 14 individuals are unquestionably children of Mercury. Not only is "Why?" their watchword, but they think along typically analytical Mercurial lines. If their lives resemble a quest for discovery (in which they are helped by their receptive, feminine polarity), they rarely let their findings go to waste, because their earthy element makes them responsible and industrious. Their mutable quadruplicity makes them versatile, so the expression of their knowledge may take many forms.

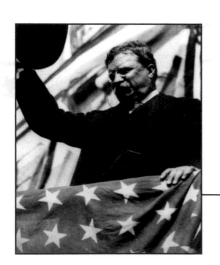

Famous Births: Michael Haydn (1737); Alexander von Humboldt (1769); Ivan Pavlov (1849); Sam Neill (1947)

Staying Power

The earthy perseverance of Theodore Roosevelt in overcoming health problems and building his political career paid off when, on this day in 1901, he became President of the United States, following the assassination of President McKinley.

VIRGO
☿ ♍

Introspective
Perceptive
Adaptable

SEPTEMBER
15

COMPLEX CHARACTERS

Having an earthy element makes you a straightforward type if you were born on this day, but that does not mean that you are shallow. Far from it! Your feminine polarity gives you a propensity to mull over problems for days, while Mercury's gifts include a brilliant combination of intelligence and perceptiveness. And while the double dose of restlessness that you receive from Mercury and your mutable quadruplicity may cause your focus to wander, these influences can also supply great adaptability.

FAMOUS BIRTHS: William H. Taft (1857); Agatha Christie (1890); Oliver Stone (1946); Tommy Lee Jones (1946); Dan Marino (1961); Prince Harry of England (1984)

VOYAGE OF DISCOVERY
Scientific discovery is aided under the influence of analytical Mercury, a ruling planet that also favors travel. On this day in 1835 the HMS Beagle, with Charles Darwin aboard, reached the Galapagos Islands.

SEPTEMBER 16

Sensual
Moody
Objective

DISPASSIONATE OBSERVERS

If you were born on September 16, you are probably a sensual type, thanks to your earthy element, but people with your birthday are also sensible individuals who do not let emotions cloud their judgment, having inherited cool objectivity from Mercury. It is from Mercury, too, that you derive your communication skills, but your mutable mode means that you are prone to occasional moodiness, and your feminine polarity gives you the need to turn inward and spend time alone once in a while.

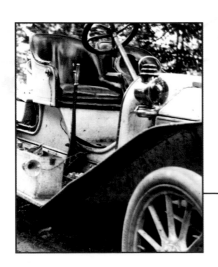

FAMOUS BIRTHS: Lauren Bacall (1924); B.B. King (1925); Peter Falk (1927); Mickey Rourke (1956); David Copperfield (1956); Jennifer Tilly (1961); Katie Melua (1984)

MOTOR MAKERS

Earth gives this day a practical flavor, while Mercury links it with travel, making it an auspicious date for William C. Durant to found the U.S. General Motors Corporation in 1908.

VIRGO
☿ ♍ ♍

Easily bored
Home-centered
Dependable

SEPTEMBER 17

NINE-TO-FIVERS

Saying that September 17 people are both restless and routine-loving may sound contradictory, but it is nevertheless true. While the combination of Mercury and their mutability is responsible for their itchy feet and constantly changing moods, the effects of their earthy element and feminine polarity cause them to feel grounded and secure when their lives are played out against a smoothly running, predictable backdrop. They may occasionally be impulsive and unpredictable, but chaos unsettles them.

FAMOUS BIRTHS: Hank Williams (1923); Stirling Moss (1929); Roddy McDowall (1928); Anne Bancroft (1931); Baz Luhrmann (1962); Anastacia (1973)

DECIPHERED!
Mercury, this day's intellectual planetary ruler, exerted his influence in 1822 on Jean-François Champollion when he delivered a lecture explaining the inscriptions on the Rosetta Stone.

SEPTEMBER 18

Restless
Travel-focused
Family oriented

RESTLESS HOMEBODIES

If you were born on September 18, chances are that you become miserable and moody if confined to one place for too long. Your mutable quadruplicity is partly responsible for this, but this syndrome is also partly due to your ruling planet, which gives you a strong desire to see the world. That said, you are an earthy character: your element is responsible for your strong desire to put down roots and settle down, and your passive polarity makes you appreciate plenty of regular domestic downtime.

FAMOUS BIRTHS: Greta Garbo (1905); Robert Blake (1933); James Gandolfini (1961); Jada Pinkett Smith, Lance Armstrong (1971)

READ ALL ABOUT IT!

Mercury infuses this day with the desire to exchange information. How appropriate that the first issue of The New-York Daily Times, which would later become The New York Times, was published on September 18, 1851.

VIRGO
☿ ♍

Knowledgeable
Articulate
Adaptable

SEPTEMBER
19

ETERNAL STUDENTS

Whatever their age, knowledge-hungry Mercury makes eternal students of September 19 people, whose prodigious appetite for learning is matched by the articulacy with which they communicate their interests to others. They have a contemplative, feminine polarity, but these are no impractical, academic types, because their earthy element provides a hands-on approach, along with determination. Their adaptable nature gives them the versatility to make numerous career changes if need be.

FAMOUS BIRTHS: Adam West (1928); David McCallum (1933); Paul Williams (1940); "Mama" Cass Elliott (1943); Jimmy Fallon (1974)

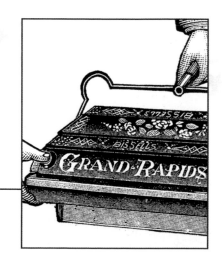

A CLEAN SWEEP
A streak of practicality runs through earthy September 19, which may have been partly responsible for the patenting of a carpet-sweeper by Melville R. Bissell, of Grand Rapids, Michigan, on this day in 1876.

September 20

♍ ☿

Ambitious
Irritable
Sociable

GREGARIOUS GO-GETTERS

September 20 people seem to spend much of their time trying to get ahead, because their earthy element fills them with the ambition to go far—and usually succeeding. Quick-witted, fast-moving Mercury both speeds up their thought processes and makes them feel twitchy and irritable when they suspect that their time is being wasted. Yet when they do slow down and make time to kick back, their earthy sensuality kicks in, as does their mutable-quadruplicity enjoyment of socializing.

FAMOUS BIRTHS: Upton Sinclair (1878); Sophia Loren (1934); Kristen Johnston (1967); Juan Pablo Montoya (1975)

A CINEMATIC CELEBRATION

It was on September 20, 1946, that the first Cannes Film Festival opened, which seems fitting, given that the day's quadruplicity is mutable, or appreciative of variety, and that its planetary ruler is the communicative Mercury.

VIRGO
☿ ♍

Talkative
Logical
Prone to mood swings

SEPTEMBER 21

COMPELLING COMMUNICATORS

Your earthy element gives you a hefty dose of realism, if you're a September 21 baby, and Mercury provides a logical outlook, along with enviable communication skills. But you also have a worry-inducing, negative polarity, and, in your mutable nature, a birth influence that can induce frequent mood swings. On the outside, you usually seem calm and composed, and you are always articulate and convincing, but sometimes the impression you convey to others bears no resemblance to how you feel inside.

FAMOUS BIRTHS: H.G. Wells (1866); Larry Hagman (1931); Leonard Cohen (1934); Stephen King (1947); Bill Murray (1950); Faith Hill (1967); Ricki Lake (1968)

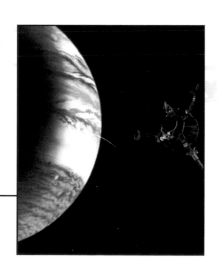

GALILEO'S DAY
The partnership of dependable earth and exploratory, information-seeking Mercury was especially evident on September 21, 2003, when Galileo, the U.S. space probe, finally completed its fourteen-year mission to Jupiter.

September 22

*Stubborn
Analytical
Practical*

CONSTANT CONTEMPLATIVES

Once you've made up your mind, you will change your viewpoint only reluctantly if you're a typical child of September 22. This tendency is mainly due to your element of earth, which also makes you tenacious. It's reinforced, too, by your passive polarity, but this also causes you to be thoughtful. Mercury blesses you with plenty of intelligence, while your other birth influence is adaptability. So, if all the logical arguments justify it, you'll revise your opinions when properly convinced that you should.

FAMOUS BIRTHS: Michael Faraday (1791); Nick Cave (1957); Andrea Bocelli (1958); Scott Baio (1961); Ronaldo (1976)

SALTY SCROLLS

Maybe it was in honor of Mercury, September 22's ruling planet, which was named for the Roman messenger god, that the ancient Dead Sea Scrolls were put on public display for the first time on this day in 1991.

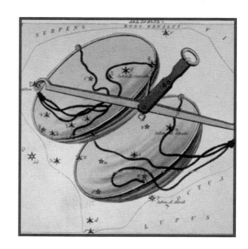

Symbol: The scales
Celestial Ruler: Venus
Element: air
Polarity: Positive (masculine)
Quadruplicity: Cardinal

Libra

September 23 to October 22 ♎

In Latin, *libra* means "a pair of scales" or "balance," and if you imagine an old-fashioned pair of weighing scales, this should give you a good idea of the Libran personality. If the four astrological ingredients that make up the characters of a Libran are evenly balanced, the result is someone who is light-hearted, thanks to Venus; who takes the initiative, due to their cardinal quadruplicity; who is outgoing, as a result of having a positive polarity; and who, under air's influence, is bright and talkative. Should any ingredient predominate, however, and Venus's vanity, a cardinal mode's bossiness, a masculine polarity's aggression, or air's fickleness—to name some examples—may prevail.

September 23

INDULGENT INITIATORS

If you're a child of September 23, you are likely to be bursting with the initiative that is the gift of your cardinal quadruplicity. This trait is reinforced by the confidence you derive from your positive polarity, but you do not thoughtlessly rush headlong into new ventures. Not only does your element of air encourage you to analyze the pros and cons of a project before you invest too much time and energy in it, but Venus gives you a laid-back approach and a susceptibility to self-indulgent distractions.

FAMOUS BIRTHS: Mickey Rooney (1920); John Coltrane (1926); Ray Charles (1930); Julio Iglesias (1943); Bruce Springsteen (1949)

SPOTTED IN SPACE
Information-seeking air, September 23's element, was evident in 1846 when German astronomer Johann Gottfried Galle, working from his Berlin Observatory, became the first human to identify the planet Neptune.

LIBRA

♀ ♎

Magnetic
Influential
Self-starting

SEPTEMBER 24

CHARMING CAMPAIGNERS

Those born on this day make good use of the double dose of charm that is the joint gift of Venus and the element of air, not least in winning others over to their point of view. These same birth influences typically cause September 24 people to be logical and tolerant types, who are always upset by perceived instances of unfairness and who, thanks to their self-starting, cardinal quadruplicity and assertive, positive polarity, are prepared to campaign energetically in the cause of justice and to defend their friends.

FAMOUS BIRTHS: F. Scott Fitzgerald (1896); Jim Henson (1936); Linda McCartney (1941); Phil Hartman (1948); Pedro Almodovar (1951)

ARABIAN ARRIVAL
The initiative with which its cardinal quadruplicity infuses this day was demonstrated on September 24, 622, when Muhammad, the founder of Islam, arrived in Medina, having fled Mecca to escape persecution and to establish a Muslim state in Arabia.

SEPTEMBER 25

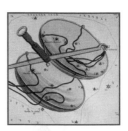

Hedonistic
Ambitious
Objective

SENSUAL SELF-STARTERS

Were you born on September 25? If so, your personality is probably a striking blend of hedonism and sensuality (thanks to the input of pleasure-loving Venus, your ruling planet) and focus and ambition (the contribution of your go-getting, cardinal quadruplicity). In your mission to get ahead, you are also helped by your pioneering, positive polarity and intelligence-heightening element of air, which gives you the streak of cool objectivity that can make you seem a little aloof at times.

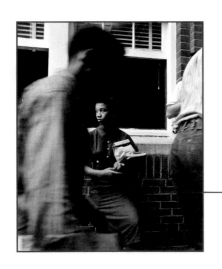

FAMOUS BIRTHS: William Faulkner (1897); Dmitri Shostakovich (1906); Michael Douglas (1944); Will Smith (1968); Catherine Zeta-Jones (1969)

YOUNG PIONEERS
On this air-governed, freethinking day in 1957, with its pioneering, cardinal qualities, nine African-American children were escorted by paratroopers to enter a segregated high school in Little Rock, Arkansas, for the first time.

LIBRA
♀ ♎

Stylish
Gregarious
Ambitious

SEPTEMBER 26

CHIC COMMUNICATORS

Venus's stylishness is evident in everything that September 26 people undertake in life, as is the goddess's tolerance of different personalities and lifestyles. A love of fun is another quality that she contributes to her protégés' personalities, boosted in this respect by air, which also causes them to be compelling communicators. It is not all play, however, for their cardinal nature makes them quite ambitious characters, and their positive polarity can make them confrontational, should forcefulness be required.

FAMOUS BIRTHS: T.S. Eliot (1888);
George Gershwin (1898);
Serena Williams (1981);
Christina Milian (1982)

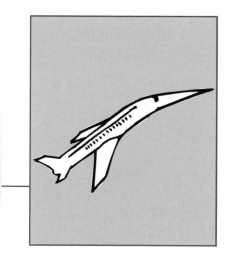

SUPERSONIC FLIGHT
It seems appropriate that Concorde, the Anglo–French supersonic airliner, should have pioneered its nonstop Atlantic crossing on September 26, 1973, a day that has air as an element and a go-getting, cardinal quadruplicity.

SEPTEMBER 27

THEATRICAL THINKERS

Because your element is air, if you were born on this day, you are an incisive and dispassionate thinker, although your Venus-inspired, dramatic façade often causes you to appear far more emotional than you actually are. Your cardinal nature predisposes you to put number one above all else, too, while your positive polarity provides the vigor and energy that fuels your drive to get ahead. Somewhat self-promoting you may be, but your considerable charm sweetens your determination and wins others over.

FAMOUS BIRTHS: Samuel Adams (1722); Jayne Meadows (1920); Arthur Penn (1922); Meat Loaf (1947); Avril Lavigne (1984)

STEAMING AHEAD

Its trailblazing, cardinal quadruplicity suggests that all kinds of "firsts" are likely on September 27, such as the introduction, by George Stephenson, of the first steam locomotive designed to haul a passenger train, which occurred in England in 1825.

LIBRA

♀ ♎

Self-assured
Decisive
Polite

SEPTEMBER 28

SWEET, BUT STEELY

Gracious Venus may be behind September 28 people's exquisite manners, polished appearance, and dislike of unpleasantness, but these are no spineless esthetes. Far from it: their masculine polarity makes them highly assertive, and their cardinal nature provides initiative and decisiveness, while their element of air prompts them to think along rigorously rational lines. And if thwarted or disrespected, they will not hesitate to peel off the kid gloves in order to demonstrate decisively who's boss.

FAMOUS BIRTHS: Ed Sullivan (1901); Brigitte Bardot (1934); Janeane Garofalo (1964); Mira Sorvino (1967); Gwyneth Paltrow (1972); Hilary Duff (1987)

CAPITAL CITY
Perhaps September 28's enterprising and self-promoting, cardinal quadruplicity was at work on this day in 1867, when Toronto was formally proclaimed the capital of Ontario, Canada.

SEPTEMBER 29

LIBRA

♎ ♀

Thoughtful
Placid
Self-possessed

PEOPLE-PLEASERS

Their Venusian inheritance is particularly pronounced in those born on September 29, for they get a buzz from giving others pleasure, especially when it comes to indulging their senses or providing them with a delightful, entertaining diversion. They are natural peacemakers, too, which is not to say that they won't stand up for their own interests, however, for their cardinal quadruplicity makes them self-centered, their masculine polarity, self-confident, and their airy element, fundamentally unsentimental types.

FAMOUS BIRTHS: Miguel de Cervantes (1547); Greer Garson (1908); Jerry Lee Lewis (1935); Madeline Kahn (1942)

START TO FINISH

September 29 marks both the start of construction (1907) and the completion (1990) of the Washington National Cathedral. The landmark embodies the architectural intelligence, enterprise, and confidence associated with this day's astrological influences.

LIBRA
♀ ♎

Intelligent
Enterprising
Easygoing

SEPTEMBER 30

REALISTIC ROMANTICS

While you are blessed with your element of air's sharp, inquiring intellect, if you're a child of September 30, such is Venus's input that you often come across as being an indolent romantic. Yet Venus's gifts also include a shrewd way with money and a highly developed sense of materialism, while your cardinal mode gives you ambition, and your positive polarity provides enterprise and energy. This is why you're a driven, if easygoing, person who should never be mistaken for a ditsy do-nothing.

FAMOUS BIRTHS: Deborah Kerr (1921); Truman Capote (1924); Johnny Mathis (1935); Monica Bellucci (1968); Martina Hingis (1980); Kieran Culkin (1982)

BANNING THE BOMB
Maybe the League of Nations took its cue from peace-loving Venus when, on September 30, 1938, members of its international assembly unanimously resolved that "The intentional bombing of civilian populations is illegal."

OCTOBER

1

LIBRA

♎ ♀

Courteous
Articulate
Self-indulgent

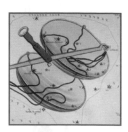

POLITE PLEASURE-SEEKERS

October 1's four birth influences interact intriguingly. The merging of articulate air and well-mannered Venus results in exquisitely polite individuals, for example, albeit ones with a tendency to please themselves, due to the coming-together of their ego-emphasizing, cardinal quadruplicity and their uninhibited, masculine polarity. But peaceable Venus is queen of the October 1 personality, so that however self-indulgent her children may be at times, they remain loath to upset others through their actions.

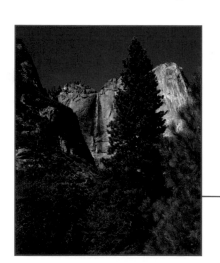

FAMOUS BIRTHS: Walter Matthau (1920); Jimmy Carter (1924); George Peppard (1928); Richard Harris (1932); Julie Andrews (1935)

AS FREE AS AIR
The air, this day's element, is clean and unpolluted at Yosemite, California, thanks to the pioneering naturalists who campaigned for its preservation as a natural haven: on this day in 1890, it became the third U.S. national park.

LIBRA
♀ ♎

Critical
Well-groomed
Adept networker

OCTOBER 2

SOCIABLE CRITICS

If you were born on this day, you're undoubtedly a child of Venus, in that you place great store on immaculate appearances and understand the dramatic value of staging a scene in order to convey a message effectively. Many of your air-derived characteristics complement those of Venus, notably your gregariousness and love of fun, but you also have a tough side, due to your forceful, masculine polarity and go-getting, cardinal nature, as well as the urge to criticize—again, this is an air characteristic.

FAMOUS BIRTHS: Mahatma Gandhi (1869); Groucho Marx (1890); Don McLean (1945); Donna Karan (1948); Sting (1951)

MISSION ACCOMPLISHED!
It was on this day in 1836 that Charles Darwin returned to England after five years of exploring the natural world, his home-coming demonstrating the successful partnership of information-seeking air and a goal-oriented, cardinal quadruplicity.

OCTOBER 3

LIBRA
♎ ♀

Clever
Style-conscious
Extrovert

IMAGE-CONSCIOUS INTELLECTUALS

The presence of air among their birth influences suggests that those born on October 3 are very bright individuals, as well as inventive, playful, and articulate. Take Venus into consideration, and they are likely to be as stylishly smart as they are intellectually smart, despite often appearing indolent to the point of laziness. Appearances can be deceptive, however, for behind their laid-back façade, these positive-polarity, cardinal-quadruplicity extroverts are buzzing with energy and fizzing with initiative.

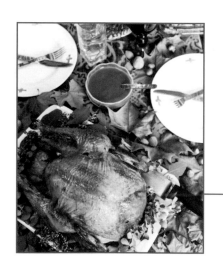

FAMOUS BIRTHS: Gore Vidal (1925); Chubby Checker (1941); Tommy Lee (1962); Gwen Stefani (1969); Neve Campbell (1973); Ashlee Simpson (1984)

GIVING THANKS

Venus, October 3's ruling planet, favors feasting, and may have influenced George Washington in his decision to sign the Thanksiving Proclamation on this day in 1789, designating its official national celebration for the first time.

LIBRA
♀ ♎

Polite
Confrontational
Dominant

OCTOBER
4

MANIPULATIVE CHARMERS

Although, due to the influence of your airy element, you probably regard yourself as being first and foremost an intellectually sharp, objective thinker, if you're a typical October 4 child you are perceived quite differently. Others may, for instance, appreciate the courtesy that is Venus's contribution to your character, but may be disconcerted when exposed to your masculine-polarity aggression and cardinal-mode bossiness, as may happen when you turn off the charm and go for the forceful approach.

FAMOUS BIRTHS: Buster Keaton (1895); Charlton Heston (1924); Susan Sarandon (1946); Alicia Silverstone (1976)

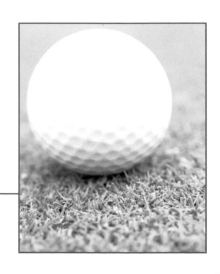

STRIKING A PRECEDENT
Given this day's pioneering, cardinal quadruplicity, enterprising, positive polarity, and airy element, perhaps it is not surprising that the first shot in a U.S. Open Men's Golf Championship was played on this day in 1895.

OCTOBER 5

ENERGETIC ENTERTAINERS

October 5 individuals are especially influenced by their cerebral, airy element and go-getting, cardinal nature, so that when their bright minds are fully engaged by the possibilities they see in a project or plan, they will throw the full force of their formidable, masculine-polarity energy into following it up. And what sorts of ventures excite their interest? Well, having Venus as their ruling planet suggests that these are likely to combine artistic, design-related, media, or dramatic themes with material rewards.

FAMOUS BIRTHS: Larry Fine (1902); Karen Allen (1951); Bob Geldof (1954); Bernie Mac (1957); Guy Pearce (1967); Kate Winslet (1975); Nikki Hilton (1983)

CYCLONE CITY

Air, this day's element, can be whipped up to devastating effect, as occurred on this day in 1864, when a cyclone caused by the collision of polar and equatorial air decimated the Indian city of Calcutta, killing 60,000 people.

LIBRA
♀ ♎

Stylish
Dynamic
Clever

OCTOBER
6

IMAGE-CONSCIOUS INTELLECTS

The presence of Venus, the artistic, beauty-emphasizing planet, is easily discernible in the October 6 personality, because those born on this day are typically concerned with image-projection, whatever their blank canvas may be (and it is often they themselves). Also evident are their dynamic, positive polarity, go-getting, cardinal nature, and the cleverness, emotional detachment, and knack of getting across their ideas easily and instantly that are part and parcel of having air as an element.

FAMOUS BIRTHS: Le Corbusier (1887); Carole Lombard (1908); Britt Ekland (1942); Elisabeth Shue (1963)

AN OPERATIC DEBUT
This day has strong pioneering influences, while Venus infuses it with an appreciation of artistry. Small wonder, then, that Italian composer Jacopo Peri's experimental opera *Euridice* should have been premiered in Florence on October 6, 1600.

OCTOBER 7

CHARISMATIC CRITICS

Of all your birth influences, if you were born on this day, air and Venus usually interact the most powerfully, for while your element is responsible for your objectivity and critical tongue, your planetary ruler tempers your coolness with kindness, courtesy, and charm. When working in harmony, air and Venus are responsible for your amiability, too, but there may also be times when your masculine polarity provokes your confrontational tendencies, or when your cardinal nature promotes selfish behavior.

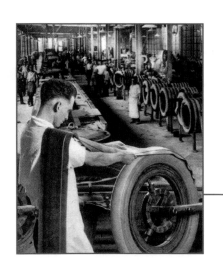

FAMOUS BIRTHS: Heinrich Himmler (1900); Desmond Tutu (1931); Vladimir Putin (1952); Yo-Yo Ma (1955); Simon Cowell (1959); Toni Braxton (1968)

FACTORY FLOOR

Air gives this day a logical, analytical flavor, which may have made it an auspicious date in 1913 for Henry Ford to introduce the radical, but hugely influential, assembly line, a method that transformed many industries.

LIBRA
♀ ♎

Original
Motivated
Adventurous

OCTOBER 8

FREETHINKING FORERUNNERS

It is not just because their go-getting, cardinal quadruplicity provides initiative and prompts them to set themselves ambitious targets that self-motivated October 8 individuals tend to act as forerunners. Add freethinking air and an uninhibited, positive polarity to the mix, and you have personalities who refuse to be bound by convention and are brave enough to follow their own path in life. It's not all go, go, go, though, for Venus encourages plenty of relaxation and a good deal of self-indulgence, too.

FAMOUS BIRTHS: Juan Peron (1895); Jesse Jackson (1941); Chevy Chase (1943); Sigourney Weaver (1949); Matt Damon (1970)

MIND YOUR MANNERS!
Reflecting the emphasis that Venus, this day's ruling planet, is said to place on the importance of good manners, October 8, 1952, was the first U.S. publication date of Amy Vanderbilt's Complete Book of Etiquette.

October 9

DYNAMIC CHARMERS

When acting independently, Venus provides your playful charm, if today is your birthday, and your masculine polarity supplies your dynamism and a positive outlook. But when these influences merge, you can radiate the sort of mesmerizing, compelling energy that draws all eyes upon you. Because you have a self-promoting, cardinal nature as well as an intellect-sharpening, communicative element in air, you are not in the least bit shy about pushing yourself forward, and you're rarely lost for words.

FAMOUS BIRTHS: John Lennon (1940); Jackson Browne (1948); Sharon Osbourne (1952); Scott Bakula (1954)

A PIONEERING PILOT

On landing in Glendale, California, on October 9, 1930, Laura Ingalls became the first woman to fly solo across the U.S.A. Did feminine Venus, air, and this day's enterprising nature aid her pioneering flight?

LIBRA
♀ ♎

Focused
Relaxed
Communicative

OCTOBER 10

RELAXED PERFORMERS

There is often a distinct difference between the public and private personas projected by those born on October 10. When engaged in the "performance" side of life, their cardinal quadruplicity and masculine polarity typically dominate, so that the October 10 personality can appear driven, pioneering, and determined to get ahead. Behind the scenes, however, Venus and air are likely to prevail, so that the same person's character then seems gentle, relaxed, fun-loving, and talkative.

fAMOUS BIRTHS: Giuseppe Verdi (1813); Helen Hayes (1900); Thelonious Monk (1917); Harold Pinter (1930); Charles Dance (1946); Mya (1979)

AMOROUS ACTORS
This day's ruling planet is Venus, whose namesake is the Roman goddess of love, so maybe it had a hand in the remarriage of the legendary lovers Richard Burton and Elizabeth Taylor in Africa on this day in 1975.

OCTOBER 11

LIBRA
♎ ♀

Original
Lively
Materialistic

ENERGETIC LIVE WIRES

Your ruling planet, Venus, ensures that you let your hair down and have a good time every so often, and also gives you your talent for making money, if this is your birthday. However, you tend to be so full of energy, due to your active polarity, that you rarely sit still. Not only that, but your cardinal quadruplicity causes you to be target-driven and, with your Venusian love of material things, makes you quite ambitious. Because you have an airy element, you also hate to be hemmed in by convention.

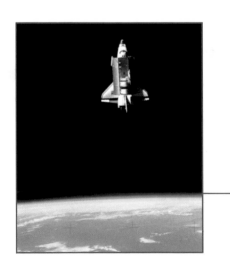

FAMOUS BIRTHS: Henry John Heinz (1844); Eleanor Roosevelt (1884); Joan Cusack (1962); Luke Perry (1966); Michelle Wie (1989)

SPACE STEPS
Kathryn D. Sullivan became the first woman to space-walk on this day in 1984, deep within its airy element in the U.S. space shuttle Challenger, and egged on, maybe, by October 11's enterprising polarity and quadruplicity and femininity-favoring Venus.

LIBRA
♀ ♎

Sociable
People oriented
Independent-minded

OCTOBER
12

GREGARIOUS GO-GETTERS

The potent combination of convivial Venus, amiable air, and their outgoing, positive polarity causes those born on this day to be sociable types who enjoy being surrounded by others and generally feel restless and dissatisfied if left to their own devices. But when working toward a cherished ambition, October 12 individuals are capable of an impressive degree of cardinal single-mindedness, and also demonstrate the ingenuity and independence of mind that are attributes of the element of air.

FAMOUS BIRTHS: Ann Petry (1908);
Luciano Pavarotti (1935);
Hugh Jackman (1968);
Marion Jones (1975)

BEER FESTIVITIES
Venus favors love and indulgence, and both were evident on October 12, 1810, when Prince Ludwig of Bavaria married Princess Therese of Saxony-Hildburghausen. This event was celebrated with the first Oktoberfest ("October festival").

OCTOBER 13

OUTSPOKEN ORIGINALS

Although having Venus as a ruling planet means that you often demonstrate remarkable kindness and tact, particularly in your personal dealings, if this is your birthday, you're more notable for your bluntness. This is partly because air makes you an articulate, "tell-it-how-it-is" type, and partly because your positive polarity removes any inhibitions you might have. And when freethinking air and your enterprising, cardinal quadruplicity merge, you have the potential to be uniquely original and progressive.

FAMOUS BIRTHS: Margaret Thatcher, Paul Simon (1941); Marie Osmond (1959); Sacha Baron Cohen (1971); Ashanti (1980)

MAGIC NUMBERS

That light-hearted Venus and playful air fill this day with fun was emphasized on October 13, 1995, when Florida's Walt Disney World Resort welcomed its 500-millionth visitor.

LIBRA
♀ ♎

Polite
Quick-witted
Elegant

OCTOBER
14

STYLISH ECCENTRICS

Stylish October 14 individuals may appear conformist types, for Venus's gifts to them include sartorial elegance, beautiful manners, and an aversion to causing offense, yet they often think along highly unusual lines. When their airy element sets their minds musing on a certain subject, they will often shoot off at an extraordinary tangent, at which point their initiative-bestowing, cardinal nature and dynamic, positive polarity may kick in, and often with quite unorthodox, sometimes bizarre, results.

fAMOUS BIRTHS: William Penn (1644); Dwight Eisenhower (1890); e.e. cummings (1894); Roger Moore (1927); Ralph Lauren (1939); Usher (1979)

PRIZE PEACEMAKER
Venus encourages—and rewards—peacemaking, which may be why it was on this day in 1964 that U.S. civil-rights leader Dr. Martin Luther King, Jr., an advocate of non-violent protest, was awarded the Nobel Prize for Peace.

OCTOBER 15

Shrewd
Well-mannered
Goal-driven

ASTUTE ANALYSTS

October 15 people's Venusian courtesy enchants, but they also have their planetary ruler's hard head when it comes to money matters. Couple their feel for finances with the analytical mindset supplied by their airy element, and they have money-making potential, particularly given their goal-oriented, cardinal quadruplicity and masculine-polarity willingness to take risks. Yet refined Venus encourages them to favor artistic ventures over commercial ones, unless someone else is grafting on their behalf!

FAMOUS BIRTHS: John Kenneth Galbraith (1908); Mario Puzo (1920); Lee Iacocca (1924); Penny Marshall (1942); Richard Carpenter (1946)

PEACE PROTEST

The interaction between peace-loving Venus and this day's energetic, positive polarity was very powerful on October 15, 1969, when 2 million Americans participated in a "Peace Moratorium" opposing the Vietnam War.

LIBRA

♀ ♎

Ambitious
Communicative
Stylish

OCTOBER 16

ARTICULATE OBSERVERS

If you were born on October 16, you share Venus's sense of style, you are driven by your cardinal ambition to get ahead in life, and you tackle everything that you undertake with positive-polarity vigor. But of all of your birth influences, the element of air is the most evident in your personality. You are someone who reads, observes, and learns almost compulsively, noting everything that occurs around you with a perceptive, dispassionate eye. You are also blessed with impressive communication skills.

fAMOUS BIRTHS: Noah Webster (1758); Oscar Wilde (1854); Eugene O'Neill (1888); Angela Lansbury (1925); Tim Robbins (1958); Flea (1962)

WINDS OF CHANGE

Air, October 16's element, is associated with change, and may have had something do to with the election of the first non-Italian pope for over four hundred years on this day in 1978, namely the Polish cardinal Karol Wojtyla.

OCTOBER 17

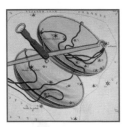

SOCIABLE SELF-STARTERS

If you were born on this day, your birth influences gave you some tremendous traits: Venus gave you her charming demeanor, for example, with your positive polarity providing your energy and enthusiasm. Your cardinal quadruplicity contributed plenty of initiative and your self-motivation. But the characteristics that define you are air's gifts, especially your hunger to learn, your rational, analytical way of thinking, your articulacy, and the enviable ability to communicate with almost anyone you meet.

FAMOUS BIRTHS: Arthur Miller (1915); Rita Hayworth (1918); Montgomery Clift (1920); Evel Knievel (1938); Wyclef Jean (1972); Eminem (1972)

OVER THE AIRWAVES
October 17's element is air, which promotes the gathering and dissemination of information—not least over the airwaves—so this was a very good day for the Radio Corporation of America (R.C.A.) to be incorporated, in 1917.

LIBRA
♀ ♎

Driven
Fun-loving
Gregarious

OCTOBER 18

PARTY PEOPLE

Because they have an energy-bestowing, positive polarity, October 18 people both work hard and play hard, although rarely simultaneously! When "on duty," or furthering their careers, they display the determination and drive that comes of having a go-getting, cardinal quadruplicity, but when they can relax, their hedonistic, Venusian side comes to the fore. Air is a steady presence, however, contributing on the one hand intelligence and logic, and, on the other, playfulness and easy sociability.

FAMOUS BIRTHS: Chuck Berry (1926); Lee Harvey Oswald (1939); Martina Navratilova (1956); Jean-Claude Van Damme (1960)

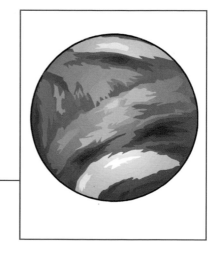

EXPLORING VENUS
Venus rules this day, and it was on October 18, 1967 that a probe—Venera 4—launched by the Soviet Union became the first spacecraft to penetrate this planet's atmosphere, whereupon it beamed its findings back to Earth.

OCTOBER 19

LOGICAL LEADERS

Your masculine-polarity confidence and dynamism, cardinal-quadruplicity initiative and ambition, and airy element's independent and rational mindset together give you leadership potential, if today is your birthday. But whether you actually assume such a role in life depends on the input of your ruling planet. If tolerant, easygoing Venus's influence gives you an aversion to ordering others around, your enterprising energy still makes you likely to be a pioneer or leading light in your chosen field.

FAMOUS BIRTHS: John Le Carre (1931); Robert Reed (1932); Peter Max (1937); John Lithgow (1945); Evander Holyfield (1962)

SUING FOR PEACE

Venus, its ruling planet, exerted a peacemaking influence over this day in 1781, when the British general Lord Cornwallis surrendered his troops to the American commander, George Washington, at Yorktown, Virginia, ending the Revolutionary War.

LIBRA
♀ ♎

Energetic
Open-minded
Intelligent

OCTOBER 20

ACTIVE AVANT-GARDISTS

Two traits are often particularly noticeable in those born on October 20: their vigorous, "can-do" attitude—the gift of their positive polarity—and their willingness to experiment, which is partly down to the airy element that makes them curious, and partly their self-motivating, cardinal quadruplicity. Although these bright sparks are often regarded as being highly intelligent, light-hearted, pleasure-loving Venus, their planetary ruler, ensures that they don't become too serious or neglect simple pleasures.

FAMOUS BIRTHS: Christopher Wren (1632); Arthur Rimbaud (1854); Bela Lugosi (1882); Mickey Mantle (1931); Tom Petty (1950); Snoop Dogg (1972)

OPERA-TIONAL
The Sydney Opera House opened on October 20, 1973, a fitting date, given that this day's ruler is Venus, a planet—and goddess—associated with a heightened appreciation of artistry.

OCTOBER 21

RATIONAL ROMANTICS

The characters of those born on October 21 often seem to comprise a curious combination of soft-heartedness and hard-headedness, which comes of having sentimental Venus as a ruling planet and unemotional air as an element. But because their results-oriented, cardinal quadruplicity and assertive, masculine polarity tend to side with rational air in daily life, the harder side is more in evidence, and the influence of Venus may be confined to the domestic sphere and personal relationships.

FAMOUS BIRTHS: Samuel Taylor Coleridge (1772); Alfred Nobel (1833); Dizzy Gillespie (1917); Benjamin Netanyahu (1949); Carrie Fisher (1956)

ART HOUSE
Venus exerts her influence by making art accessible, as was demonstrated on October 21, 1959, when the Solomon R. Guggenheim Museum (the vision of U.S. architect Frank Lloyd Wright) opened to the public in New York.

LIBRA

♀ ♎

Approachable
Purposeful
Well-presented

OCTOBER 22

SMOOTH OPERATORS

That charm-enhancing Venus is your ruling planet, if today is your birthday, is usually very apparent, for you have a delightful demeanor, take great trouble over your appearance, and hate unpleasantness. But you are not a shallow, superficial type, because your pushy, cardinal quadruplicity gives you purpose, and your masculine polarity provides boldness. Your airy element also makes you an astute, objective thinker with a playful streak, and your quirkiness surprises and engages others.

FAMOUS BIRTHS: Franz Liszt (1811); Curly Howard (1903); Christopher Lloyd (1938); Catherine Deneuve (1943); Jeff Goldblum (1952)

PIONEERING PARACHUTIST
Benefiting from its masculine-polarity fearlessness and its airy element, it was on this day in 1797 that André-Jacques Garnerin made the first parachute jump, leaping from a hot-air balloon 3,200 feet above Paris, France.

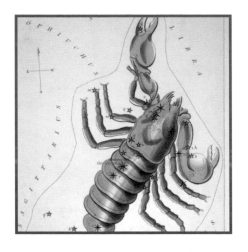

Symbol: The scorpion
Celestial Ruler: Pluto
Element: Water
Polarity: Negative (feminine)
Quadruplicity: Fixed

Scorpio

October 23 to November 21 ♏

Scorpios are often perceived negatively. Yet while they may lash out with a painful sting in their tails (demonstrating the aggression of Mars, Scorpio's former planetary ruler), they usually only do so in self-defense. In fact, their passive polarity makes Scorpios shy, contemplative types, with a tendency to be negative, but their fixed quadruplicity provides commitment and stubbornness. Under their watery element's influence, they are caring and creative, yet oversensitive, while Pluto gives them endurance, but also secretive instincts. All in all, if scorpions are misunderstood, it is because it is simply not in their natures to be flexible, forthcoming, or transparent.

SCORPIO

♇ ♏

Private
Steady
Sensitive

OCTOBER 23

SENSITIVE STICKLERS

Your element of water has blessed you with sensitivity, if this is your birthday, but while you seem able to "read" others intuitively, you yourself are a closed book. Your reticence, especially about personal matters, is down to the combination of Pluto, your secretive planetary ruler, and your passive polarity, which gives you unforthcoming instincts. Perhaps the key to gaining some insight into your character lies in your fixed-nature steadiness, which makes you a stickler for routine.

FAMOUS BIRTHS: Gummo Marx (1892); Frank Rizzo (1920); Johnny Carson (1925); Pelé (1940); Michael Crichton (1942)

A DARK DESTINATION

When he committed suicide on October 23, 42 B.C., vanquished Roman soldier Marcus Junius Brutus would have believed that he was destined for the underworld realm of Pluto, the Greco–Roman god for whom this day's ruling planet is named.

OCTOBER 24

Quiet
Creative
Strong-willed

COMMITTED CREATIVES

If you were born on October 24, the influence of Pluto and your feminine polarity infuses you with the powerful urge to preserve your privacy, with the result that you usually only relax your guard with those whom you know well, and trust. Your water-bestowed creativity does, however, offer tantalizing glimpses of the complex characters that lie behind the typically inscrutable face that you present to the world, while your fixed-quadruplicity commitment is indicative of your considerable willpower.

FAMOUS BIRTHS: Moss Hart (1904); J.P. "Big Bopper" Richardson (1930); Bill Wyman (1936); F. Murray Abraham (1939); Kevin Kline (1947)

A WATERPROOF WOMAN?

Taking advantage of the protective influence of this day's element of water and feminine nature, it was on October 24, 1901, that Annie Edson Taylor became the first person successfully to negotiate Niagara Falls in a barrel.

SCORPIO

♇ ♏

Reserved
Evasive
Determined

OCTOBER 25

OPAQUE ORIGINALS

Such is the privacy protecting barrier that you throw up around yourself at the joint behest of Pluto and your negative polarity, if this is your birthday, that your personality may be a complete mystery to those who try to work out what makes you tick. The original ideas that your creativity-nurturing element of water encourages to flow from your fertile imagination are what most attract others to you. You also impress because of your focused, fixed-quadruplicity concentration and sheer commitment.

FAMOUS BIRTHS: Johan Strauss (1825); Georges Bizet (1838); Sarah Bernhardt (1844); Pablo Picasso (1881); Nancy Cartwright (1959)

RUSSIAN REVOLUTION
The joint influence of this day's current and former rulers—Pluto, planet of transformations, and Mars, that of violent confrontation—was potent on this day in 1917, when the Bolsheviks instigated the Russian Revolution.

OCTOBER 26

RESILIENT REVOLUTIONARIES

Although their stable, fixed quadruplicity makes them resistant to change in some areas of their lives—usually their domestic arrangements, thanks to their cautious, privacy-prizing, feminine polarity—their ruling planet exerts a forceful influence over those born on this day. Pluto is associated with total transformations, as well as toughness and power bases, while water strengthens their caring and giving qualities, so that October 26 people have the potential to be social or political revolutionaries.

FAMOUS BIRTHS: Leon Trotsky (1879); Mahalia Jackson (1911); Bob Hoskins (1942); Hillary Rodham Clinton (1947)

A LIQUID LINK

October 26's element is water, making it an auspicious day for water-related ventures, like the opening of the Erie Canal, the waterway linking Lake Erie and the Hudson River, which occurred in New York State on this day in 1825.

SCORPIO

♇ ♏

Determined
Insightful
Highly strung

OCTOBER 27

IRON-WILLED INTUITIVES

If this is your birthday, you give the impression of being a tough cookie, as, indeed, you are to some extent. Pluto supplies your stamina that you need for survival in difficult circumstances, while your fixed quadruplicity provides your fierce determination. But you are vulnerable, too, as well as a compassionate person. This is because your feminine polarity makes you a worrier, your watery element increases your sensitivity, and the influence of both of these factors gives rise to profound intuition.

FAMOUS BIRTHS: Captain James Cook (1728); Theodore Roosevelt (1858); Dylan Thomas (1914); Roy Lichtenstein (1923); John Cleese (1939); Kelly Osbourne (1984)

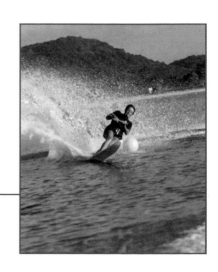

WALKING ON WATER
Could water, October 27's element, have aided the inventive Fred Waller on this day in 1925, when he was granted a U.S. patent for the water skis (or "Dolphin Akwa-Skees," as he called them) that he had developed?

OCTOBER 28

♏ ♇

Caring
Reserved
Helpful

SHY SENSITIVES

There is often a central dilemma in the lives of those born on October 28, who may feel painfully torn between the pull exerted on them by Pluto and their feminine polarity on the one hand, and their fixed quadruplicity and water, on the other. They are conflicted about whether to turn their back on the world and retreat inward in solitary pursuits, or instead to express their fellow-feeling in practical ways, by working in caring professions, dedicating themselves to helping and supporting others.

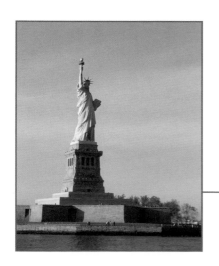

FAMOUS BIRTHS: Evelyn Waugh (1903); Cleo Laine (1927); Bill Gates (1955); Julia Roberts (1967); Joaquin Phoenix (1974)

LADY LIBERTY

Given that October 28 has a feminine polarity and water as an element, it seems an eminently appropriate date for the dedication, by President Cleveland in 1886, of the Statue of Liberty, which rises 152 feet above New York Harbor.

Scorpio

♇ ♏

Quiet
Thoughtful
Hardworking

OCTOBER 29

COMPLEX CHARACTERS

Is this your birthday? If your passive polarity and watery element make you receptive and intuitive, and the same birth influences promote contemplation and introspection, it is secrecy-advocating Pluto that ensures that much of this internal activity is hidden beneath your calm exterior. But your fixed nature also gives you productive instincts and the determination to stick by your principles, so that your beliefs, ideas, and innermost thoughts may emerge, after all, through your work, behavior, or actions.

FAMOUS BIRTHS: James Boswell (1740); Joseph Goebbels (1897); Richard Dreyfuss (1947); Kate Jackson (1948); Winona Ryder (1971)

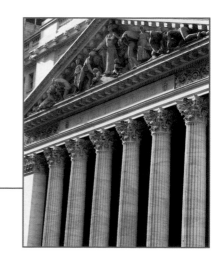

BLACK TUESDAY

Pluto named for the god of the underworld and the planet associated with money and transformations, rules October 29. "Black Tuesday" in 1929, when panic selling caused the New York Stock Exchange to crash.

OCTOBER 30

QUIET SOFTIES

If you were born on October 30, your personality is an intriguing blend of "hard" and "soft" characteristics, although your gentle side is by no means always obvious to others. For while your fixed quadruplicity is responsible for your unbending determination, you derive your secretive instincts from Pluto. As a result, few would guess that beneath your somewhat forbidding, aloof façade lies a shy and sensitive soul, thanks to the input of your "soft" astrological influences—your feminine polarity and water.

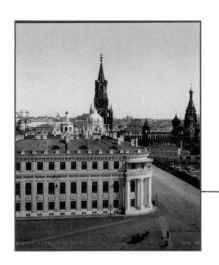

FAMOUS BIRTHS: John Adams (1735); Fyodor Dostoevsky (1821); Ezra Pound (1885); Henry Winkler (1945); Diego Maradona (1960)

REAPPRAISAL AND REBURIAL
Pluto governs the dead's resting places. Small wonder that Russia's Soviet Party Congress should have decreed that the disgraced Josef Stalin's remains be removed from Lenin's Red Square tomb on this day in 1961.

SCORPIO
♇ ♏

Stubborn
Sensitive
Empathetic

OCTOBER 31

STRONG, SUPPORTIVE TYPES

Their passive polarity may make those born on October 31 thoughtful types, while their watery element's gifts include empathy, sensitivity, and supportiveness, but these are not faint-hearted individuals who will let themselves be exploited or pushed around. While their fixed quadruplicity strengthens their will to the extent that they often become notorious for their stubbornness, Pluto provides the resilience that enables them to stick grimly to their guns, no matter how unpopular their stance.

FAMOUS BIRTHS: Jan Vermeer (1632); John Keats (1795); Chiang Kai-shek (1887); Peter Jackson (1961); Adam Horovitz (1966)

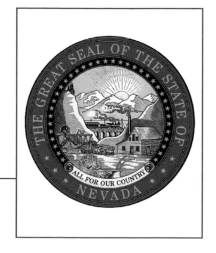

NEVADA DAY

October 31 has a fixed quadruplicity, a mode that favors consolidation and commitment, both of which were demonstrated on this day in 1864, when the territory of Nevada joined the Union of the United States of America.

NOVEMBER 1

♏ ♇

Intuitive
Moody
Tenacious

CAPABLE DREAMERS

Such is the influence of water, if you were born on this day, that you are at heart a dreamy, intuitive type, whose heightened sensitivity makes you prone to changing emotions. Although the fusion of guarded Pluto and your reticent, passive polarity makes you keep your sentiments to yourself in your everyday encounters, your creativity often acts as an outlet for your feelings. Your fixed quadruplicity supplies the necessary stability and concentration for you to develop and make the most of your talents.

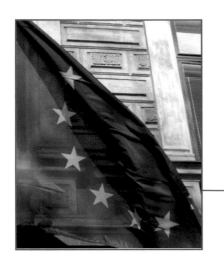

FAMOUS BIRTHS: Stephen Crane (1871); Gary Player (1935); Larry Flynt (1942); Lyle Lovett (1957); Jenny McCarthy (1972); Aishwarya Rai (1973)

NATIONS UNITED
Maybe November 1's fixed quadruplicity provided solidarity on this day in 1993, when the European Union came into being, comprised initially of twelve member states.

Scorpio
♇ ♏

Cliquey
Reticent
Stubborn

November 2

Inscrutable, but Obstinate

Their love of intrigue makes November 2 people true children of Pluto, and because their ruling planet also blesses them with the ability to keep a secret—a gift enhanced by their feminine-polarity tendency to withdraw into themselves—others are fascinated by their inscrutable image. Water heightens their mysterious air by boosting their intuitive powers, but there is nothing enigmatic about the traits bestowed on them by their fixed quadruplicity, which include obstinacy and dedication.

Famous Births: Daniel Boone (1734); Marie Antoinette (1755); Burt Lancaster (1913); k.d. lang (1961); Nelly (1978)

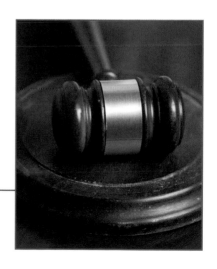

Uncensored Reading
Its rulership by Pluto suggests that controversy is likely to occur on November 2, the day on which, in 1960, Penguin Books was found not guilty of obscenity in the trial over the novel Lady Chatterley's Lover.

NOVEMBER 3

♏ ♇

Shy
Guarded
Sentimental

SENSITIVE SURVIVORS

That you are a true survivor, if you were born on this day, is partly due to protective Pluto, which gives you the resilience to withstand the hardest of knocks, and partly to the characteristics imparted by your fixed quadruplicity—especially your purpose and persistence. But when easier circumstances encourage you to relax your guard, your feminine polarity brings out your caring nature, and the sentimental side that is part and parcel of having water as an element also comes to the fore.

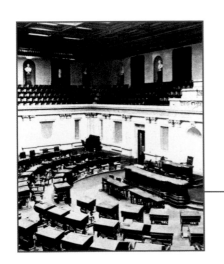

FAMOUS BIRTHS: Vincenzo Bellini (1801); Charles Bronson (1921); Lulu (1948); Roseanne Barr (1952); Dolph Lundgren (1959)

A LADY LEGISLATOR

It was on November 3, 1993, that Carol Moseley-Braun became the first African-American woman to be elected a U.S. senator, a fitting date, for this day's polarity is feminine, and Pluto links it with power bases.

SCORPIO
♇ ♏

Focused
Dreamy
Remote

NOVEMBER
4

INTENSE INTROVERTS

November 4 people tackle almost everything that they do with a rare intensity that is born of the powerful interaction between their planetary ruler, the grimly resolute Pluto, and their concentration-sharpening, fixed quadruplicity. Their formidable focus is boosted by their watery tendency to immerse themselves totally in an idea or activity, and their feminine-polarity habit of becoming completely engrossed in it. Small wonder, then, that others often find them both impressive and unapproachable.

FAMOUS BIRTHS: Will Rogers (1879); Loretta Swit (1937); Laura W. Bush (1946); Matthew McConaughey (1969); Sean Combs (1970)

DISCOVERING THE DEAD
Pluto governs both this day and the realm of the dead—a good day for British archaeologist Howard Carter to discover the entrance to Pharaoh Tutankhamen's tomb, in Egypt's Valley of the Kings, on November 4, 1922.

NOVEMBER 5

♏ ♇

Talented
Surprising
Reticent

VIVID IMAGINATIONS

It is the fusion of your sensitivity-sharpening, watery element and receptive and reflective, feminine polarity that makes you so imaginative, if this is your birthday. You have a particular talent for relating to others' emotions, too. But both birth influences can also give you a tendency to clam up, a trait that is intensified by your ruling planet, Pluto, which encourages secrecy. Your unyielding, fixed quadruplicity reinforces this even more, so that when the floodgates open, others may be amazed by your passion.

FAMOUS BIRTHS: Roy Rogers (1911); Vivien Leigh (1913); Ike Turner (1931); Art Garfunkel (1941); Bryan Adams (1959)

"TREASON AND PLOT"

Pluto, an inciter of plots, may have encouraged Guy Fawkes and others to hatch their "Gunpowder Plot" to blow up Britain's king and parliament on this day in 1605. Its failure has been celebrated ever since.

NOVEMBER
6

LYRICAL LONERS

With guarded Pluto, a reticent, passive polarity, introspective water, and an unbending, fixed quadruplicity for birth influences, it seems as though it was written in the stars that November 6 individuals should be privacy-obsessed loners to some extent. Their rich inner life nevertheless gives these sensitive souls evocative imaginations and plenty of insightful ideas. They don't communicate easily, but may sometimes get through to others via the medium of music or other forms of artistic expression.

FAMOUS BIRTHS: John Philip Sousa (1854); James Naismith (1861); Mike Nichols (1931); Sally Field (1946); Glenn Frey (1948); Ethan Hawke (1970)

SECRET MISSION
That this day's watchword is secrecy was illustrated on November 6, 1971, when a U.S. underground nuclear test, codenamed "Cannikin," took place on Amchitka Island in the Aleutians.

NOVEMBER 7

♏ ♇

Kind
Modest
Supportive

CONCERNED CHARACTERS

Although you November 7 babies are rarely extroverts—for Pluto, water, and your passive polarity together give you inward-looking instincts—the merging of your element and polarity causes you to be compassionate people who care deeply about others. And because you have a fixed quadruplicity, you typically dedicate yourselves wholeheartedly to your family and your work, often quietly and unassumingly, thanks to the veil of reserve that Pluto encourages you to draw around yourselves.

FAMOUS BIRTHS: Marie Curie (1867); Leon Trotsky (1879); Albert Camus (1913); Billy Graham (1918); Joni Mitchell (1943)

FIRST LADY

Having a feminine polarity, this day favors female endeavors; its fixed nature also rewards dedication, and it was on November 7 that Hillary Clinton became the first U.S. senator to have been a first lady (in 2000).

SCORPIO

♇ ♏

Loyal
Independent
Strong-willed

NOVEMBER 8

CANNY CONTEMPLATIVES

Having a secretive planetary ruler in Pluto, a receptive, feminine polarity, and an introspective, intuitive, and imagination-enhancing, watery element means that November 8 individuals are more likely to be reclusive than outgoing. But it also means that when they do have something to say, you can be certain that it will be well-considered, perceptive, and original. And if challenged, they will typically stick to their guns, for their fixed quadruplicity makes them surprisingly stubborn.

FAMOUS BIRTHS: Bram Stoker (1847); Margaret Mitchell (1900); Katharine Hepburn (1907); Bonnie Raitt (1949); Tara Reid (1975); Jack Osbourne (1985)

THE RIVER RUNS

November 8 is appropriate for ventures concerned with its element of water, like the diversion of China's mighty Yangtze River in preparation for the creation of the Three Gorges Dam, a project that began on this day in 1997.

NOVEMBER 9

*Committed
Caring
Pessimistic*

LOYAL SUPPORTERS

November 9 people may have a pessimistic streak—it would be surprising if they didn't, for Pluto, their planetary ruler, also governs the dark realms, and their polarity is negative—but their lives are emphatically not all doom and gloom. Their polarity also gives them nurturing instincts, their watery element supplies the supportive side to their personalities, and their fixed nature makes them loyal, so that they will always derive much happiness from looking after their loved ones.

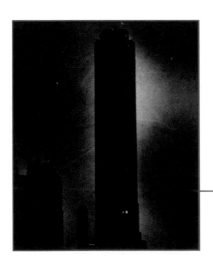

FAMOUS BIRTHS: Hedy Lamarr (1913); Spiro Agnew (1918); Lou Ferrigno (1951); Sisqó (1978); Delta Goodrem (1984)

THE DARKNESS

Distant Pluto is associated with darkness, and may have had something to do with the "Great Northeast Blackout," a power failure that caused chaos in a large section of the U.S. and Canadian Northeast on November 9, 1965.

SCORPIO

♇ ♏

Sensitive
Passionate
Creative

NOVEMBER 10

UNCOMPROMISING CREATIVES

If today is your birthday, you are a sensitive character. You may allow your creativity to flow unreservedly in your work, but your water-element characteristics are much less evident in your day-to-day dealings with people. Privacy-promoting Pluto and your cautious, passive polarity can make you very guarded in expressing your feelings. But when you feel strongly about something, you can inspire shock and awe in others by the strength of your fixed-quadruplicity determination to stick to your guns.

FAMOUS BIRTHS: Martin Luther (1483); Richard Burton (1925); Ennio Morricone (1928); Roy Scheider (1935); Tim Rice (1944)

PROTECTIVE PATRIOTS
Not only is this day's element water, but it has a loyalty-promoting, fixed quadruplicity. November 10, 1775, was therefore a highly appropriate date for the founding of the U.S. Marine Corps, whose motto is Semper Fidelis ("Always Faithful").

NOVEMBER 11

♏ ♇

Loyal
Shy
Committed

QUIET WORRIERS

There are two sides to the November 11 personality: a public one that has a Scorpionic, passive-polarity flavor, and a private one influenced by water and a fixed quadruplicity. When interacting with new acquaintances and colleagues, those born on this day generally appear quite reserved, but they are nevertheless quietly observing—and absorbing—others' behavior. When with trusted friends and loved ones, however, their compassion and commitment are unmistakable, as is also their self-doubt.

FAMOUS BIRTHS: Fyodor Mikhailovich Dostoyevsky (1821); Kurt Vonnegut, Jr. (1922); Demi Moore (1962); Calista Flockhart (1964); Leonardo DiCaprio (1974)

RESTING IN PEACE

World War I ended on November 11, 1918, a day ruled by Pluto, guardian of the dead. So what better date for the dedication of the Tomb of the Unknowns in the USA's Arlington Cemetery, Virginia, in 1921?

SCORPIO

♇ ♏

Artistic
Intense
Reserved

NOVEMBER
12

PRIVATE, BUT PASSIONATE

If this is your birthday, the blending of intense Pluto, emotional water, and your dedication-supplying, fixed quadruplicity makes you a passionate person, but you certainly don't wear your heart on your sleeve. The combination of reticent Pluto and another birth influence—your reserved, passive polarity—causes you to believe that neither your feelings nor your vulnerability should be subject to public scrutiny. Your artistic talents may provide tantalizing hints of the sensitive, complex person you are inside.

FAMOUS BIRTHS: Auguste Rodin (1840); Grace Kelly (1929); Neil Young (1945); Nadia Comaneci (1961); David Schwimmer (1966); Anne Hathaway (1982)

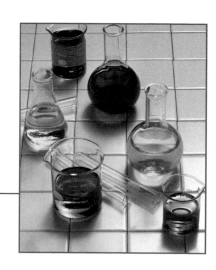

ASTROLOGICAL CHEMISTRY?
In 1915, Theodore W. Richards became the first American to be awarded the Nobel Prize for Chemistry, a branch of science concerned with reactions and transformations, as are this day's passive polarity and ruling planet.

November 13

Scorpio
♏ ♇

Caring
Determined
Anxious

SENSITIVE DOUBTERS

If you were born on this day, you were given a strong backbone by your fixed quadruplicity. Your circumspect, feminine polarity and the influence of wary, secretive Pluto together encourage you to think long and hard before revealing too much of yourself, so others are often led to believe that you are completely certain of yourself and can be inflexible. In fact, because of your watery element, underneath you are a sensitive and sympathetic soul who is frequently beset by worries and misgivings.

FAMOUS BIRTHS: Robert Louis Stevenson (1850); Eugène Ionescu (1912); Whoopi Goldberg (1955); Rachel Bilson (1981)

HONORING THE DEAD

Pluto, the planet named for a guardian god of the dead, encourages us to remember the dear departed, making November 13, 1982, an apt date for the dedication of the Vietnam Veterans' Memorial in Washington, D.C.

SCORPIO

♇ ♏

Aloof
Introspective
Compassionate

NOVEMBER 14

COMPASSIONATE CONSOLIDATORS

That November 14 people are often misunderstood is down to Pluto, which makes them suspect others' motives and guard against being exploited by keeping themselves to themselves. They may sometimes come across as being disinterested loners, but because they have a feminine polarity and watery element, they're actually contemplative, caring, and compassionate people who will draw on their fixed powers of concentration and commitment when helping out or caring for those they love.

FAMOUS BIRTHS: Claude Monet (1840); Pandit Nehru (1889); King Hussein of Jordan (1935); Charles, Prince of Wales (1948); Condoleezza Rice (1954)

IN THEIR ELEMENT?

It was on November 14, 1851, that U.S. author Herman Melville's novel Moby-Dick was first published. Could its subsequent success have been linked to the fact that both this day's element, and that of the whale, is water?

NOVEMBER 15

CREATIVE CATALYSTS

So powerful is the influence that your receptive, feminine polarity and creativity-nurturing, watery element wield over you, if this is your birthday, that it is as though you are a human catalyst. Given to absorbing everything you hear and read, mulling it over, and then coming out with a different take on it, your innovative ideas can be truly amazing when you harness Pluto's transformational potential. Add your fixed quadruplicity to the mix, and you are as committed as you are creative—and caring, too.

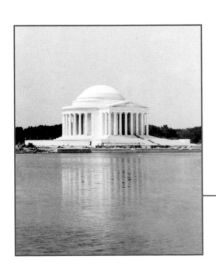

FAMOUS BIRTHS: Georgia O'Keeffe (1887); J.G. Ballard (1930); Petula Clark (1932); Daniel Barenboim (1942); Anni-Frid Lyngstad (1945); Beverly D'Angelo (1951)

MAKING A MEMORIAL
On this day in 1939, U.S. President Franklin D. Roosevelt laid the cornerstone of the Jefferson Memorial in Washington, D.C.—an appropriate day given that Pluto, the ruling planet, governs the realm of the dead.

SCORPIO

ে ♏

Moody
Sympathetic
Determined

NOVEMBER
16

COMPLEX CHARACTERS

It is not just because they have a changeable, emotional element in water that November 16 people's characters resemble multifaceted, intricately patterned, ever-shifting kaleidoscopes. Secretive Pluto prompts them to hide their inner selves from public view for a start, but when a trusted person is allowed a glimpse of what lies within, he or she will find a great deal of empathy (the gift of water), thoughtfulness (provided by their passive polarity), and tenacity (their fixed quadruplicity's contribution).

FAMOUS BIRTHS: King David Kalakaua of Hawaii (1836); Shigeru Miyamoto (1952); Diana Krall (1964); Lisa Bonet (1967); Maggie Gyllenhaal (1977)

PAKISTAN PREMIER
Its feminine polarity suggests that women are likely to be in the spotlight on this day, as, indeed, was Benazir Bhutto, of the Pakistan People's Party, who was elected prime minister of Pakistan on November 16, 1988.

NOVEMBER 17

INSCRUTABLE INDIVIDUALS

If you were born on this day, you have the unnerving knack of instantly understanding what makes others tick, without giving away much about yourself. This is due on the one hand to your intuition (from your watery element) and passive polarity, and, on the other, to your secretive planetary ruler—a combination that is intense because Pluto encourages your withholding, passive instincts. That you are persistent to the point of pigheadedness, because of your fixed nature, can often be annoying to others.

FAMOUS BIRTHS: Rock Husdson (1925); Martin Scorsese (1942); Lauren Hutton (1943); Danny DeVito (1944); RuPaul (1960)

A FLUID CONNECTION

November 17 is a day whose element is water, and also marks the anniversary, in 1869, of the official opening of the Suez Canal, the Egyptian waterway that was constructed to link the Mediterranean and Red seas.

SCORPIO
♇ ♏

Loyal
Supportive
Inscrutable

NOVEMBER 18

SHY AND SELF-CONTAINED

Having water as an element makes November 18 individuals innately sympathetic and supportive, while their fixed quadruplicity prompts them to stick by loved ones through thick and thin. And because their ruling planet is reticence-encouraging Pluto, they can always be relied upon to keep a secret. They themselves are not always easy to fathom, however, partly due to Pluto's influence and partly because the additional input of their passive polarity can make them utterly unforthcoming.

FAMOUS BIRTHS: Eugene Ormandy (1899); Alan Shepard, Jr. (1923); Margaret Atwood (1939); Linda Evans (1942); Graham Parker (1950); Owen Wilson (1968)

A DEADLY DELUSION
That Pluto, this day's planetary ruler, can have a dark, even deadly, influence was demonstrated on November 18, 1978, when over 900 members of Jim Jones's People's Temple cult committed suicide in Jonestown, Guyana.

NOVEMBER 19

Kind
Courageous
Resilient

BRAVE SOLDIERS

Although caring water and their nurturing, feminine polarity ensure that November 19 people show compassion and kindness in their private lives, and are devoted to their loved ones, thanks to their fixed quadruplicity, their professional image is completely different. For here Pluto's influence prevails, infusing them with the belief that knowledge is power and giving them the resilience to endure hard knocks. Their fixed quadruplicity gives them the tenacity to soldier on when times are tough.

FAMOUS BIRTHS: Indira Gandhi (1917); Larry King (1933); Calvin Klein (1942); Meg Ryan (1961); Jodie Foster (1962)

ADDRESS THE NATION

November 19's passive polarity predominated on this day in 1863, when Union President Abraham Lincoln delivered the Gettysburg Address dedication at the military cemetery dedication ceremony in Gettysburg, Pennsylvania

SCORPIO

♇ ♏

Caring
Intuitive
Impractical

NOVEMBER 20

DEDICATED DREAMERS

At heart, if you were born on November 20, you are a true child of your element of water and passive polarity: you're intuitive, receptive, thoughtful, and caring, and, on occasions, decidedly dreamy. That said, your fixed quadruplicity gives you both determination and obstinacy when needs be, while Pluto, your planetary ruler, provides resilience and your firm belief in the possibility of transformation, so that you are better psychologically equipped than most to make your dreams come true.

FAMOUS BIRTHS: Edwin Hubble (1889); Emilio Pucci (1914); Robert F. Kennedy (1925); Don DeLillo (1936); Bo Derek (1956); Mike Diamond (1965)

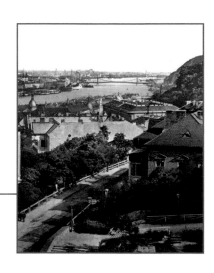

TWO BECOME ONE

November 20 has a consolidating, fixed quadruplicity and water for an element. These influences were at work in 1872, when the cities of Buda and Pest, on the Danube River, were amalgamated as Budapest, Hungary.

NOVEMBER 21

ENIGMATIC EMPATHIZERS

If you were born on this day, you are interested in, and sympathetic to, others. This is down to knowledge-valuing Scorpio and water, which heightens your sensitivity, imagination, and compassion. But while you are ready to reach out to others, others may find you somewhat emotionally closed, due to the joint influence of guarded Scorpio and your circumspect, defensive, negative polarity. Indeed, it may only be when in the grip of your fixed-quadruplicity stubbornness that you ever make their feelings clear.

FAMOUS BIRTHS: Voltaire (1694); René Magritte (1898); Harold Ramis (1944); Goldie Hawn (1945); Björk (1965)

SECRET AGENT

Pluto, a planet that is associated with secrecy and plotting, rules this day, on which, in 1985, Jonathan Jay Pollard, a U.S. citizen in the employ of the U.S. Navy, was arrested on charges (later proven) of spying for Israel.

SYMBOL: THE CENTAUR/ARCHER
CELESTIAL RULER: JUPITER
ELEMENT: FIRE
POLARITY: POSITIVE (MASCULINE)
QUADRUPLICITY: MUTABLE

SAGITTARIUS

NOVEMBER 22 TO DECEMBER 21

Sagittarius is the Latin for "archer," this one being Chiron, a centaur in Roman mythology—an imaginary, hybrid being. But the symbolism underlying its description tells us much about Sagittarians, for they combine human intelligence with animal energy. Jupiter, their ruling planet, provides wisdom and broad-mindedness (and a sense of superiority); the element of fire supplies spontaneity and passion (or a quick, fiery temper); a positive polarity adds extroversion and dynamism (or aggression); and a mutable quadruplicity imparts versatility (or changeability).

NOVEMBER 22

SAGITTARIUS

♐ ♃

Lively
Aggressive
Competitive

COOPERATIVE COMPETITORS

The combined influence of your passion- and courage-bestowing element of fire and your assertive, positive polarity is particularly noticeable in you, if you were born on November 22. You appear to know no fear and will unhesitatingly fight for your heart's desire. Having such an aggressive, competitive streak, it is, perhaps, just as well that your mutable nature also gives you sociable and cooperative instincts, and that Jupiter supplies both a jovial attitude and a pronounced sense of fair play.

FAMOUS BIRTHS: Charles de Gaulle (1890); Terry Gilliam (1940); Billie-Jean King (1943); Jamie Lee Curtis (1958); Boris Becker (1967); Scarlet Johansson (1984)

A DEADLY AIM

This day's aggressive flavor and fiery tendencies were tragically demonstrated on November 22, 1963, when Lee Harvey Oswald shot, and killed, the U.S. president, John F. Kennedy, in Dallas, Texas.

EXPANSIVE EXTROVERTS

Although broad-minded Jupiter and your variety enjoying, mutable quadruplicity encourage you to have many interests, if this is your birthday, solitary pursuits do not usually number among them, because all four of your birth influences suggest that you are an outgoing person who is stimulated by the company of others. What's more, your fiery element can give you exuberant, attention-seeking, exhibitionist tendencies, while your masculine polarity prompts you to behave in an uninhibited fashion.

FAMOUS BIRTHS: Franklin Pierce (1804); William H. Bonney, "Billy the Kid" (1859); Boris Karloff (1887); Harpo Marx (1888); Maxwell Caulfield (1959)

LESSONS IN LIFE
Influenced, by Jupiter, November 23's mind-broadening ruling planet, and its variety-loving mutability, it was on this day in 1936 that the first issue of the U.S. magazine Life *was published.*

NOVEMBER 24

Lively
Creative
Egotistical

CONFIDENT CREATIVES

November 24 people rarely lack self-confidence, thanks to their daring, positive polarity and fearless, fiery element. Although the additional input of Jupiter, whose namesake was the chief Roman god, can incite rampant egotism, such imperious phases rarely last for long, for their ruling planet also fosters an all-embracing urge. Their gregarious, mutable nature moreover causes them to take an interest in everyone, not least because behavioral quirks fascinate them and spark their fiery creativity.

FAMOUS BIRTHS: Henri de Toulouse-Lautrec (1864); Scott Joplin (1868); Dale Carnegie (1888); Billy Connolly (1942)

CHALLENGING CONVENTION
Charles Darwin's On the Origin of Species by Natural Selection—*introducing his controversial theory of evolution—was first published on this day in 1859, an apt date, given that Jupiter, its planetary ruler, encourages openmindedness and learning.*

Flexible
Generous
Original

NOVEMBER 25

GENEROUS GENERATORS

There are typically three facets to November 25 people's personalities. The first is their positive urge to pursue their personal or professional interests, when their fiery creativity may come to the fore. The second is their generosity—the product of the coming-together of warm-hearted fire and big-hearted Jupiter—which encourages them to share any good fortune that may come their way with others. And, finally, the third is their mutable-mode versatility, which sometimes transmutes into sheer fickleness.

FAMOUS BIRTHS: Andrew Carnegie (1835); Joe DiMaggio (1914); Etta Jones (1928); Percy Sledge (1941); John F. Kennedy, Jr. (1960)

AN INCENDIARY INVENTION
November 25's pioneering polarity, fiery element, and expansionary planetary ruler, make it appropriate that the Swedish chemist Alfred Nobel patented dynamite (an explosive substance) on this day in 1867.

NOVEMBER 26

♐ ♃

Fiery
Sociable
Theatrical

CONVIVIAL CHARACTERS

If you were born on November 26, you can be quite moody and hot-tempered on occasion—you have a changeable, mutable quadruplicity and a fiery element, after all. But this same pair of birth influences, reinforced by the authority of ruling Jupiter, ensures that you are usually sociable, warm, and jovial when in others' company. And it is partly because you have an extroverted, positive polarity, and partly because fire gives you a love of the limelight, that you clearly love playing to an audience.

FAMOUS BIRTHS: Cyril Cusack (1910); Charles M. Schulz (1922); Robert Goulet (1933); Rich Little (1938); Tina Turner (1939)

AN OLYMPIAN GESTURE

Jupiter contributes generosity of spirit to the Sagittarian month. This may have been a factor in the International Olympic Committee's decision, made on this day in 1979, to readmit China, following over twenty years of exclusion.

SAGITTARIUS
4 ♐

Unconventional
Outgoing
Risk-taking

NOVEMBER 27

PIONEERING ADVENTURERS

The fusion of fire, a positive polarity, and powerful Jupiter within the November 27 personality has a potent effect, typically resulting in exuberant, experimental individuals who are burning to push back the boundaries of convention to see how far they can go—and what they'll learn when in new territory. Having a mutable quadruplicity means that they are also versatile people whose interests are many and varied, including, perhaps, artistic, scientific, philosophical, and physical pursuits.

FAMOUS BIRTHS: Anders Celsius (1701); Chaim Weizmann (1874); Bruce Lee (1940); Jimi Hendrix (1942); Robin Givens (1964)

UNIVERSALLY ESTABLISHED
Astrological influences may have aided the founding of the University of Pennsylvania on November 27, 1779: its cooperative, mutable quadruplicity and optimistic Jupiter.

November 28

Sagittarius

↗ ♃

*Radical
Energetic
Impatient*

Vigorous Visionaries

It is thanks to your dynamic, masculine polarity and vibrant, fiery element that you are such a livewire, if November 28 is your birthday. And due to far-sighted, expansionist Jupiter, you are always trying to broaden your horizons, whether through learning, traveling, work, or widening your social circle. That said, the combination of impulsive fire and your changeable, mutable quadruplicity may frequently cause you to lose patience and focus whenever an interesting distraction presents itself.

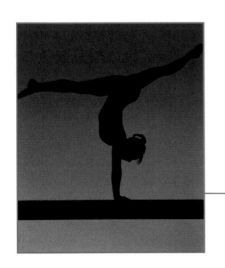

Famous Births: William Blake (1757); Friedrich Engels (1820); Claude Lévi-Strauss (1908); Randy Newman (1943); Alexander Godunov (1949)

Spirit of Cooperation
Maybe this day's mutability prevailed in 1989 when Romanian gymnast Nadia Comaneci arrived in New York having fled her homeland, detouring through Hungary.

Optimistic
Fair-minded
Easily bored

NOVEMBER 29

LIBERAL LIVEWIRES

November 29 protégés of Jupiter display many qualities associated with their planetary ruler, including a sense of justice, a liberal outlook, and a jovial manner. Add the adventurousness and optimism imparted by their fiery element, along with the assertiveness and vigor provided by their positive polarity, and they have the potential to be innovators, performers, and campaigners. But despite supplying adaptability, their restlessness-inducing, mutable quadruplicity can play havoc with their staying power.

FAMOUS BIRTHS: Christian Johann Doppler (1803); Louisa May Alcott (1832); C. S. Lewis (1898); Jacques Chirac (1932); John Mayall (1933); Joel Coen (1954)

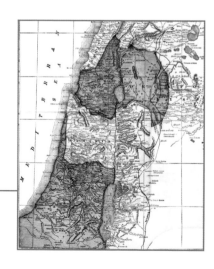

PLAYING FAIR

Jupiter is associated with fairness, and may have been at work on this day in 1947, when the General Assembly of the United Nations approved a resolution that advocated the division of Palestine between Jews and Arabs.

NOVEMBER 30

Sociable
Inspirational
Attention-seeking

DRAMATIC PERFORMERS

Your fiery element blesses you with creativity, if this is your birthday, as well as with an appetite for being the center of attention, and a performer's flair. It also ensures that your performances are inspirational, while Jupiter reinforces your positive-polarity optimism and provides an inclusive, warm attitude to others. Your generous impulses are boosted by the sociability that you derive from your mutable quadruplicity, but this tends to make you prone to sulking and moodiness, too.

FAMOUS BIRTHS: Jonathan Swift (1667); Mark Twain (1835); Winston Churchill (1874); Virginia May (1920); Billy Idol (1955); Ben Stiller (1965)

A FIERY END

November 30, a fire-governed day, marks the anniversary of the fiery destruction of the Crystal Palace (1936), in London, England, an iconic building that had been created for the International Exhibition of 1851.

SAGITTARIUS

4 ♐

Witty
Knowledgeable
Extroverted

DECEMBER

1

ERUDITE ENTERTAINERS

Jupiter and fire together have the strongest influence on the December 1 personality. The ruling planet gives those born on this day the desire to learn, often through self-education, while fire supplies passion, the urge to experiment, and a taste for others' company. Their remaining two birth influences typically reinforce all these characteristics: their mutable quadruplicity encourages them to pursue a varied range of interests, and their active polarity boosts their extroverted, uninhibited side.

FAMOUS BIRTHS: Marie Tussaud (1761); Mary Martin (1913); Woody Allen (1935); Lee Trevino (1939); Richard Pryor (1940); Bette Midler (1945)

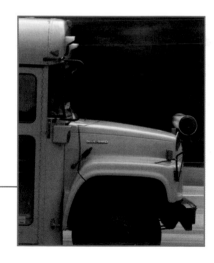

A CHANGE IS GONNA COME

Mutable quadruplicity gives December 1 changeability. This was illustrated when, in 1955, Rosa Parks refused to give up her seat on a bus to a white man and, in the process, enabled progress in the civil rights movement.

December 2

♐ ♃

Bossy
Excitable
Tolerant

ENERGETIC EXHIBITIONISTS

It's your active polarity that supplies your energy, as well as your confrontational tendencies, if you were born on this day. Your fiery element fuels your enthusiasm and delivers the electrifying jolt that fires you up whenever you take center stage, prompting you to give your all to your audience. And while your mutable nature provides versatility (but can also make you moody), Jupiter encourages you to be tolerant of others. However, your ruling planet is also responsible for your occasional bossiness.

FAMOUS BIRTHS: Georges Seurat (1859); Maria Callas (1922); Cathy Lee Crosby (1944); Tracy Austin (1962); Monica Seles (1973); Britney Spears (1981)

THIRD WORLD DONATION

Jupiter commands dignity and tolerance, and on December 2, 1998, Microsoft Corp chairman Bill Gates donated $100 million to help immunize children in developing countries.

Sagittarius

4 ♐

Adventurous
Outgoing
Fearless

December

3

Versatile Voyagers

A striking aspect of the December 3 character is the versatility of those born on this day, for their mutable quadruplicity blesses them with flexibility and a craving for variety. Jupiter's gifts include a wide-ranging outlook and a zest for voyages of discovery, whether they are literal or metaphorical forays into the unknown. But while their fiery element heightens their adventurousness, and their active polarity increases their fearlessness, these influences can combine to provoke reckless behavior, too.

Famous Births: Joseph Conrad (1857); Andy Williams (1930); Ozzy Osbourne (1948); Daryl Hannah (1960); Julianne Moore (1960); Brendan Fraser (1968)

By Jove!
December 3 is ruled by Jupiter, making it a fitting date (in 1973) for the U.S. space probe Pioneer 10 to fly by this gas giant and relay the first close-up images of the planet to Earth.

DECEMBER
4

Restless
Inquisitive
Strong-willed

EXPANSIVE EXPERIMENTERS

All of your birth influences contribute to your desire to experiment, if today is your birthday. Your mutable quadruplicity makes you restless; your active polarity gives you pioneering impulses; your fiery element makes you want to explore; and Jupiter, your planetary ruler, encourages you to broaden your experience, knowledge, and understanding—especially of the "meaning of life." Your quadruplicity makes you multitalented, so your interests are likely to be many and varied, but often short-lived.

FAMOUS BIRTHS: Thomas Carlyle (1795); Wassily Kandinsky (1866); Rainer Maria Rilke (1875); Deanna Durbin (1921); Jeff Bridges (1949)

GRAND GESTURES
Jupiter's influence of grand gestures may be illustrated by Terry Anderson's release on this day in 1991, after 2,454 days held captive by the Islamic Jihad.

SAGITTARIUS

4 ♐

Sociable
Original
Influential

DECEMBER
5

PIONEERING PERSONALITIES

December 5 people are pioneers in more than one sense of the word: while having a fiery element makes them trendsetters, their positive polarity pushes them to explore uncharted territory, and their planetary ruler gives them expansive instincts. These influences may motivate them to travel the world, or simply to broaden their minds. The influence of fire can be particularly powerful on some, so that they constantly try to seek others' attention, but all are sociable, thanks to their mutable quadruplicity.

fAMOUS BIRTHS: Martin Van Buren (1782); George Armstrong Custer (1839); Walt Disney (1901); Little Richard (Penniman) (1935); José Carreras (1946)

GOING GREAT GUNS
Demonstrating the pioneering nature of December 5, U.S. inventor Richard Gatling patented his rapid-fire gun in 1861. The Gatling gun was an early form of machine gun.

December 6

TOLERANT TRENDSETTERS

The moral tolerance that comes of having broad-minded Jupiter as your planetary ruler plays a large part in making you a trendsetter, if this is your birthday. Your positive-polarity self-confidence and fiery experimentalism are also important factors in your habit of blazing your own trail through life, whether you are best known for innovation at work or for your stylish image. And because you have an adaptable, mutable nature, you can impress different audiences by telling your story in a variety of ways.

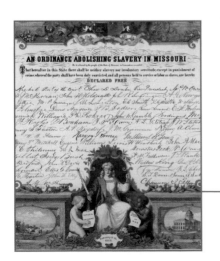

AN ORDINANCE ABOLISHING SLAVERY IN MISSOURI

FAMOUS BIRTHS: Warren Hastings (1732); Osbert Sitwell (1892); Ira Gershwin (1896); Dave Brubeck (1920); Janine Turner (1962)

RIGHTING A WRONG
This day is ruled by Jupiter, the planet whose sphere of astrological influence includes decent, liberal behavior. It seems fitting that the Thirteenth Amendment of the U.S. Constitution, was ratified in 1865, abolishing slavery.

Inquiring
Talkative
Attention-seeking

DECEMBER

7

DIDACTIC DECLAIMERS

One thing's certain: December 7 people have plenty to say. Not only does their active polarity make them forthcoming, but their fiery element causes them to feel comfortable at the center of a circle of listeners. In addition, their mutable mode gives them wide-ranging interests, while Jupiter sharpens their desire to increase the depth and breadth of their knowledge. They are consequently both informative and well-informed, but they sometimes come across as being tedious know-alls.

FAMOUS BIRTHS: Giovanni Lorenzo Bernini (1598); Eli Wallach (1915); Noam Chomsky (1928); Ellen Burstyn (1932); Gregg Allman (1947)

AN ACT OF WAR
Japan attacked the U.S. naval base at Pearl Harbor on the Hawaiian island of Oahu on this day in 1941. They may have been harnessing the aggression inherent in this day's fiery element and masculine polarity.

DECEMBER 8

SAGITTARIUS

✓ ♐ 4

Spontaneous
Confident
Amiable

INSPIRATIONAL INNOVATORS

It is your inspirational element of fire that is mainly responsible for your spontaneity, adventurousness, and creativity, if this is your birthday. Your positive polarity ensures that you're self-confident and have no inhibitions about shocking other people. There is inevitably a danger that your habit of challenging convention may rub others up the wrong way. However, jovial Jupiter, your amiable, mutable nature, and your fiery warmth and liveliness generally prove to be a winning combination.

FAMOUS BIRTHS: Diego Rivera (1886); Lucian Freud (1922); Sammy Davis Jr. (1925); Jim Morrison (1943); Kim Basinger (1953); Sinead O'Connor (1966)

DISSEMINATING A DOGMA
That Jupiter infuses this day with religious sensitivity was illustrated on December 8, 1854, when Pope Pius IX proclaimed the Immaculate Conception of the Blessed Virgin Mary to be an article of faith for Roman Catholics.

SAGITTARIUS

4 ✗

Charismatic
Talkative
Open-minded

DECEMBER
9

CHARISMATIC CHARACTERS

With magnetic fire, a dynamic, positive polarity, and integrity-providing Jupiter among their birth influences, it is hardly surprising that December 9 people are such charismatic characters. Although it is true that their presence can be intimidating to some, this is usually not their intention. Jupiter blesses them with a convivial personality, and fire, with warmth, while their mutable nature makes them gregarious as well as encouraging their willingness to be flexible when working as part of a team.

FAMOUS BIRTHS: John Milton (1608); Kirk Douglas (1916); Judi Dench (1934); Joan Armatrading (1950); John Malkovich (1953); Donny Osmond (1957)

SURVEYING SPACE

On December 9, 1993, U.S. astronauts finished repairing the Hubble Space Telescope, enabling it to relay images from space to Earth—an apt date, given its rulership by Jupiter, which encourages us to broaden our horizons.

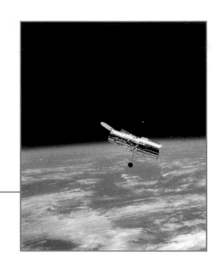

DECEMBER 10

DARING DEMOCRATS

The fact that you children of all-embracing Jupiter who were born on this day have inclusive instincts is unmistakeable. Having a sociable, variety-loving, mutable quadruplicity heightens your enjoyment of working, playing, and living alongside all kinds of people. Open to every influence, you tend to be daringly experimental types, thanks to your positive polarity and fiery element, but your impulsiveness may sometimes push you into going too far (in others' eyes, at least).

FAMOUS BIRTHS: Emily Dickinson (1830); Olivier Messiaen (1908); Dorothy Lamour (1914); Kenneth Branagh (1960)

GOING UP IN SMOKE
The influence of Jupiter encourages interest in religion, evident on this day in 1520 in Wittenberg, Germany, when German religious reformer Martin Luther publicly burned the papal bull proclaiming his excommunication.

SAGITTARIUS

4 ♐

Assertive
Individual
Open-minded

DECEMBER
11

FLEXIBLE FREE-THINKERS

Although your mutable mode makes you cooperative, if you were born on this day, it is your ruling planet that is responsible for your intellectual flexibility, because Jupiter encourages you to be broad-minded and to form your own opinions. It is therefore just as well that your masculine polarity provides the necessary assertiveness for you to advance—and strongly defend—your own beliefs, and that your fiery element causes you to savor being different and standing out from the crowd.

FAMOUS BIRTHS: Hector Berlioz (1803); Alexandr Solzhenitzyn (1918); Donna Mills (1943); Booker T. Jones (1944); Brenda Lee (1944)

ADDING TO AMERICA
December 11 is ruled by Jupiter, which expands; perhaps its influence prompted President Madison to approve Indiana's admission into the Union as the USA's nineteenth state on this day in 1816.

DECEMBER 12

♐ ♃

Moody
Dramatic
Indecisive

THEATRICAL TRAILBLAZERS

If today is your birthday, your element of fire breathes passion and drama into your actions and creations—whether or not you are a professional performer. That Jupiter, your expansionist, planetary ruler, encourages you to think big is also obvious, as are your pioneering, positive-polarity instincts and your mutable versatility. It is your mutable quadruplicity that can make you complex and changeable, however, because this birth influence can induce feelings of restlessness, indecisiveness, and instability.

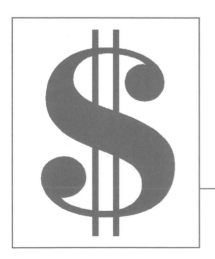

FAMOUS BIRTHS: Gustave Flaubert (1821); Edvard Munch (1863); Frank Sinatra (1915); Dionne Warwick (1941); Jennifer Connelly (1970)

PRIDE AND PUNISHMENT
The Jovian characteristic of justice was highlighted on this day in 1989, when U.S. billionairess Leona Helmsley was sentenced to four years' imprisonment and fined $7 million for tax evasion.

SAGITTARIUS

♃ ♐

Optimistic
Exuberant
Creative

DECEMBER 13

CHEERFUL CHARACTERIZERS

Although having a changeable, mutable nature means that December 13 people can be moody, their default mode is cheerfulness, thanks to jovial Jupiter, their good-humor-encouraging planetary ruler, and also to their positive polarity and fiery element, both of which promote an optimistic outlook. And it is mainly down to their element of fire that these ardent and exuberant types are blessed with great creative potential. Fire also stokes their infectious enthusiasm for the grand passions that burn within them.

FAMOUS BIRTHS: Heinrich Heine (1797); Dick Van Dyke (1925); Christopher Plummer (1927); Ted Nugent (1948); Robert Lindsay (1949)

BENDING A BOUNDARY

Harnessing December 13's element and Jupiter's boundary-stretching spirit, in 1964 Mexican President Gustavo Diaz Ordaz and U.S. President Lyndon B. Johnson altered the Mexican–American border.

DECEMBER 14

Visionary
Assertive
Enthusiastic

FAR-SIGHTED FREE SPIRITS

If today is your birthday, your personality is multifaceted, but the respective influences of your ruling planet, a positive polarity, a mutable mode, and fire are nevertheless evident. You are blessed with Jupiter's wide-ranging vision—both metaphysical and literal, if you enjoy traveling. You are assertive because of your active polarity, and highly adaptable. Your element of fire gives you a great deal of generosity, enthusiasm, and initiative, but you can't stand to be constrained or dictated to by anyone.

FAMOUS BIRTHS: Michel de Nostraedame, "Nostradamus" (1503); Tycho Brahe (1546); Lee Remick (1935); Jane Birkin (1946)

A POLITICAL PRELATE

Considering its rulership by Jupiter, the planet named after the Roman god that highlights religious matters, it is appropriate that in 1959, Archbishop Makarios was elected the first president of the Cyprus Republic.

SAGITTARIUS

4 ♐

Cooperative
Generous
Vibrant

DECEMBER
15

OPEN-HEARTED ORIGINALS

Those born on December 15 often display the effects of two powerful astrological affinities. The attraction between Jupiter, their planetary ruler, and their mutability results in their sociable and cooperative mutable traits reinforcing the inclusiveness and generosity that emanate from the planet. The kinship between fire and their positive polarity means that their element's inspirational attributes and vibrancy are given direction by their polarity's pioneering and assertive "go-for-it" tendencies.

FAMOUS BIRTHS: Gustave Eiffel (1832); John Paul Getty (1892); Friedensreich Hundertwasser (1928); Edna O'Brien (1936); Don Johnson (1949)

A GOODWILL GESTURE
Jupiter's broad-minded influence was perhaps responsible for the Spanish government's decision to open the border between Spain and Gibraltar, which had been closed for thirteen years, to pedestrians on December 15, 1982.

DECEMBER 16

SAGITTARIUS

↗ ♃

Extroverted
Creative
Jovial

PASSIONATE PHILOSOPHERS

If you were born on this day, having a mutable mode means that as well as being adaptable and flexible, you're subject to changeable moods. Your positive polarity generally causes you to remain extroverted, but fire and Jupiter can trigger bewildering mood swings. When your element is in the ascendant, you can appear incandescent with creativity and passion, to the point of seeming to be spiraling out of control. But when your planetary ruler predominates, your philosophical, jovial side emerges.

FAMOUS BIRTHS: Ludwig van Beethoven (1770); Jane Austen (1775); Noel Coward (1899); Arthur C. Clarke (1917); Liv Ullmann (1938)

A DEFIANT DEED

Demonstrating fiery aggression and daring, in Massachusetts in 1773, American colonists disguised as Native Americans boarded three British ships and consigned over three hundred chests of tea to the depths of Boston Harbor.

SAGITTARIUS

♃ ↗

Restless
Adventurous
Spontaneous

DECEMBER 17

PROGRESSIVE PERFORMERS

Is today your birthday? If so, it is only partly because of your mutable mode that you're always on the go and rarely seem to rest. Take your outgoing, active polarity into consideration, as well as the characteristics with which your fiery element endows you—adventurousness, spontaneity, and a zest for performing—and it may seem amazing that you ever sleep! Mature Jupiter provides a calming influence on you, however, while still encouraging you to broaden your horizons at every opportunity.

FAMOUS BIRTHS: Ford Madox Ford (1873); Erskine Caldwell (1903); Christopher Casenove (1945); Paul Rodgers (1949); Milla Jovovich (1975)

A HEALING HEART

Jupiter promotes healing, while this day's positive polarity has pioneering qualities, making December 17, 1986, an apt date for the first heart, lungs, and liver transplant.

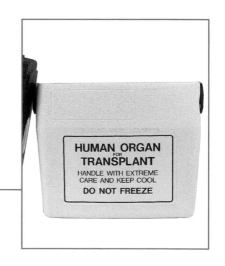

HUMAN ORGAN
FOR
TRANSPLANT
HANDLE WITH EXTREME
CARE AND KEEP COOL
DO NOT FREEZE

December 18

Sagittarius

↗ ♃

Energetic
Liberal
Experimental

Experimental Exhibitionists

If December 18 people are driven by their energetic, active polarity, there's no question that they are motivated by the urge to experiment with new interests and diversions. They also love to bask in others' attention and approval, another classic fire-element trait. They derive their liberal outlook, desire to broaden their knowledge, and interest in philosophical matters from Jupiter, while their mutable nature is the source of their adaptability, but also of their sudden, sometimes excessive, mood swings.

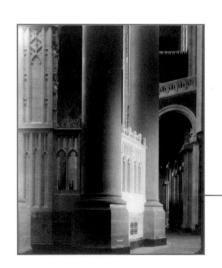

Famous Births: Paul Klee (1879); Keith Richards (1943); Steven Spielberg (1947); Brad Pitt (1964); Katie Holmes (1978); Christina Aguilera (1980)

Holy Smoke!

There is a danger that its element of fire may burn out of control on this day, as occurred on December 18, 2001, when a blaze damaged New York City's St. John the Divine Cathedral.

SAGITTARIUS

4 ♐

Sociable
Emotional
Adventurous

DECEMBER
19

ARDENT ATTENTION-SEEKERS

If this is your birthday, all of your birth influences suggest that you are outgoing and vibrant. Your positive polarity pushes you toward the extroverted end of the personality spectrum, while your mutable mode makes you highly sociable. Jupiter encourages you to broaden your horizons, and your fiery element fills you with the spirit of adventure. And it is fire, too, that is behind your heated emotions, especially the warm glow that you experience when others' attention is focused on you.

fAMOUS BiRTHS: Ralph Richardson (1902); Jean Genet (1910); Edith Piaf (1915); Alyssa Milano (1973); Jake Gyllenhall (1980)

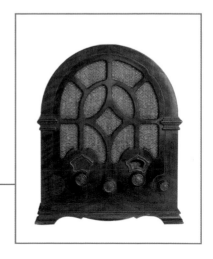

A fAR-REACHiNG INITIATIVE
Jupiter encourages expansion, as was evident on December 19, 1932, when the British Broadcasting Corporation launched its Empire Service, which transmitted as far as Australia. It now broadcasts to over 150 million people.

DECEMBER 20

SAGITTARIUS

Exuberant
Dynamic
Generous

MAGNANIMOUS MAGNETS

Those born on December 20 typically have a magnetic quality that attracts others to them. It may be because their fiery element fills them with such infectious exuberance and passion that they are impossible to ignore, or perhaps it is down to their active-polarity dynamism. Once you're within December 20 people's orbit, other attractive characteristics become apparent, too, notably their mutable gift for getting along with all kinds of people and their Jovian tolerance and generosity of spirit.

FAMOUS BIRTHS: Harvey Firestone (1868); Uri Geller (1946); Jenny Agutter (1952); Kris Tyler (1964); Chris Robinson (1966)

A FRESH START

Was this day's changeable, mutable quadruplicity at work in 1699 when, in his drive to modernize Russia, Czar Peter the Great decreed that the date of the Russian New Year be changed from September 1 to January 1?

SAGITTARIUS

4 ♐

Dynamic
Magnanimous
Warm

DECEMBER 21

PERSONALITIES WITH PRESENCE

If you were born on this day, you have a moody, mutable personality, so that others may not always be able to predict which side of your character will manifest itself at any given time. The sheer strength of your personality remains a constant, though, thanks in part to your dynamic, active polarity. Your family, friends, and colleagues may enjoy your Jovian magnanimity and fiery warmth one day, but then be upset by your egotistical, superior attitude and hot-tempered outbursts the next.

FAMOUS BIRTHS: Josef Stalin (1879); Heinrich Böll (1917); Jane Fonda (1937); Frank Zappa (1940); Samuel L. Jackson (1948); Kiefer Sutherland (1967)

A HEARTENING HAPPENING

Encouraged by December 21's influences—optimistic Jupiter, enthusiasm-enhancing fire, and a positive polarity—it was in 1946 that Frank Capra's classic movie, It's a Wonderful Life, *was premiered in New York City.*

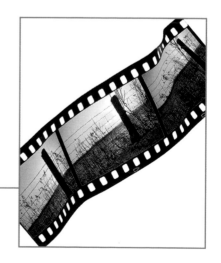

SYMBOL: THE GOAT-FISH
CELESTIAL RULER: SATURN
ELEMENT: EARTH
POLARITY: NEGATIVE (FEMININE)
QUADRUPLICITY: CARDINAL

CAPRICORN

DECEMBER 22 TO JANUARY 19 ♑

Capricorn was traditionally represented as a hybrid goat-fish, with a goat's top half and a fish's tail. Nowadays it is portrayed as a goat, a very real creature of the earth—Capricorn's element—which makes human goats practical and prudent, responsible and steady. Their passive polarity redoubles their caution and is also responsible for their thoughtfulness. Saturn, the ruling planet, whose namesake was the father of the Roman gods, instills such values as seriousness and self-discipline in its children, yet their cardinal quadruplicity is an altogether pushier influence that gives them initiative, self-absorption, and drive.

CAPRICORN
♄ ♑

Ambitious
Focused
Introverted

DECEMBER 22

COMMITTED CAREERISTS

Your cardinal mode supplies your go-getting impulses (along with a flicker of fire, the influence of the Sagittarius cusp), if this is your birthday. But it is serious Saturn that commits you to longer-term aims, especially earning both financial security and respect for your achievements. Not that you're a flashy or vain person, however, because your inward-looking, feminine polarity makes you interested in what goes on beneath the surface, while your element makes you refreshingly down-to-earth and hands-on.

FAMOUS BIRTHS: Frank Billings Kellogg (1856); Giacomo Puccini (1858); Maurice and Robin Gibb (1949); Ralph Fiennes (1962); Heather Donahue (1974)

AN EXTRAORDINARY X-RAY
This day is imbued with pioneering promise, which was realized in Würzburg, Germany, on December 22, 1895, when German physicist Wilhelm Röntgen produced the world's first X-ray, a radiograph of his wife's hand.

December 23

VS ♄

Sensible
Determined
Ambitious

INTROVERTS WITH INITIATIVE

If you were born on this day, you come across to others as a sensible, grounded sort of person. You have maturity-bestowing Saturn as a ruling planet and level-headed earth as an element, which ensures that you are generally straightforward and steady. However, this does not mean that you lack dreams or ambitions. Your feminine polarity encourages you to draw inspiration from your rich inner resources, and your initiative-sharpening, cardinal quadruplicity makes you a determined self-starter.

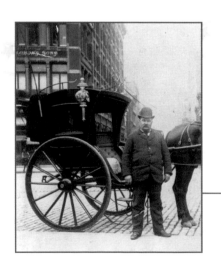

FAMOUS BIRTHS: Joseph Smith (1805); Yousuf Karsh (1908); Maurice Denham (1909); Harry Shearer (1943)

PATENT PRUDENCE

December 23's element is practical earth, associated with prudence and a negative polarity. It seems apt that English architect Joseph Hansom should have patented his horse-drawn "safety cab" on this date in 1834.

CAPRICORN
ち ♑

Driven
Persistent
Patient

DECEMBER 24

PRODUCTIVE WORKERS

One of the most striking qualities about December 24 individuals is their tenacity. This is, perhaps, inevitable, given their single-mindedness and drive, their earthy firmness and persistence, and their Saturnine patience and resolve. This trio of influences causes those born on this day to be goal-oriented, diligent, and productive characters. Their passive polarity promotes thoughtfulness, so the upshot is that they are prepared to work hard to achieve both material and personal stability and satisfaction.

FAMOUS BIRTHS: Ignatius Loyola (1491); Howard Hughes (1905); Ava Gardner (1922); Ricky Martin (1971)

A CYCLIST'S CONSTRAINT
Earth gives this day a practical flavor, and Saturn advocates restraint, which may be why it was on December 24, 1889, that Illinois inventors Daniel Stover and William Hance patented a bicycle with a back-pedal brake.

December 25

♑ ♄

Rational
Logical
Realistic

LOGICAL LEADERS

December 25 people are realists with a resolutely logical outlook, due to having stoical Saturn as a planetary ruler and rational earth as an element. This is a potentially pessimistic combination, particularly when their worrisome polarity exerts a negative influence over those born on this day. Their cardinal nature generally helps to lift them out of the doldrums, however. Instead of dwelling on their worries, they are more inclined to seize the initiative and work their way toward a rewarding or fulfilling goal.

FAMOUS BIRTHS: Jesus Christ (*c.*4 B.C.); Isaac Newton (1642); Humphrey Bogart (1899); Sissy Spacek (1949); Annie Lennox (1954); Shane McGowan (1957)

A CHRISTMAS CATASTROPHE
Days whose element is earth are particularly prone to earth-related disasters, as on December 25, 1975, when Managua, the capital of Nicaragua, was rocked by an earthquake that left more than ten thousand people dead.

ℏ ♑

Productive
Contemplative
Conscientious

DECEMBER 26

PIONEERING PRODUCERS

If you were born on this day, your earthy element encourages you to savor sensual pleasures, but you're sensible—neither a natural-born hedonist nor often truly at rest. While diligent earth and responsible Saturn cause you to enjoy being productive, and to feel guilty when frittering away your time, your passive polarity promotes contemplation, especially when you are relaxing. The combination of your conscientiousness, thoughtfulness, and motivation often results in pioneering achievements.

fAMOUS BIRTHS: Charles Babbage (1792); Mao Tse-tung (1893); Phil Spector (1940); Lars Ulrich (1963); Jared Leto (1971)

A TERRIBLE TREMOR
The tsunami that devastated Southeast Asia on December 26, 2004, was a massive ocean wave triggered by an underwater earthquake. Was it coincidence that this day's element is earth, or could there have been a causative connection?

DECEMBER 27

CAPRICORN
♑ ♄

Thorough
Motivated
Intuitive

RESOLUTE RESEARCHERS

If you were born on December 27, you are well equipped to make an excellent researcher. Your purpose-providing, cardinal nature gives you motivation, while your earthy element supplies thoroughness and an enjoyment of working with facts. Saturn adds determination, patience, and a long-term outlook. You have an instinctive, meditative, feminine polarity and you often use the information that you have amassed as a launching pad from which to make intuitive leaps in pioneering directions.

FAMOUS BIRTHS: Johannes Kepler (1571); Louis Pasteur (1822); Marlene Dietrich (1901); Gerard Depardieu (1948); David Knopfler (1952); Maryam D'Abo (1960)

BANKING ON BETTERMENT
Saturn, which rules this day, is linked with desire for financial security, making December 27, 1945, an auspicious date for the creation of the World Bank, an organization that fights poverty in the developing world.

CAPRICORN
ħ ♑

Diligent
Receptive
Progressive

DECEMBER 28

HARDWORKING PROGRESSIVES

Two distinct streaks can usually be seen running through the personalities of December 28 individuals. The first is diligence (a double dose of which they receive from Saturn, their commitment-increasing planetary ruler, and their earthy element), and the second is their progressive, forward-moving tendency, the gift of their go-getting, cardinal quadruplicity. Those born on this day are progressive in another sense, too, in that their passive polarity causes them to be open to all manner of influences.

FAMOUS BIRTHS: Woodrow Wilson (1856); Johnny Otis (1924); Maggie Smith (1934); Denzel Washington (1954); Nigel Kennedy (1956)

A PATRIOTIC PLEDGE

Saturn, this day's ruling planet, and earth, its element, are both loyalty-enhancing influences, which may be why it was on December 28, 1945, that the U.S. Congress officially approved the Pledge of Allegiance to the flag.

December 29

SENSUAL SURVIVORS

It may seem surprising that people who are so straightforward can be led astray, but the earthy element that is at the root of December 29 people's level-headedness also makes them sensual and susceptible to seduction, while their receptive, passive polarity can be a confusing influence. But when experience and stern Saturn, their backbone-stiffening ruling planet, have taught them some tough life lessons, these resilient survivors can draw on their cardinal quadruplicity's drive to get back on track.

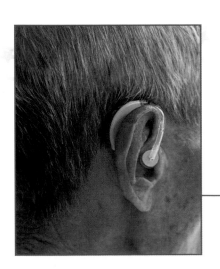

FAMOUS BIRTHS: Andrew Johnson (1808); Jon Voight (1938); Marianne Faithfull (1946); Ted Danson (1947); Jude Law (1972)

HEAR, HEAR!

December 29's passive polarity encourages receptiveness, and it was on this day in 1952 that the first transistor hearing aid, the model 1010, was put on sale in the USA by the Sonotone Corporation of Elmsford, New York.

CAPRICORN
♄ ♑

Driven
Patient
Diligent

DECEMBER 30

DILIGENT DELIVERERS

If today is your birthday, not only are you driven to achieve the demanding targets that you set yourself, but you are also equipped with the requisite characteristics. Saturn causes you to understand that, although there are no short-cuts to success, the rewards will be long-lasting. Your feminine polarity encourages you to be sensitive and to think your plans through thoroughly, and your earthy element gives you diligence. Your family, friends, and colleagues can always depend on you to deliver.

FAMOUS BIRTHS: Rudyard Kipling (1865); Bo Didley (1928); Patti Smith (1946); Jay Kay (1969); Tiger Woods (1975)

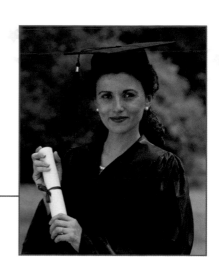

A LADY LAWYER

Not only does this day have a feminine polarity, but Saturn highlights careers, making December 30, 1919, a fitting date for Lincoln's Inn (an inn of court in London, England) to admit the first female to study for the bar.

DECEMBER 31

℣ ♄

Ambitious
Practical
Pragmatic

RESILIENT REALISTS

Others admire December 31 people's apparent ability to cope with all that life throws at them. They may not appreciate that behind the earthy, matter-of-fact front that they present to the world lie worry-prone, feminine-polarity souls. That said, their cardinal nature makes them very ambitious, their element makes them level-headed and practical, and Saturn supplies pragmatism and commitment, so that their concerns will disappear when they are focused on furthering their careers or helping others.

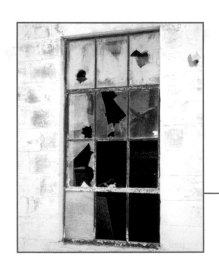

FAMOUS BIRTHS: Henri Matisse (1869); Anthony Hopkins (1937); John Denver (1943); Donna Summer (1948); Val Kilmer (1959)

WALLED IN

On this day in 1695, a window tax was introduced to Britain, prompting many citizens to brick up their windows. Could this have been related to the day's rulership by repressive Saturn and its inward-looking tendency?

CAPRICORN

♄ ♑

Sensible
Careful
Pioneering

JANUARY

1

LONG-SIGHTED LEADERS

January 1 individuals are often at the forefront of their fields, perhaps because their birthday kicks off a new year, or maybe because their cardinal nature gives them an affinity for the avant-garde. That said, their passive polarity encourages thoughtfulness, their earthy element makes them sensible, and Saturn forces them to acknowledge that there are no short-cuts to enduring success. Unlikely to take risks, these people's pioneering projects are usually the result of careful, detailed planning.

FAMOUS BIRTHS: Alfred Stieglitz (1864); E.M. Forster (1879); J. Edgar Hoover (1895); J.D. Salinger (1919); Joe Orton (1933)

PENSIONS DAY
Saturn rules this day and imbues it with a sense of responsibility and commitment, particularly within the realm of financial security. This may be why on January 1, 1909, state-funded old-age pensions were instituted in Britain.

January 2

♑ ♄

Sensible
Realistic
Thoughtful

GROUNDED GRAFTERS

Your cardinal quadruplicity may push you into setting yourself stellar goals, if today is your birthday, but your feet are nevertheless planted firmly on the ground. While having earth as an element makes you sensible and hardworking, your passive polarity is at the root of your tendency to think long and hard before you take action, and Saturn gives you a realistic, no-frills outlook. With these influences, even though your aims may be ambitious, you have an excellent chance of achieving them.

FAMOUS BIRTHS: Isaac Asimov (1920); David Bailey (1938); Christy Turlington (1969); Kate Bosworth (1983)

A LIMITING INFLUENCE

On January 2, 1974, President Nixon imposed a speed limit of 55m.p.h. on U.S. drivers, a gas-conserving measure prompted by an Organization of Petroleum Exporting Countries' embargo, but also, perhaps, by repressive Saturn.

CAPRICORN

♄ ♑

Focused
Dedicated
Cautious

JANUARY 3

COMPULSIVE CONSERVATIVES

People born on this day may be cautious, but the combination of committed, conservative Saturn and constant, upright earth indicates that once January 3 individuals have decided to devote themselves to realizing an aim, they will not rest until they have completed their self-imposed task (without cheating!). And because they have a target-oriented, cardinal quadruplicity and a career-minded ruling planet, the chances are that their formidable sights will be focused on furthering their life's work.

FAMOUS BIRTHS: J.R.R. Tolkien (1892); Victor Borge (1909); Victoria Principal (1946); Mel Gibson (1956)

AN ELECTRICAL ERA

It was on January 3, 1957—a day that has a ruling planet whose name (Saturn) is synonymous with Father Time—that the U.S. Hamilton Watch Company introduced the first electric (battery-powered) watch, the Ventura.

January 4

COMMITTED CONSTRUCTORS

Although your passive polarity makes you thoughtful, if you were born on this day, aimless idleness is out of the question. You are a self-starter and you're self-motivated, thanks to your cardinal nature, and you derive satisfaction from being productive and helpful. Your industriousness results from having earth as an element and Saturn as a planetary ruler. These birth influences are also behind your patient commitment to creating security for your family and making a solid contribution at work.

FAMOUS BIRTHS: Jakob Grimm (1785); Louis Braille (1809); Augustus John (1878); Jane Wyman (1914); Michael Stipe (1960); Deana Carter (1966)

A CUTTING-EDGE OPERATION
Its pioneering influence suggests that January 4 is a date for "firsts," such as the first successful appendectomy, performed in Davenport, Iowa, by Dr. William Grant on this day in 1885.

CAPRICORN
♄ ♑

Serious
Prudent
Progressive

JANUARY
5

UNCONVENTIONAL CONFORMISTS

At heart, January 5 people are the sensible children of Saturn who cherish their traditional values and are intent on achieving career success and financial and emotional security. Take their passive polarity and earthy element into account, and these are serious individuals who give much thought to planning their lives, and then follow through their plans patiently and productively. But it is their cardinal nature that is behind their sometimes surprisingly bold, pioneering, and progressive approach.

fAMOUS BIRTHS: Konrad Adenauer (1876); Stella Gibbons (1902); Robert Duvall (1931); Diane Keaton (1946); Brian Warner, "Marilyn Manson" (1969)

YOU GOVERN, GIRL!
Female ventures are favored on this feminine, go-getting, cardinal day. It was on January 5, 1925, that Nellie Tayloe Ross was inaugurated as the USA's first female governor (of Wyoming).

JANUARY 6

STEADY SUCCESSES

January 6 people's birth influences divide into pairs to produce a distinctive combination of personality traits. The conjunction of sober Saturn and earnest earth creates responsible, straightforward, and tenacious types who have concrete ambitions and are set on seeing them become a reality. The fusion of their profoundly contemplative—sometimes almost dreamy—passive polarity and go-getting qualities results in committed individuals who are very determined and always loyal to their loved ones.

FAMOUS BIRTHS: Joan of Arc (1412); Loretta Young (1912); Rowan Atkinson (1957); John Singleton (1968)

A CAPITAL CREATION

The influence of this day's element, earth, which is associated with enduring foundations, must have been pronounced on January 6, 1535, when the conquistador Francisco Pizarro founded the city of Lima, now Peru's capital.

CAPRICORN

♄ ♑

Wise
Straightforward
Ambitious

JANUARY
7

VIGOROUS VISIONARIES

Your passive polarity predisposes you to being wise, thoughtful, and caring, if this is your birthday. Earth, your element, and Saturn, your ruling planet, may together encourage you to steer a steady and straightforward course through life. You are emphatically not an inactive or plodding type, however. While the combination of earth and Saturn makes you ambitious and diligent, your cardinal nature gives you the drive and initiative to make your enterprising visions come true.

FAMOUS BIRTHS: St. Bernadette of Lourdes (1844); Charles Addams (1912); Erin Gray (1950); Nicolas Cage (1964)

A SATURNINE SIEGE

Saturn and earth inject a double dose of tenacity into this day, and may have inlfuenced events in World War II: January 7, 1942, marks the start of the four-month-long siege of the Bataan Peninsula.

January 8

Capricorn

♑ ♄

Introspective
Innovative
Self-disciplined

Introverted Initiators

It may not be obvious, but January 8 individuals are deep thinkers, even introverts, at heart, often welcoming the opportunity for some solitary introspection. But their feminine-polarity introversion may well be masked by their cardinal-quadruplicity ability to be innovative without either cutting corners or doing a sloppy job. It is sober Saturn that is the source of their self-discipline and dutiful work ethic, while their earthy element is responsible for their thoroughness, as well as their sensuality.

Famous Births: Wilkie Collins (1824); Elvis Presley (1935); Stephen Hawking (1942); David Bowie (1947)

Tunnel Vision

Emphasizing that January 8's element and quadruplicity are earth and cardinal, or pioneering, it was on this day in 1886 that Britain's longest rail tunnel, the Severn Tunnel (which is over 4 miles long), was officially opened.

CAPRICORN
♄ ♑

Goal-driven
Tenacious
Reticent

JANUARY
9

PRACTICAL ACHIEVERS

If you were born on this day, your birth influences cause you to focus on getting results, although your cautious feminine polarity can slow you down. This is because you have a tendency to hold back until you feel certain that your actions will have a successful outcome, whether at work or in your personal life. Otherwise, the fusion of careerist Saturn, a cardinal quadruplicity, and grounding earth makes you aspire to ambitious targets and work so single-mindedly at achieving them that you rarely fail.

FAMOUS BIRTHS: Simone de Beauvoir (1908); Richard Nixon (1913); Joan Baez (1941); Jimmy Page (1944)

HANGING ON IN THERE!
Saturn, Capricorn's planetary ruler and a supplier of tenacity, may have aided Russian cosmonaut Valeri Poliakov aboard the space station Mir, in becoming the first person to spend 366 days in space on January 9, 1995.

JANUARY 10

VS ♄

Enterprising
Receptive
Anxious

TENACIOUS TYPES

The action of their four birth influences on each January 10 individual inevitably varies, with some displaying more cardinal, enterprising drive than others, or, if their element predominates, being more earthy. All, however, are receptive people with a tendency to worry too much, especially about their families or their careers (due to their negative polarity and the influence of Saturn). But they usually overcome both their real and imagined problems with the help of their earth-and-Saturn-derived tenacity.

FAMOUS BIRTHS: Jesse James (1843); Barbara Hepworth (1903); Rod Stewart (1945); George Foreman (1949)

A SENSIBLE CONCLUSION?

Was it just a coincidence that it was on January 10—a day whose element is associated with level-headedness—that the English-born writer Thomas Paine published (in 1776) an influential pamphlet entitled "Common Sense"?

CAPRICORN

♄ ♑

Serious
Hard working
Productive

JANUARY
11

PRODUCTIVE PERSONALITIES

If you were born on this day, you like to keep busy. Maybe this is because serious Saturn and your worry-prone, negative polarity cause you to feel guilty when you are not doing something useful for yourself or others, or perhaps it is because your cardinal nature gives you an interest in attaining your goals as swiftly as possible. Either way, your earthy element's contribution is to make you hardworking, loyal, and responsible, and you want your loved ones to be able to enjoy the fruits of your labor.

FAMOUS BIRTHS: Ellery Queen (1905); Naomi Judd (1946); Ben Crenshaw (1952); Mary J. Blige (1971); Amanda Peet (1972)

LAND LEGISLATION

January 11's element is earth, so it is an appropriate date for events relating to land and territory, and it was on this day in 1805 that U.S. President Thomas Jefferson signed the act that created the Michigan Territory.

JANUARY 12

♑ ♄

*Professional
Diligent
Practical*

PRACTICAL PROFESSIONALS

Those born on January 12 are known for the professionalism with which they approach tasks and duties. They have been blessed by both Saturn and earth with patience, diligence, thoroughness, and staying power. While earth makes them practical, hands-on types, their careful feminine polarity ensures that they think over their decisions in great detail before they start a project. Once they commit themselves to a goal, they will dedicate themselves to achieving it with typical cardinal determination.

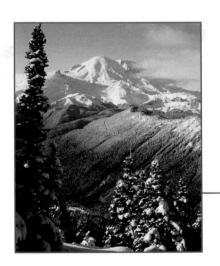

FAMOUS BIRTHS: Edmund Burke (1729); John Singer Sargent (1856); Joe Frazier (1944); Howard Stern (1954); Kirstie Alley (1955)

NATIONALIZING NATURE
This was the day, in 1915, when the U.S. Congress voted in favor of establishing the Rocky Mountain National Park. Could they have been influenced by January 12's earthy element?

CAPRICORN

♄ ♑

Dedicated
Motivated
Thoughtful

JANUARY
13

STEADY CHARACTERS

Because their cardinal nature motivates them to work hard for the things they value, and because their earthy element encourages them to be calm, responsible, and constant, it may seem as though January 13 people know exactly where they are going in life, and how to get there. Yet while Saturn encourages them to be true to their life plan, others may be surprised to know that their passive polarity causes them to think deeply about others, and often fills them with worries or self-doubt.

FAMOUS BIRTHS: Horatio Alger (1832); Gwen Verdon (1925); Richard Moll (1943); Penelope Ann Miller (1964); Patrick Dempsey (1966)

AN AUTOMOTIVE ADVANCE
Practical innovations are likely on January 13, a day with earth as an element and an enterprising quality. It was on January 13, 1942, that U.S. car-manufacturer Henry Ford patented a plastic-bodied automobile.

JANUARY 14

CAPRICORN

VS ♄

Supportive
Practical
Nurturing

HANDS-ON HELPERS

Of your four birth influences, earth probably has the greatest effect on your personality, if this is your birthday. You are a practical, level-headed, and supportive person, and others know that they can depend on you. While your feminine polarity gives you nurturing, family-minded impulses, you may also have strong self-promoting instincts, which can make you somewhat self-centered and pushy. However, this is partly due to your belief that you owe it to your loved ones to build a successful career.

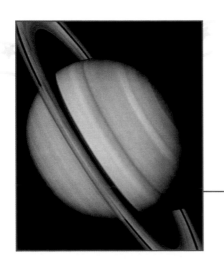

FAMOUS BIRTHS: Albert Schweitzer (1875); Cecil Beaton (1904); Billy Jo Spears (1937); Faye Dunaway (1941)

A TITANIC MISSION

This day is ruled by Saturn, and it was on January 14, 2005, that N.A.S.A.'s *Huygens Probe* landed on Titan, a moon orbiting Saturn, and began beaming images back to Earth.

CAPRICORN
♄ ♑

Self-disciplined
Responsible
Thoughtful

JANUARY
15

THOUGHTFUL PROBLEM-SOLVERS

January 15 people tend to have high standards, which is, perhaps, inevitable when one has earth as an element and Saturn as a planetary ruler, both of which encourage moral behavior and self-discipline. These birth influences supply a sense of responsibility to others and a caring, nurturing outlook, too. When these individuals identify someone who needs support, their feminine-polarity thoughtfulness and initiative kick in, prompting them to come up with practical solutions and a steady helping hand.

FAMOUS BIRTHS: Pierre S. DuPont (1870); Ivor Novello (1893); Martin Luther King, Jr. (1929); Regina King (1971)

ONWARD AND UPWARD!
Maybe January 15's cardinal quadruplicity and practical, earthy element were at work on this day in 1861, when U.S. inventor Elisha Otis was granted a patent for his steam-powered elevator.

JANUARY 16

SELF-DISCIPLINED SENSUALISTS

If you were born on January 16, you are blessed with remarkable long-term vision and the focus required to attain your goals. While Saturn encourages you to succeed in your career, your cardinal nature helps you by giving you single-minded determination. Although your earthy element contributes diligence, it also makes you highly sensual. Your passive polarity provides common sense and some self-doubt, so that life is not all work—or plain sailing—so you should always try to find the right balance.

FAMOUS BIRTHS: André Michelin (1853); Susan Sontag (1933); Sade Adu (1959); Kate Moss (1974); Aaliyah Haughton (1979)

BOOZING BANNED

Saturn, this day's planetary ruler, encourages discipline. Its influence may have been especially potent on January 16, 1920, when Prohibition, which effectively made alcoholic drinks illegal, began in the USA.

CAPRICORN

♄ ♑

Driven
Robust
Diligent

JANUARY
17

DETERMINED DISCIPLINARIANS

Such is their drive and Saturn-derived strictness in pursuing an undeviating course toward their personal goals that it seems as though January 17 individuals are fueled by willpower alone. Yet not only does their doubt-inducing, feminine polarity often make them hesitant, but restrictive Saturn forces them to recognize that hard graft is required before rewards can be reaped. With these influences, they mainly rely on their earthy robustness, diligence, and perseverance to help them succeed.

fAMOUS BIRTHS: Benjamin Franklin (1706); Al Capone (1899); Eartha Kitt (1927); Muhammad Ali (1942); Jim Carrey (1962)

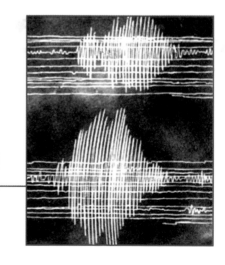

A TERRIBLE TREND
Perhaps because January 17's element is earth, it is prone to earthquakes, as occurred on this day in 1994, when the Northridge Earthquake shook Los Angeles, California, and again in 1995, when thousands died in Kobe, Japan.

January 18

Capricorn

♑ ♄

Persistent
Sensible
Dynamic

Tenacious Traditionalists

The conservative influence that Saturn, their restrictive planetary ruler, wields over January 18 people can make them rather conventional characters, sometimes even downright traditionalist types. Take their earthy element into account as well, and the picture taking shape is of upright, straightforward, and persistent individuals who have cautious personalities. Dull they are not, however, because their cardinal nature injects a dynamic and driven streak into their sometimes surprising characters.

Famous Births: Peter Mark Roget (1779); A. A. Milne (1882); Oliver Hardy (1892); Cary Grant (1904); Danny Kaye (1913); Kevin Costner (1955)

A Fabulous Finding

Perhaps there was a special interaction between January 18's enterprising, inward-looking, and earthy qualities in 1995, when the Chauvet Cave network, and its ancient decorations, were discovered in Vallon-Pont-d'Arc, France.

CAPRICORN

♄ ♑

Patient
Thoughtful
Steadfast

JANUARY 19

EARTHY ENABLERS

It is not just your practical skills—the gift of your earthy element—that make you a "can-do" character, if you were born on this day. You have the qualities you need to achieve your aims, including a down-to-earth approach to problem-solving and seemingly inexhaustible supplies of patience. Your passive polarity provides compassion, Saturn donates self-discipline and steadfastness, and your cardinal quadruplicity contributes initiative. As you are on the cusp, you also display a little Aquarian gregariousness.

FAMOUS BIRTHS: Robert E. Lee (1807); Edgar Allan Poe (1809); Paul Cézanne (1839); Janis Joplin (1942); Dolly Parton (1946); Stefan Edberg (1966)

INDIA'S FIRST LADY

Reaping the benefit of the combination of a feminine polarity and a cardinal quadruplicity, it was on January 19, 1966, that Indira Gandhi was elected prime minister of India, becoming the nation's first female premier.

SYMBOL: THE WATER CARRIER
CELESTIAL RULER: URANUS
  (TRADITIONALLY SATURN)
ELEMENT: AIR
POLARITY: POSITIVE (MASCULINE)
QUADRUPLICITY: FIXED

AQUARIUS

JANUARY 20 TO FEBRUARY 18 ♒

The English translation of the Latin word *aquarius* is "water-carrier," and Greco–Roman myth says that this was Ganymede, whom Zeus (Jupiter) appointed cup-bearer to the Olympian deities. Saturn, Aquarius's traditional planetary ruler, was ousted by Uranus during the nineteenth century, an appropriate decision, given that this sign's element is air. It is from Uranus and air that Aquarians derive their intelligence and independence, with Uranus adding eccentricity and rebelliousness, and air providing sociability and playfulness. Their positive polarity makes them extroverts, while their fixed mode provides staying power.

AQUARIUS

♅ ♒♒

Confrontational
Enterprising
Questioning

JANUARY 20

ENTERPRISING EXPERIMENTERS

If this is your birthday, you are quite consistent when it comes to your personal beliefs and habits (the result of having a fixed quadruplicity), but you love to challenge other people's certainties and customs. Your confrontational tendencies, as well as your enterprising outlook, may be part and parcel of having an active polarity, but your questioning nature is the inevitable result of having curious, analytical air as your element and experimental, revolutionary Uranus as your ruling planet.

FAMOUS BIRTHS: Aristotle Onassis (1906); Federico Fellini (1920); Edwin "Buzz" Aldrin (1930); David Lynch (1946); Malcolm McLaren (1947)

A LONG-AWAITED LIBERATION

Two Aquarian influences—Uranus and air—disseminate a demand for freedom, so maybe Iranian authorities were obeying when they released fifty-two Americans whom they had held hostage for 444 days on January 20, 1981.

JANUARY 21

COMMITTED CHARACTERS

The unconventional, experimental qualities imparted by Uranus, the planet that rules those born on this day, may be quite pronounced in some January 21 people, while others may appear to have received more than their fair share of airy charm. The traits that characterize their remaining two birth influences are common to all, however. While their active polarity makes them assertive, their fixed mode is responsible for their unwavering commitment and occasional obstinacy.

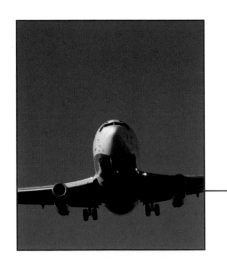

fAMOUS BIRTHS: Thomas "Stonewall" Jackson (1824); Christian Dior (1905); Jack Nicklaus (1940); Geena Davis (1957)

TRANSATLANTIC TRANSPORT
This day's element is air, so January 21, 1970, was an auspicious date for the Boeing 747-100 to begin as a commercial aircraft, when it flew from New York to London for Pan American Airways.

AQUARIUS
♒ ♒
♒ ♒

Curious
Independent
Innovative

JANUARY
22

INDEPENDENT INNOVATORS

If you were born on January 22, you rarely hesitate, because your fixed nature gives you the courage of your firmly held convictions. Your active polarity provides you with self-belief, initiative, and daring. Your airy element causes you to be curious, while Uranus, your planetary ruler, makes you very willful. Another consequence of this combination of birth influences is that you are an independent thinker. You're never afraid to take risks, so that you have the potential to be an innovator, too.

FAMOUS BIRTHS: Lord George Byron (1788); August Strindberg (1849); John Hurt (1940); Diane Lane (1965); Balthazar Getty (1975)

AN INNOVATIVE INTRODUCTION
Demonstrating air's propensity to broadcast information and Uranus's technology link, Apple advertised the then ultra-innovative GUI (graphic user interface) Macintosh on January 22, 1984, during the Super Bowl.

JANUARY 23

AQUARIUS

♒ ♅

Independent
Radical
Determined

RESOLUTE REVOLUTIONARIES

Interaction between their birth influences within the January 23 character gives those born on this day revolutionary potential. They derive their propensity to think for themselves, rather than according to convention, from their independence and intelligence-sharpening element of air. Their rebellious individualism and radical outlook come from Uranus, but their positive polarity provides forcefulness when promoting their ideas. Their fixed mode makes them unshakable in their determination.

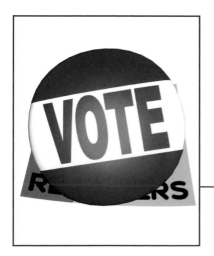

FAMOUS BIRTHS: John Hancock (1737); Edouard Manet (1832); Django Reinhardt (1910); Jeanne Moreau (1928); Rutger Hauer (1944)

FIXING A DATE

This day's quadruplicity is change-resistant, which may be why it was in 1845 that U.S. Congress decreed that the USA's national elections should always be held on the first Tuesday after the first Monday in November.

Aquarius

♒ ♒
♅ ♒

Sociable
Inquisitive
Gregarious

JANUARY 24

STRONG-WILLED SOCIALIZERS

There are usually two sides to the January 24 personality: those born on this day generally exhibit remarkable strength of will on the one hand, and great sociability on the other. They have the influence of radical Uranus, their planetary ruler, and the stubbornness of their fixed mode to thank for their sometimes maddening willfulness. But their outgoing, positive polarity and inquisitive and communicative element of air are together responsible for their appealing, uninhibited gregariousness.

FAMOUS BIRTHS: Edith Wharton (1862); Neil Diamond (1941); John Belushi (1949); Nastassja Kinski (1959); Tatyana Ali (1979)

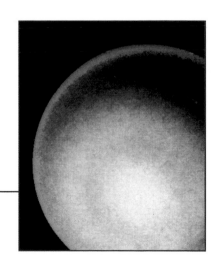

A VISITING VOYAGER
When they launched their Voyager 2 space probe, did N.A.S.A. scientists know that it would fly past Uranus on a Uranus-ruled day, namely January 24, 1986? In doing so, the spacecraft came within 50,679 miles of the planet.

JANUARY 25

AQUARIUS

♒ ♅

Extroverted
Analytical
Intellectual

AMIABLE ANALYSTS

If this is your birthday, you're sociable because air, your element, predisposes you to enjoy company and take an interest in others. In addition, your masculine polarity ensures that you are usually at the extrovert end of the personality spectrum. But you are often just as happy when engaged in solitary intellectual pursuits as you are in company. Both air and Uranus give you an analytical, experimental mind, but there are times when you don't feel inclined to compromise, because of your fixed mode.

FAMOUS BIRTHS: Robert Burns (1759); William Somerset Maugham (1874); Virginia Woolf (1882); Corazon Aquino (1933); Alicia Keys (1981)

A CUNNING COUP

General Idi Amin seized leadership of Uganda when he overthrew Milton Obote on January 25, 1971, exhibiting the aggression associated with this day's masculine polarity, and the rebelliousness that is the hallmark of Uranus.

AQUARIUS

♅ ♒

Dedicated
Challenging
Enterprising

JANUARY 26

DEDICATED DEVELOPERS

If you're a January 26 baby, your fixed nature gives you dedication and determination—and often stubbornness as well. The combined action of your remaining birth influences ensures that you don't become stale or set in your ways, however. Your challenging, outward-focused, active polarity, added to experimental Uranus and inquisitive air, give you an enterprising attitude and interest in the potential of the new. You are focused enough, too, to concentrate on and develop the ideas that capture your interest.

FAMOUS BIRTHS: Douglas MacArthur (1880); Paul Newman (1925); Jacqueline du Pré (1945); Ellen DeGeneres (1958); Wayne Gretzky (1961)

AFFIRMATIVE ACTION

Influenced, perhaps, by this day's radical, forward-looking Uranus and communicative air, January 26, 1948, was the day President Truman signed Executive Order 9981, putting an end to segregation in the U.S. Armed Forces.

JANUARY 27

♒ ♅

Inventive
Easygoing
Unconventional

ORIGINAL THINKERS

Given that January 27 people have a masculine polarity that removes their inhibitions, an inventive element in air, and a ruling planet that encourages unconventional thinking, it is almost inevitable that they should be original thinkers. Their fixed nature makes them stick to their guns, too. They can be unyielding to the point of mutiny, especially when challenged, thanks to the interaction between their quadruplicity, Uranus, and their polarity. Their easygoing, airy charm normally prevails, however.

FAMOUS BIRTHS: Wolfgang Amadeus Mozart (1756); Lewis Carroll (1832); Mimi Rogers (1956); Bridget Fonda (1964)

GET THE PICTURE?

Uranus disseminates a fascination with technology that was evident in 1926, when Scottish engineer John Logie Baird demonstrated his prototypal television to members of the Royal Institution in London, England.

AQUARIUS

♒ ♒♒♒

Dynamic
Curious
Inventive

JANUARY 28

EXPERIMENTAL EXPLORERS

If you were born on this day, it is Uranus, your planetary ruler, that is responsible for your fascination with the new. Your positive polarity gives you daring dynamism that pushes you to explore the possibilities inherent in a new idea, a cutting-edge gadget, or even virgin territory. And because your fixed nature gives you tremendous concentration when your interest has been piqued, and your airy element's gifts include curiosity and inventiveness, you are always experimenting in one way or another.

FAMOUS BIRTHS: Henry Morton Stanley (1841); William Burroughs (1855): Jackson Pollock (1912); Alan Alda (1936); Elijah Wood (1981)

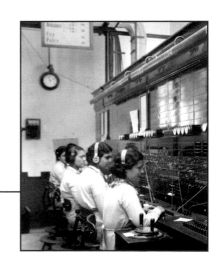

AN ENTERPRISING EXCHANGE

Air encourages communication, while Uranus promotes technology, making January 28, 1878, a fitting date for the introduction of the first commercial telephone switchboard by the District Telephone Company in Connecticut.

JANUARY 29

♒ ♅

Intelligent
Logical
Articulate

CONTRARY COMMUNICATORS

Uranus and air give those born on January 29 a double dose of intelligence, as well as a rigorously logical way of looking at life. While their ruling planet is behind their unconventional—and sometimes even contrary—conclusions and opinions, their articulacy and communication skills are down to their element. And when you take their confrontational, masculine polarity and immovable, fixed quadruplicity into consideration, you have people who love to engage in an argument and rarely back down.

FAMOUS BIRTHS: Thomas Paine (1737); Frederick Delius (1862); W. C. Fields (1880); Germaine Greer (1939); Oprah Winfrey (1954)

"FOR VALOUR"

It was on January 29, 1856—a day whose masculine polarity is linked with dynamism and courage—that Britain's Victoria Cross, perhaps the most famous medal in the world to be awarded for acts of military valor, came into being.

AQUARIUS
♒ ♒♒

Independent
Analytical
Stubborn

JANUARY
30

DARING DOGMATISTS

Your intellect-enhancing and independence emphasizing element and ruling planet—air and Uranus—encourage you to think for yourself and to form your own views, if you were born on this day. It is your fixed nature that causes you to dig in your heels and refuse to budge whenever others contradict you. Because your masculine polarity makes you an aggressive defender and promoter of your sometimes controversial beliefs, you would make a formidable (if dogmatic) political lobbyist or campaigner.

FAMOUS BIRTHS: Franklin Delano Roosevelt (1882); Gene Hackman (1930); Vanessa Redgrave (1937); Dick Cheney (1941); Phil Collins (1951)

AGGRESSIVE ASSASSIN
Indian peace activist Mahatma Gandhi was assassinated on this day in 1948. Was his killer perhaps taking advantage of the aggression imparted by this day's masculine polarity?

JANUARY 31

ENERGETIC ECCENTRICS

Those who come into the orbit of people born on this day are usually impressed by their sheer energy, which their active polarity bestows on them, along with their positive attitude. Their oddball, Uranus-inspired eccentricities are also apparent, as well as their airy charm. There are plenty of times, however, when January 31 people are infuriating because of their fixed-nature stubbornness, which typically manifests itself most strongly when they feel that they are not being taken seriously enough.

FAMOUS BIRTHS: Franz Schubert (1797); Freya Stark (1893); Norman Mailer (1923); Minnie Driver (1971); Portia de Rossi (1973); Justin Timberlake (1981)

TELEPHONE REUNION
January 31's fixed quadruplicity favors union, which is what happened when, in 1971, telephone service was re-established between East and West Berlin.

AQUARIUS

♅ ♒
♒

Radical
Individual
Stubborn

FEBRUARY

1

IDIOSYNCRATIC INDIVIDUALS

If you were born on February 1, you are emphatically "one of a kind." Not only does your airy element encourage independence of thought, but Uranus promotes a way of thinking that is radically different from the norm. Your masculine polarity gives you the courage of your convictions, while your fixed nature causes you to remain utterly unyielding when you're under pressure. This usually means that you win the respect of others, even if they don't always like you for your forcefulness.

FAMOUS BIRTHS: Clark Gable (1901); S. J. Perelman (1904); Muriel Spark (1918); Boris Yeltsin (1931); Terry Jones (1942); Lisa Marie Presley (1968)

COME TOGETHER

Perhaps the consolidating impulses supplied by this day's fix quadruplicity provoked President Lincoln, on this day in 1865, to sign the Thirteenth Amendment to the Constitution, abolishing slavery in the United States.

FEBRUARY 2

AQUARIUS
♒ ♅

Energetic
Brave
Playful

COURAGEOUS CHARMERS

If this is your birthday, you certainly don't lack courage, thanks to your masculine polarity, which is also the source of your energy and dynamism. It is just as well that you are brave, though, because Uranus gives you such a boundless appetite for experimentation that your anarchic ideas may be rebuffed by more conventional souls as being too radical. Rejection can make you highly inflexible, even angry, because of your fixed nature, but your airy, playful charm generally gets you a long way.

FAMOUS BIRTHS: Havelock Ellis (1859); James Joyce (1882); Stan Getz (1927); Farrah Fawcett (1947); Christie Brinkley (1953)

A TESTING TIME
This day is associated with innovation and communication. These qualities were evident at the summit in Yalta in 1945 that was attended by Winston Churchill, Franklin D. Roosevelt, and Josef Stalin.

AQUARIUS

♅ ♒
♒

Radical
Innovative
Persevering

FEBRUARY
3

PERSISTENT PIONEERS

There is no question that February 3 individuals are radical thinkers, for the combination of revolutionary Uranus, their ruling planet, and free-thinking air, their element, causes them to push aside the boundaries of convention. Fueled by their positive-polarity dynamism, they tend to run as far as they can with their innovative ideas. And because they have a fixed nature, they will doggedly persevere with their pioneering pursuits—often profitably—regardless of others' ridicule or disapproval.

FAMOUS BIRTHS: Felix Mendelssohn (1809); Gertrude Stein (1874); Norman Rockwell (1894); Alvar Aalto (1898); James Michener (1907)

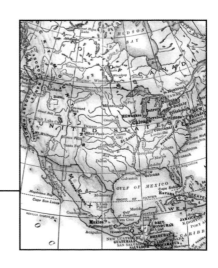

ACKNOWLEDGING AUTONOMY

Both Uranus and air are associated with independence, so could February 3's ruling planet and element have brought pressure to bear on Spain on this day in 1783, when it recognized the autonomy of the United States of America?

FEBRUARY 4

Playful
Stubborn
Radical

EASYGOING EXTREMISTS

The endearing thing about many of those born on February 4 is that although Uranus, their radical ruling planet, urges them to take a different stance to a conventional viewpoint, their airy element gives them such playfulness and easygoing charm that others tend to regard them as being quirky oddballs rather than dangerous revolutionaries. When their masculine-polarity aggression or fixed-nature stubbornness comes to the fore, though, a confrontational clash of wills may occur.

FAMOUS BIRTHS: Charles Lindbergh (1902); Betty Friedan (1921); Alice Cooper (1948); Lisa Eichhorn (1952); Natalie Imbruglia (1975)

OF ONE MIND

Displaying this day's positive-polarity decisivenes, on February 4, 1789, every elector voted for George Washington to become the first president of the USA, in the first—and currently only—unanimous presidential ballot.

AQUARIUS

♒ ♒♒
♒♒

Rational
Self-confident
Independent

fEBRUARY
5

INflEXIBlE fREE SPIRITS

It sometimes seems as though those born on February 5 are laws unto themselves. Their intellectual element of air gives them wide-ranging interests and a rational, dispassionate outlook. Uranus, their planetary ruler, encourages them to ignore convention and follow their own, idiosyncratic path, egged on by their self-confidence-bestowing, positive polarity. While they demand their independence, though, their fixed nature can make them totally inflexible when it comes to allowing others equal freedom.

fAMOUS BIRTHS: Adlai Stevenson (1900); John Carradine (1906); Charlotte Rampling (1946); Jennifer Jason Leigh (1962); Bobby Brown (1969)

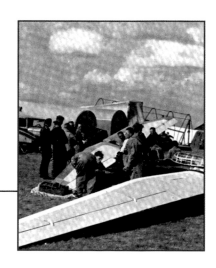

A SOARING SUCCESS

This day has a pioneering flavor, while its airy element encourages aeronautics, so could these considerations be linked to Maxine Dunlap's feat in becoming the first woman to receive a U.S. glider pilot's license on February 5, 1931?

FEBRUARY 6

AMIABLE ACTIVISTS

Appearances can be deceptive, and February 6 individuals' amiable persona typically hides a very principled, and often stubbornly determined, character. While their element of air is responsible for their friendly and relaxed demeanor (and their intelligent and detached outlook), it is their fixed quadruplicity that supplies their dogmatism. And when unpredictable, revolutionary Uranus and an active, pioneering polarity are added to the mix, the result is people with radical views who make things happen.

FAMOUS BIRTHS: Babe Ruth (1895); Ronald Reagan (1911); Zsa Zsa Gabor (1915); Bob Marley (1945); Natalie Cole (1950)

GOING BALLISTIC

Emphasizing this day's active polarity and airy element, it was on February 6, 1959, that the USA launched a Titan I intercontinental ballistic missile (I.C.B.M.) successfully for the first time, from Cape Canaveral, Florida.

AQUARIUS

♒ ♒

Independent
Articulate
Rebellious

FEBRUARY

7

OBJECTIVE OBJECTORS

Uranus and air have a powerful influence on February 7 people. The result of their combined action is individuals who are objective and independent thinkers, as well as gifted communicators (thanks to their element) who are inspired by their ruling planet's rebellious spirit. Should they consequently find themselves at odds with conventional wisdom, their active polarity arms them with the aggressive energy required to battle it, while their fixed nature supplies stubborn determination.

FAMOUS BIRTHS Thomas More (1478); Charles Dickens (1812); Frederick Douglass (1817); Laura Ingalls Wilder (1867); Ashton Kutcher (1978)

FLOATING FREE

This day's element, air, is associated with freedom, as is Uranus, its ruling planet. How apt that the first untethered space walk was made on February 7, 1984, by U.S. astronauts Bruce McCandless II and Robert L. Stewart.

FEBRUARY 8

Radical
Logical
Analytical

RATIONAL RADICALS

Should others consider February 8 people to be radical and reckless, they probably don't have Uranus as a ruling planet or an active polarity, birth influences that encourage a revolutionary outlook and banish doubts. Not that those born on this day are thoughtless, however. Their intelligence-enhancing, airy element gives them a logical and analytical approach to everything they say and all that they undertake, while their fixed nature causes them to be principled to the point of dogmatism.

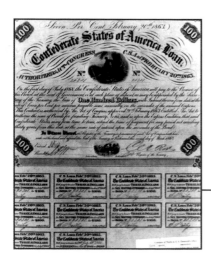

FAMOUS BIRTHS: William Tecumseh Sherman (1820); Jules Verne (1828); Jack Lemmon (1925); James Dean (1931); John Grisham (1955)

CONSOLIDATING THE CONFEDERACY

The influence of February 8's consolidation-encouraging was powerful in 1861. This date marks the anniversary of the adoption of the Constitution of Confederacy by which the Confederate States of America came into being.

AQUARIUS
♒ ♒♒

Questioning
Logical
Fearless

FEBRUARY
9

COURAGEOUS CONFRONTERS

Having individualistic Uranus and independent air among their birth influences means that February 9 people are predisposed to questioning convention, rather than merely accepting it. They do so with impeccable logic, due to the rationalizing effect that this astrological duo has on their thought processes. If they decide that convention requires challenging, they will instinctively confront its champions with typical masculine-polarity fearlessness, strengthened and sustained by their steely staying power.

FAMOUS BIRTHS: Brendan Behan (1923); Janet Suzman (1939); Carole King (1942); Alice Walker (1944); Mia Farrow (1945)

SOMETHING IN THE AIR
This day's element is air, the medium through which we experience different types of weather, making February 9, 1870, a fitting date for the creation of the United States Weather Bureau, or the National Weather Service.

FEBRUARY 10

♒♒ ♅

Rebellious
Challenging
Determined

CHARMING CHALLENGERS

Not only does their confrontation-provoking, masculine polarity wield a powerful influence over those born on February 10, but Uranus, their ruling planet, gives them the desire to stand out from the crowd. Although they have the potential to be aggressive and anarchic challengers of convention, their airy element encourages them to use their brains, charm, and highly developed powers of communication for positive purposes, while their fixed mode supplies their determination and self-discipline.

FAMOUS BIRTHS: Boris Pasternak (1890); Bertolt Brecht (1898); Roberta Flack (1940); Mark Spitz (1950); Greg Norman (1955)

AN ENTERPRISING EXODUS

Its active polarity gives this day an enterprising quality, and may have contributed to the Mormons' decision to leave Nauvoo, Illinois, on February 10, 1846 and begin their long trek west to the Valley of the Great Salt Lake, Utah.

AQUARIUS

♒ ♒♒

Articulate
Inventive
Dynamic

fEBRUARY
11

INVENTIVE INNOVATORS

February 11 individuals are very much children of their element of air, being friendly, playful, and articulate, and, above all, inventive. While air encourages their minds to roam freely until inspiration strikes, Uranus, their ruling planet, is behind their love of experimentation, an enterprising combination that is given real potential by their dynamic, active polarity. In addition, because their fixed nature makes them, persistent, they are capable of seeing their pioneering projects through to completion.

fAMOUS BIRTHS: Thomas Alva Edison (1847); Leslie Nielsen (1926); Mary Quant (1934); Burt Reynolds (1936); Sheryl Crow (1963); Jennifer Aniston (1969)

A fREE SPIRIT
The combination of independence and free-thinking infuses this day with a love of liberty, shown on February 11, 1990. The South African government released Nelson Mandela after holding him captive for twenty-seven years.

FEBRUARY 12

QUIRKY QUESTIONERS

If this is your birthday, your active polarity makes you outgoing, and your element of air is responsible for your desire to know more about (and tendency to question) almost everyone and everything that you encounter. Constant quizzing gives you a reputation for quirkiness, and this is a result of Uranus's influence, as well as air. Although you become restless when bored, once your interest is engaged by something truly unusual, your fixed mode gives you focus, concentration, and commitment.

FAMOUS BIRTHS: Charles Darwin (1809); Abraham Lincoln (1809); Franco Zeffirelli (1923); Judy Blume (1938); Christina Ricci (1980)

AN AVANT-GARDE ADDRESS
Responding to the attraction to new technology and urge to communicate that Uranus and air bestow on this day, Calvin Coolidge became the first U.S. president to broadcast a presidential speech over the radio in 1924.

AQUARIUS
♒ ♒♒

Sociable
Rebellious
Playful

FEBRUARY
13

PLAYFUL PERSISTERS

When February 13 people are relaxed, their active polarity and element of air come to the fore, so that those born on this day appear confident, sociable, and endearingly playful in their leisure time. When life becomes more serious, however, another side to the February 13 personality emerges, with Uranus being responsible for their unconventional, rebellious streak, and their fixed nature providing such unwavering persistence that others may end up cursing their sheer bloody-mindedness.

FAMOUS BIRTHS: Rosa Parks (1913); Kim Novak (1933); George Segal (1934); Jerry Springer (1944); Peter Gabriel (1950); Robbie Williams (1974)

AN AERIAL ATTACK
Some may detect the influence of this day's element of air, its aggressive polarity, and its uncompromising, fixed quadruplicity, in the British fire-bombing of Dresden, Germany, which began on February 13, 1945.

FEBRUARY 14

AQUARIUS

♒ ♅

Unconventional
Independent
Assertive

INDIVIDUALISTIC INVESTIGATORS

There are a number of astrological reasons why you are an instinctive nonconformist, if you were born on this day. One is your unconventional, Uranus-inspired way of looking at the world, and another is the independent, investigative, and curious spirit with which your element of air infuses you. And because you derive assertiveness from your masculine polarity, and also have a propensity to commit yourself totally to a certain standpoint, you are not easily manipulated or swayed by anyone else.

FAMOUS BIRTHS: Jimmy Hoffa (1913); Carl Bernstein (1944); Alan Parker (1944); Gregory Hines (1946); Meg Tilly (1960)

INCITING INTOLERANCE
Intolerance is linked with this day's fixed quadruplicity. In 1989, Iranian leader Ayatollah Khomeini proclaimed a fatwa inciting the murder of Salman Rushdie, author of the "blasphemous" novel The Satanic Verses.

AQUARIUS

♒ ♒♒
♒♒

Friendly
Adventurous
Obstinate

fEBRUARY

15

AMICABLE ADVENTURERS

If those born on this day have a default mode, it is typically their airy amicability, or the easygoing friendliness
that characterizes their approach to others. Yet certain circumstances can bring some markedly different February
15 characteristics to the fore. When presented with the
challenge of exploring new things, for instance, their
Uranian adventurousness and active-polarity energy and
lack of inhibition become evident. When crossed, their
fixed-mode obstinacy may make them angry.

fAMOUS BIRTHS: Galileo Galilei
(1564); Charles Louis Tiffany
(1812); Sir Ernest Shackleton
(1874); Cesar Romero (1907);
Jane Seymour (1951)

A STAMP OF APPROVAL

Air promotes communication; Uranus,
innovation and sticking power. With
these astrological influences, February
15, 1842, was a apt day for the introduc-
tion of adhesive postage stamps by New
York City's City Dispatch Post.

fEBRUARY 16

♒ ♅
♒

Independent
Assertive
Experimental

RESOLUTE REBELS

Others think of you as a born rebel, if today is your birthday. While it is true that Uranus, your ruling planet, attracts you to the unconventional and experimental, you don't deliberately cultivate your nonconformist image. Instead, your airy independence of thought, your active-polarity assertiveness, and your fixed resolution are often seen by friends and colleagues as contrariness and aggression. You should be careful not to let your reputation for being insubordinate and rebellious become a problem.

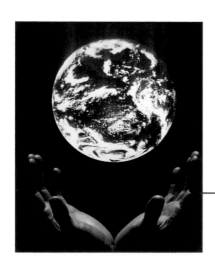

fAMOUS BIRTHS: John Schlesinger (1926); Sonny Bono (1935); Pete Postlethwaite (1946); Tracy Morrow, "Ice-T" (1958); John McEnroe (1959)

PREVENTING POLLUTION
The Kyoto Protocol, a near-global commitment to cutting emissions of greenhouse gases, came into effect in 2005, aided by the combined effect of air, a proactive, positive polarity, and a determined, fixed quadruplicity.

AQUARIUS
♒ ♒♒

Dedication
Inventive
Dynamic

FEBRUARY
17

INQUISITIVE INVENTORS

The fusion of the element of air and the ruling planet, Uranus, within the characters of February 17 individuals has some surprisingly original consequences. The dedication that they derive from their fixed nature, and the confidence and dynamism that their positive polarity bestows on them, together enable them to make the most of their unique ideas. And because air makes them curious, and Uranus gives them a taste for the new, their notions are frequently both innovative and inventive.

FAMOUS BIRTHS: Ruth Rendell (1930); Alan Bates (1934); Gene Pitney (1941); Michael Jordan (1963); Jerry O'Connell (1974)

A NEWSWORTHY DATE
Air encourages sharing of information, making February 17, 1933, a fitting date for the first publication of Newsweek, a U.S. magazine that went on to sell more than over 4 million copies each week.

FEBRUARY 18

AQUARIUS

Intense
Self-confident
Independent

POWERFUL PERSONALITIES

If today is your birthday, you may be friendly and relaxed when "off duty," thanks to your element of air. Otherwise, though, you often come across as being very intense—and sometimes even overbearing. Your masculine polarity blesses you with a powerful presence and a great deal of self-confidence, while your fixed nature supplies concentration and a level of resolution verging on rigidity. Uranus in turn increases your unwillingness to compromise and redoubles your airy detachment and independence.

FAMOUS BIRTHS: Enzo Ferrari (1898); Toni Morrison (1931); Yoko Ono (1933); John Travolta (1954); Matt Dillon (1964); Andre Young, "Dr. Dre" (1965)

A BOLT FROM THE BLUE

Because this day is ruled by Uranus, radical changes to conventional systems or beliefs are possible, as occurred in 1930, when U.S. astronomer Clyde Tombaugh discovered Pluto, arguably our solar system's ninth planet.

SYMBOL: TWO FISHES
CELESTIAL RULER: NEPTUNE
  (TRADITIONALLY JUPITER)
ELEMENT: WATER
POLARITY: NEGATIVE (FEMININE)
QUADRUPLICITY: MUTABLE

PISCES
FEBRUARY 19 TO MARCH 20 ♓

Neptune, the planet named after the Roman sea god, took over the rulership of Pisces, the sign of the fishes, following its discovery in 1846. Pisces's element is sensitive, emotional water, and it is a mutable sign, as changeable as the oceans, making its children adaptable, and sometimes restless. Its feminine polarity is linked with the Moon, which influences the tides on Earth and has goddess status in many cultures. Their polarity makes Pisceans intuitive introverts. It is Neptune that is responsible for these spiritual souls' idealistic, altruistic instincts.

FEBRUARY 19

Sensitive
Compassionate
Vulnerable

SENSITIVE SOFTIES

If you were born on February 19, you are known for being soft at heart, always full of empathy for your fellow creatures. You have your element's sensitivity, along with the compassion that both water and your ruling planet bestow on you. Experience may have taught you that others are all too ready to take advantage of your emotional vulnerability, which is why you tend to hide your true feelings, a passive-polarity characteristic. You usually display your mutable-mode adaptability when dealing with others.

FAMOUS BIRTHS: Nicolaus Copernicus (1473); Merle Oberon (1911); Lee Marvin (1924); Smokey Robinson (1940)

A PACIFIC PACT

Peace-promoting Neptune infuses this day with a pacific atmosphere. This was evident on February 19, 1674, when England and the Dutch Republic signed the Peace of Westminster, ending the Third Anglo–Dutch War.

Pisces

Ψ ♓

Creative
Compassionate
Introspective

FEBRUARY 20

CHANGEABLE CREATIVES

It is easy to be confused by the February 20 character, for the mutable nature and watery element of those born on this day can sometimes trigger moodiness. Two constant qualities, however, are their creativity and enormous compassion, the joint gifts of water and Neptune, their ruling planet, which flourish during the periods of introspection that their feminine polarity encourages in them. Their variable moods may manifest themselves as anything from idealism to sadness, thanks to Neptune's influence.

FAMOUS BIRTHS: Ansel Adams (1902); Sidney Poitier (1924); Cindy Crawford (1966); Kurt Cobain (1967)

BATTLING BARRED
The combined influence of February 20's gentleness-granting element of water, and Neptune, its peaceable ruling planet, prevailed in 1839, for it was on this day that the U.S. Congress banned dueling in the District of Columbia.

FEBRUARY 21

Sociable
Receptive
Empathetic

SENSITIVE SOCIALIZERS

If this is your birthday, the effect that your mutable quadruplicity has on you is often especially evident, notably
in your sociable and versatile personality, but also in your
moodiness. You are especially prone to mood swings that
others may find completely baffling, thanks to three of
your birth influences. Your passive polarity makes you an
ultrareceptive type, too, influenced by your changing
environment. The upshot is that, as a watery, Neptunian
soul, you are highly empathetic, if sometimes self-pitying.

FAMOUS BIRTHS: W. H. Auden
(1907); Nina Simone (1933);
Alan Rickman (1946);
Kelsey Grammer (1955);
Charlotte Church (1986)

COMMUNAL CONCERNS

Neptune is linked with idealism, mak-
ing February 21, 1848, an appropriate
date for the publication of The
Communist Manifesto, by German the-
orists Karl Marx and Friedrich Engels.

Pisces
Ψ ♓

Introverted
Receptive
Intuitive

fEBRUARY
22

INSECURE IDEALISTS

Your introspective, passive polarity underpins your character, if your birthday is February 22, perhaps causing you to be an introvert, and certainly making you receptive to the influence of others. The fusion of Neptune (your ruling planet) and water (your element) means that your mutable, changeable nature is more noticeable, because the qualities they impart tend to reinforce one another. This is why you may well be idealistic and intuitive one day, and hopelessly indecisive and insecure, the next.

fAMOUS BIRTHS: George Washington (1732); Robert Baden-Powell (1857); Luis Buñuel (1900); Edward Kennedy (1932); Drew Barrymore (1975)

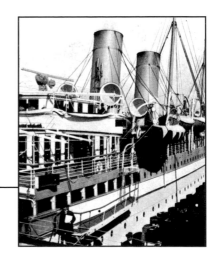

A MARINE MERCHANT
Because February 22's element is water, marine ventures are well starred on this day, on which, in 1784, the Empress of China, *the first U.S. merchant ship to trade with China, set sail for the East from New York.*

FEBRUARY 23

RESTLESS ROMANTICS

The combination of idealistic Neptune, emotional water, and their thoughtful feminine polarity often results in February 23 people being incurable romantics, as well as deeply caring types. These birth influences can also make them despondent and oversensitive—particularly when reality shatters their cherished illusions—and restless, too, thanks largely to their mutability. Small wonder that they may veer from viewing the world through rose-tinted glasses to contemplating it from a darker viewpoint.

FAMOUS BIRTHS: Samuel Pepys (1633); George Frederic Handel (1685); Peter Fonda (1939); Kristin Davis (1965)

A SUPPORTIVE SOCIETY
Responding to the spirit of supportiveness with which its element of water imbues this day, it was on February 23, 1905, that four businessmen convened in Chicago, Illinois, to found the Rotary Club for networking and mutual aid.

Pisces
♆ ♓

Altruistic
Adaptability
Compassionate

FEBRUARY 24

ADAPTABLE ALTRUISTS

If you were born on this day, you have a highly developed sense of social responsibility. This is due partly to your ruling planet's altruistic influence, partly to the compassion that you derive from both Neptune and your watery element, and partly to the love of variety—and of others' company—that your mutability bestows on you. Your mutable nature also makes you a flexible person, but it is your passive polarity that prompts you to devote so much thought to how best to help and support others.

FAMOUS BIRTHS: Wilhelm Grimm (1786); Winslow Homer (1836); Enrico Caruso (1873); Chester Nimitz (1885); George Harrison (1943)

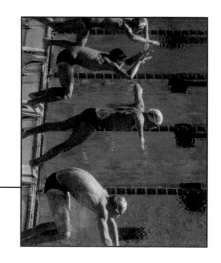

AN ENCOURAGING ELEMENT
His path eased, and strength boosted, by February 24's element of water, U.S. swimmer Johnny Weissmuller set a world record for swimming 100m in Miami, Florida, on this day in 1924.

fEBRUARY 25

Sociable
Volatile
Unpredictable

VOLATILE VISIONARIES

Although the combination of caring water, unselfish Neptune, and an inward-looking, passive polarity makes February 25 individuals gentle types who shrink from confrontation, they are certainly not colorless characters. Not only does their mutable nature give them a zest for socializing, it is also responsible for their volatile moods and unpredictable behavior. And as for their other three birth influences, they give rise to a dreamy creativity that can sometimes verge on the visionary.

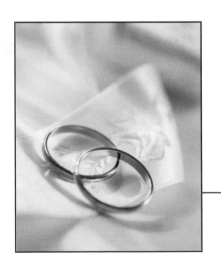

fAMOUS BIRTHS: Pierre Auguste Renoir (1841); Zeppo Marx (1901); Anthony Burgess (1917); Téa Leoni (1966)

MASS MATRIMONY
This day's element and ruling planet are both emotional influences, with Neptune adding a spiritual flavor. February 25, 1968, was an apt date for the Unification Church's mass marriage, in Korea, of 430 couples.

Pisces
♆ ♓

Sensitive
Contemplative
Idealistic

FEBRUARY 26

PRINCIPLED PERSONALITIES

The action of insecure water and nebulous Neptune on young February 26 people may confuse their emotions, especially when these veer from sunny to stormy, thanks to their moody mutability. Age, and the domestic stability that these sensitive individuals crave, has a settling effect on them, and as they mature, they often develop into deeply principled, thoughtful personalities, thanks to their contemplative, feminine polarity, as well as their Neptunian idealism and watery compassion.

FAMOUS BIRTHS: Victor Hugo (1802); William "Buffalo Bill" Cody (1846); "Fats" Domino (1928); Johnny Cash (1932); Sandie Shaw (1947)

AN EVER-CHANGING SCENE
Not only is this day's element water, but its mutability is linked with restlessness and changeability. It was on February 26, 1881, that the S.S. Ceylon set sail from Liverpool, England, thereby initiating the first round-the-world cruise.

FEBRUARY 27

♓ ♆

Introverted
Intuitive
Sensitive

EMOTIONAL EMPATHIZERS

If today is your birthday, your feminine polarity predisposes you to be introverted, but your mutability gives you a real enjoyment of others' company. Thus, you may be shy, but you are not necessarily retiring. A triple dose of intuition, sensitivity, and sympathy from your polarity, watery element, and Neptune makes you popular and implicitly trusted as a good listener. Sometimes, though, you can confuse people by sending mixed messages in response to your own rapidly changing emotions.

FAMOUS BIRTHS: Rudolf Steiner (1861); John Steinbeck (1902); Joanne Woodward (1930); Elizabeth Taylor (1932)

FAIRNESS FOR FEMALES

Because its polarity is feminine, women may be favored on February 27. In 1998 in Britain, the House of Lords decided that if a British monarch's firstborn was a daughter, she would inherit the throne before a younger son.

Pisces
♆ ♓

*Contemplative
Idealistic
Creative*

FEBRUARY 28

DISTRACTED DREAMERS

Were you born on February 28? There are occasions when your contemplative feminine polarity, mutability, fantasy-spinning ruling planet, and creative watery element all merge and make magic. But the ceaseless demands of everyday existence mean that such moments are wonderful rarities. Your mutable nature gives you an appetite for diversions and distraction, which can be fun, but you may sometimes appear to have lost your way in life, when, deep down, you are a profoundly idealistic soul.

FAMOUS BIRTHS: Stephen Spender (1909); Vicente Minnelli (1910); Mario Andretti (1940); Brian Jones (1942); Stephanie Beacham (1947)

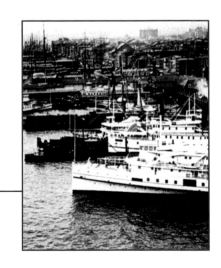

STEAMBOAT TO CALIFORNIA
This day's ruling element is water, and it was on February 28, 1849, that the first steamboat service to California arrived in San Francisco. The S.S California left New York Harbor on October 6, 1848; the trip had taken 4 months and 21 days.

fEBRUARY 29

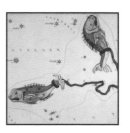

SPIRITUAL SOCIALISTS

February 29 people are special, and not just because their birthday falls but once every four years. Typically profoundly influenced by Neptune, their ruling planet, they have, on the one hand, an otherworldly, spiritual streak, and, on the other, an altruistic concern for the common good. This makes them lovely people to know, but sometimes their passive polarity can cause them to be too negative. Their mutability can provoke spells of restlessness, and their watery element can induce insecurity.

fAMOUS BIRTHS: Ann Lee (1736);
Gioacchino Rossini (1792);
Jimmy Dorsey (1904);
Joss Ackland (1928);
Antonio Sabato, Jr. (1972)

A CHANGE OF CONVENTION
Its emotion-deepening element and ruling planet and feminine polarity make February 29 a fitting day for the Scottish Parliament to select for its decree, in 1288, that women could legally propose marriage on this date.

Pisces
♆ ♓

Idealistic
Adaptable
Optimistic

MARCH
1

POETIC PURISTS

It sometimes seems as though March 1 children are doomed to disappointment. While idealistic Neptune gives them a purist's high standards, their emotional element of water fills them with romantic daydreams—but when real life is imperfect, their polarity can encourage negative thinking. That said, their passive polarity is the catalyst that helps these artistic types to create poetry from disillusionment, while their adaptable, mutable nature enables them to make the most of their lot and be a good friend to others.

FAMOUS BIRTHS: Frédéric Chopin (1810); Oskar Kokoschka (1886); Glenn Miller (1904); Harry Belafonte (1927); Roger Daltrey (1944)

HELPING HUMANITY
It was in 1872 that the U.S. Congress authorized the creation of Yellowstone National Park, the world's first national park. Could Congress's decision be attributed to the influence of idealistic Neptune, March 1's planetary ruler?

MARCH 2

PISCES

♓ ♆

Sensitive
Idealistic
Thoughtful

IRREPRESSIBLE IDEALISTS

If this is your birthday, it is your ruling planet that acts as your inspiration and guides you through life. Whatever the world throws at you, and however much your fickle, mutable nature prompts you to change course—or your sensitive element of water makes you drift and doubt yourself—you always seem to retain some of Neptune's idealism and optimism. Thoughtfulness is another of your attractive qualities, the gift of your passive polarity. You are a caring, considerate, and imaginative soul.

FAMOUS BIRTHS: Kurt Weill (1900); Mikhail Gorbachev (1931); Tom Wolfe (1931); Lou Reed (1944); Karen Carpenter (1950); Jon Bon Jovi (1962)

EXCLUSIVE ACCOMMODATION
March 2 has a nurturing polarity, while Neptune and water imbue it with caring characteristics, which may be why the first women-only hotel, New York's Martha Washington Hotel, opened on this day in 1903.

Pisces
♆ ♓

Caring
Altruistic
Idealistic

MARCH
3

UNSELFISH UPHOLDERS

Others depend upon March 3 people for support, for these are caring types, thanks to their watery element, while their adaptability is due to their mutability. And when their Neptune-derived altruism is taken into account, they can be characterized as exceptionally unselfish people who set great store on upholding their deeply held ideals. Yet while their feminine polarity reinforces their nurturing qualities, both that and water can produce worriers who bottle up their feelings and are prone to anxiety.

FAMOUS BIRTHS: Alexander Graham Bell (1847); Jean Harlow (1911); Mary Page Keller (1961); David Faustino (1974): Jessica Biel (1982**)**

CONGRESSIONAL COMPASSION
This day's influences, Neptune and water, are associated with compassion, demonstrated by the U.S. Congress on March 3, 1812, when it passed its first foreign-aid bill (to assist victims of an earthquake in Venezuela).

MARCH 4

*Insightful
Imaginative
Cooperative*

INTUITIVE INDIVIDUALS

However you use the intuition with which your psychic ruling planet, sensitive element, and receptive, feminine polarity have blessed you, there is no doubt that you March 4 children are deeply insightful. Your mutability encourages you to be cooperative, and you often use this gift, along with your Neptunian compassion and watery sympathy, to help others. Your empathetic and imaginative qualities may permeate your creative endeavors, too, typically evoking an emotional response in others.

Cover of LIBERTY, this Plate is humbly dedicated by her true bo...

FAMOUS BIRTHS: Antonio Vivaldi (1768); Bernard Haitink (1929); Bobby Womack (1944); Chris Rea (1951); Emilio Estefan (1953)

TAKING IT BACK
The British Parliament repealed the Stamp Act—which had incited rebellion among American colonists—on March 4, 1766, an apt date due to Neptune's peaceable influence and its passive polarity.

Pisces
♆ ♓

Emotional
Idealistic
Empathetic

MARCH
5

EMPATHETIC EXTREMISTS

If you were born on this day, your element of water makes you an emotional person, while your passive polarity prompts you to internalize your feelings. This sometimes magnifies your preoccupations. Because you have a mutable, changeable nature, the combination of your heightened concerns and mood swings can push you to take extreme positions. You rarely push people about your own concerns, though, because Neptune fills you with the altruistic desire to help others, especially the disadvantaged.

FAMOUS BIRTHS: Giovanni Battista Tiepolo (1696); Rosa Luxemburg (1871); Rex Harrison (1908); Samantha Eggar (1939); Eddy Grant (1948)

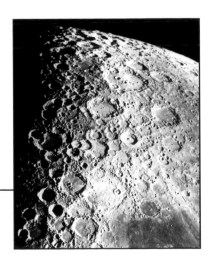

AN ELEMENTAL DISCOVERY
March 5's element is water, so it seems fitting that it was on this day in 1998 that N.A.S.A., the U.S. space agency, should have announced that a survey spacecraft had discovered ice crystals beneath the Moon's surface.

March 6

Flexible
Creative
Generous

Flexible Fantasists

March 6 people's flexibility on the one hand enables them to get along with others, and, on the other, allows their creativity to flow in different directions. Their mutable quadruplicity supplies their adaptability and versatility, but it is Neptune, their ruling planet, that is the source of their unselfishness. Their element of water feeds their imaginations, while their passive polarity encourages them to turn inward to allow their ideals and ideas to take shape. They may be dreamers, but they are lovable, loving people.

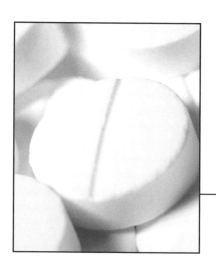

Famous Births: Michelangelo Buonarroti (1475); Elizabeth Barrett Browning (1806); Gabriel García-Márquez (1928); Kiri Te Kanawa (1944)

A Calming Combination
Neptune, water, and a feminine polarity exude a comforting and caring influence, and maybe it was due to their action that German pharmaceutical company Bayer was able to patent the painkiller aspirin on this day in 1899.

Pisces
♆ ♓

Pacifist
Idealistic
Thoughtful

MARCH
7

PROFOUND PACIFISTS

If this is your birthday, your passive polarity means that you are a pacifist, with an inborn belief that humans should live in harmony with each other—even though you are probably not a strident campaigner. Optimistic, idealistic Neptune may help you to see the good in others, while your mutability supplies your cooperative instincts. But it is the quiet fusion of your thoughtful polarity and the sensitivity-enhancing element of water that gives you mysterious—and sometimes magical—hidden depths.

FAMOUS BIRTHS: Piet Mondrian (1872); Maurice Ravel (1875); Ivan Lendl (1960); Rachel Weisz (1971); Laura Prepon (1980)

A FEMININE FEAT
March 7 has a feminine polarity, and maybe its influence contributed to a feminine "first" that occurred in Israel on this day in 1969, when Golda Meir became that Middle Eastern nation's first female prime minister.

MARCH 8

CONVIVIAL CONTEMPLATIVES

Thoughtfulness is typically the hallmark of the March 8 personality. Those born on this day are especially susceptible to the contemplative influence of their passive polarity. The additional input of their ruling planet, and of the intuitive, introspective element of water, may produce dreamy characters, but not people who are disengaged from others—far from it. Having a mutable nature means that they love company and effortlessly adapt to people from all walks of life, forming deep bonds with many.

FAMOUS BIRTHS: Kenneth Grahame (1859); Cyd Charisse (1923); Lynn Redgrave (1943); Gary Numan (1958)

A FISHY BUSINESS

March 8, 1887, was an auspicious day for Everett Horton, of Connecticut, to patent the telescopic fishing rod, for this day of the zodiacal fishes has a watery element and, in Neptune, a ruling planet named for a marine deity.

Pisces
♅ ♓

Imaginative
Idealistic
Creative

MARCH
9

BOUNDLESS VISIONARIES

It sometimes seems as though there are no restrictions limiting your vivid imagination, if you were born on this day—except, perhaps, those imposed by the self-doubt, insecurity, and caution that are part and parcel of having a watery element, a mutable nature, and a passive polarity. The idealistic, optimistic spirit of Neptune flourishes within these self-imposed parameters, however, as do your creativity, your versatility, your profound capacity for deep thinking, and your caring concern for others.

FAMOUS BIRTHS: Amerigo Vespucci (1454); Yuri Alekseyevich Gagarin (1934); Bobby Fischer (1943); Juliette Binoche (1964)

SWITCHING SIDES
Responding, perhaps, to the fickleness-inducing influence that its mutability wields over March 9, it was on this Cold War day in 1967 that Svetlana Alliluyeva, daughter of Soviet dictator Josef Stalin, defected to the USA.

MARCH 10

Pisces
♓ ♆

Gregarious
Nurturing
Instinctive

GREGARIOUS GIVERS

Their emotion-confusing, watery element and changeable mutability can subject March 10 people to the occasional moody moment, but they are better known for other qualities associated with these birth influences. Their element makes them generous, both materially and emotionally, and they are gregarious. Because their feminine polarity reinforces their nurturing impulses, and Neptune gives them a tendency to focus on the best in people, they in turn usually bring out the best in those around them.

FAMOUS BIRTHS: Wyatt Earp (1848); Bix Beiderbecke (1903); Sharon Stone (1958); Neneh Cherry (1964); Shannon Miller (1977)

A SACRED COMMITMENT
Neptune gives March 10 a spirituality. This was emphasized in 515 B.C. in Jerusalem, when, according to the Old Testament Book of Ezra (6:15–18), the Jewish Second Temple, or Zerubbabel's Temple, was dedicated.

Pisces
ψ ♓

Intuitive
Introspective
Perceptive

COMPLEX CHARACTERS

If this is your birthday, you're an excellent judge of character, thanks to Neptune, water, and your feminine polarity, which together supply an almost spookily perceptive level of intuition, as well as empathy. However, you yourself are often misunderstood. Your sociable mutability can give you the appearance of being a straightforward extrovert, when you are anything but: you're quite shy. The combination of your ruling planet, element, and polarity makes you a private person, sometimes prone to confusion.

FAMOUS BIRTHS: Malcolm Campbell (1885); Rupert Murdoch (1931); Bobby McFerrin (1950); Douglas Adams (1952); Alex Kingston (1963)

ARMING AN ALLY
Demonstrating this day's mutable quadruplicity's cooperative instincts, U.S. President Franklin D. Roosevelt signed the Lend Lease Act on March 11, 1941, thereby boosting Britain's stand against Nazi Germany during World War II.

MARCH 12

OPTIMISTIC ONE-OFFS

When you were born, one of Neptune's gifts to you was optimism, and you may retain this hopeful personality throughout your life. This is just as well, because your element can make you thin-skinned and insecure. Your negative polarity redoubles your tendency to worry too much, and your mutability aggravates your indecisiveness. That said, it is precisely this variable astrological trio that makes you a fascinatingly complex, ever-changing character, and you always care deeply for the people around you.

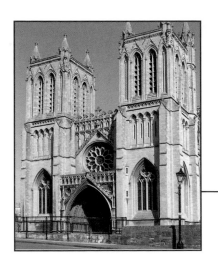

fAMOUS BiRTHS: Kemal Atatürk (1881); Vaslav Nijinsky (1888); Jack Kerouac (1922); Al Jarreau (1940); Liza Minnelli (1946)

DEDICATING DEACONS

Rulership by Neptune and a feminine polarity highlight issues relating to spirituality and women, as was demonstrated in England in 1994, when the first Church of England women priests were ordained at Bristol Cathedral.

Pisces
♆ ♓

Thoughtful
Sociable
Insecure

MARCH
13

SPIRITUAL SEEKERS

Insecurity is an attribute of all four of March 13 people's birth influences, which may be why they sometimes seem to be searching for a rock to cling to, be it the solace of spiritual certainty, due to the influence of Neptune, or the emotional comfort of being loved and having loved ones to care for, thanks to their element of water. Whatever their personal quest may be, they are helped in it by their feminine-polarity thoughtfulness and mutable, sociable personality, both of which making them more giving than needy.

FAMOUS BIRTHS: Joseph Priestley (1733); Percival Lowell (1855); L. Ron Hubbard (1911); Neil Sedaka (1939); Joe Bugner (1950)

A DEADLY DELUGE
Days with a watery element are prone to exceptional water-related events—this one being no exception. It was on March 13, 1928, that the St. Francis Dam burst catastrophically in California, killing around five hundred people.

March 14

Open-minded Optimists

Having a ruling planet that promotes psychic abilities, an element that heightens emotional responsiveness, and a passive polarity that provides receptiveness causes March 14 people to be intuitive, sensitive, and open-minded. Because their mutability also makes them sociable, they are typically surrounded, and influenced, by a variety of people. Impressionable they may be, but Neptune blesses them with such powerful optimism that this quality ultimately prevails, making them engaging, warm people.

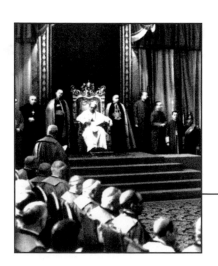

Famous Births: Johann Strauss the Elder (1804); Maxim Gorky (1868); Albert Einstein (1879); Michael Caine (1933); Quincy Jones (1933)

A Spiritual Selection

Astrologically speaking, March 14, 1800, was a fitting date for the Roman Catholic conclave of cardinals to elect Luigi Chiaramonti, an Italian, as Pope Pius VII, because Neptune, this day's ruling planet, is linked with spirituality.

Pisces
ψ ♓

Sociable
Emotional
Realistic

MARCH 15

FANCIFUL FREE SPIRITS

If you were born on this day, the influence that fantasy-encouraging Neptune wields over you can sometimes make it seem as though you inhabit another planet. And because you have a passive polarity, you do indeed often retreat into your own world to ponder the emotions with which you are often awash, thanks to your element of water. People may think of you as otherworldly, but you remain connected to the real world through your mutable sociability and your deep bonds with those around you.

FAMOUS BIRTHS: Andrew Jackson (1767); Sly Stone (1944); Judd Hirsch (1945); Ry Cooder (1947); Terence Trent D'Arby (1962)

AN ACT OF RESIGNATION
Complying, perhaps at least in part, with this day's passive-polarity instinct to withdraw from active engagement with the wider world, it was on March 15, 1917, that Czar Nicholas II abdicated the throne of Russia.

MARCH 16

PISCES
♓ ♆

*Sociable
Idealistic
Sentimental*

OUTGOING INTROVERTS

If this is your birthday, you bridge the dividing line between extroversion and introversion almost seamlessly. Although your feminine polarity makes you prone to introspection, your mutability gives you sociable instincts and a love of variety and distractions. And while spiritual Neptune and emotional water can both fill your head with idealistic longings, these usually focus on your relationships with your loved ones, who mean the world to you, or on the state of the wider world and its problems.

FAMOUS BIRTHS: James Madison (1751); Jerry Lewis (1926); Bernardo Bertolucci (1940); Isabelle Huppert (1953); Lauren Graham (1967)

RATIFYING RELIEF

The merging of Neptune and water gives this day a caring character, which may explain why it was on March 16, 1882, that the U.S. Senate ratified the Treaty of Geneva, establishing the Red Cross, the international relief agency.

PISCES
♆ ♓

Emotional
Empathetic
Gregarious

MARCH
17

SENSITIVE SYMPATHIZERS

You may learn to conceal your vulnerability, but you March 17 people are heavily influenced by water in being deeply emotional, hypersensitive souls. And because you are also extremely empathetic, due to the additional input of compassionate Neptune, you experience others' pain almost as if it were your own. When you feel wounded, you tend to turn inward to brood, negative-polarity-style, but when things are going well for you, your mutable gregariousness becomes apparent and you surround yourself with others.

FAMOUS BIRTHS: Gottlieb Daimler (1834); Nat "King" Cole (1919); Rudolf Nureyev (1938); Kurt Russell (1951); Rob Lowe (1964)

WITHDRAWAL BY WATER
Maybe March 17's withdrawn, negative polarity gave the British general William Howe the final push he needed in order to evacuate his troops from Boston, Massachusetts, by sea on this Revolutionary War day in 1776.

MARCH 18

EMPATHETIC EXPRESSIONISTS

March 18 individuals are typically introspective, passive-polarity types, with a rich inner life. And because dreamy Neptune sows the seeds of fantasy in their fertile imaginations, which their emotional element of water nourishes and sustains, it sometimes seems as though they are channeling evocative messages of beauty and pain from an otherworldly source. That they are very much of this world, however, is evident in their fellow-feeling, as well as their mutable love of socializing with, and nurturing, others.

FAMOUS BIRTHS: Grover Cleveland (1837); Stéphane Mallarmé (1842); John Updike (1932); Wilson Pickett (1941)

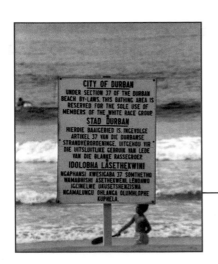

CONDONING CHANGE

Was the South African electorate's vote to abolish apartheid (a racial segregation policy that had prevailed in their country since 1948), in a referendum held in 1992, a response to this day's change-encouraging Neptune?

Pisces

ψ ♓

Optimistic
Sociable
Meditative

MARCH
19

MOODY MEDITATORS

If this is your birthday, it is the fusion of your emotional element and your mutable changeability that can predispose you to moodiness. But your default emotion is sunny optimism, the gift of your ruling planet, which makes others seek you out. While your mutability causes you to enjoy others' company, your feminine polarity gives you a need to withdraw into yourself periodically, in order to explore, or meditate on, the imaginative fantasies and deep feelings with which Neptune and water fill you.

FAMOUS BIRTHS: Tobias Smollett (1721); David Livingstone (1813); Philip Roth (1933); Ursula Andress (1936); Glenn Close (1947); Bruce Willis (1955)

A PACT FOR PEACE

Perhaps peaceable, spiritual Neptune and gentle, sympathetic water prevailed on March 19, 1563, for this day saw the signing of the Peace of Amboise, which ended the First War of Religion in France and gave the Huguenots limited rights.

MARCH 20

Idealistic
Moody
Intuitive

DESPAIRING DREAMERS

The merging of idealistic Neptune and romantic water within your character makes you March 20 people long for a perfect world, in which love reigns supreme. Life's setbacks can cast you into the depths of despair, however, when your mutable nature makes you moody and your passive polarity encourages you to turn inward. But the flicker of fire that comes from being on the cusp of Aries can modify water's influence and help light up your mindset, enabling you to focus on action rather than sadness.

FAMOUS BIRTHS: Henrik Ibsen (1828); William Hurt (1950); Spike Lee (1957); Holly Hunter (1958); Tracy Chapman (1964)

SYMPATHY FOR SLAVES

Water, this day's element, and Neptune, its ruling planet encourage empathy, as did the U.S. author Harriet Beecher Stowe, whose book Uncle Tom's Cabin, *detailing the plight of African-American slaves, was published in 1852.*

Acknowledgments

The publisher would like to thank the following individuals for their assistance in creating this book: Sara Hunt, editor; Debbie Hayes, art director; Clare Gibson, for the introduction; Fiona Fox, editorial and production assistant; and Claire Girvan and Sarah Beech. In addition, grateful acknowledgment is made for permission to reproduce the illustrations. All images are copyright © 2006 JUPITERIMAGES unless listed below, by page number:

Author's Collection: 363, 132; Courtesy of Corel Inc: 218; Library of Congress, Prints and Photographs Division: 34, 43, 47, 51, 53, 54, 62, 63, 64, 65, 66, 67, 82, 83, 96, 99, 101, 102, 103, 104, 105, 115, 118, 119, 121, 124, 130, 137, 142, 146, 153, 154, 156, 160, 161, 162, 171, 173, 175, 176, 177, 180, 181, 182, 185, 188, 192, 193, 201, 203, 209, 213, 215, 216, 220, 222, 228, 232, 237, 239, 251, 253, 256, 258, 259, 268, 276, 277, 280, 282, 284, 288, 289, 292, 306, 307, 308, 310, 313, 318, 320, 323, 324, 329, 336, 337, 338, 342, 343, 345, 348, 351, 358, 359, 361, 366, 368, 372, 373, 376, 385, 386, 388, 398, 401, 403, 405, 411, 414; The National Archives: 190; NASA: 169, 200, 242, 303, 309, 357; Planet Art: 14, 17, 27, 28; Saraband Image Library: 6, 12, 23, 38, 55, 61, 362, 397; Wikipedia/iFaqeer: 285; Wikipedia/T. Gilligan 194; Wikipedia/John Mullen: 412 (www.johnmullen.org.uk); WikipediaA.R. Pingstone 406; The World Fact Book: 327

Sources

The author would like to acknowledge the following sources that were used in the research for this book:

The BBC, On This Day: http://news.bbc.co.uk/onthisday/

The History Channel, This Day in History: http://www.historychannel.com/tdih/

On–This–Day.com: http://www.on–this–day.com/

INDEX